RELIGIOUS LIFE AND THE POOR

Liberation Theology Perspectives

Alejandro Cussiánovich, S.D.B.

Translated by John Drury

ORBIS BOOKS
Maryknoll, New York 10545

Second Printing, May 1981

Library of Congress Cataloging in Publication data

Cussiánovich, Alejandro.
  Religious life and the poor.

  Translation of Desde los pobres de la tierra.
  Includes bibliographical references and index.
  1. Monastic and religious life.   2.   Church and the poor.   3.   Liberation
theology.   I.   Title
BX2435.C8813   255   78-167140
  ISBN 0-88344-429-1

The Catholic Foreign Mission Society of America (Maryknoll) recruits and trains people for overseas missionary service. Through Orbis Books Maryknoll aims to foster the international dialogue that is essential to mission. The books published, however, reflect the opinions of their authors and are not meant to represent the official position of the Society.

First published in 1975 as *Desde los pobres de la tierra, Perspectivas de vida religiosa* by Centro de Estudios y Publicaciones, Apdo. 6118, Lima, Peru

English translation copyright ©   1979 by Orbis Books, Maryknoll, New York 10545

Printed in the United States of America

To Gerardo Poblete, a Salesian priest,
who died under torture in Iquique, Chile,
on October 25, 1973.

To Carlos Dornak, a Salesian priest,
who was assassinated in Bahía Blanca, Argentina,
on March 21, 1975.

To all the activists
in Christian communities among the common people.
It is in such communities
that new ways of following Christ
are now coming to birth.

Contents

Abbreviations

CELAM   Consejo Episcopal Latinoamericano,
Latin American Episcopal Conference

CEPAL   Comisión Económica para América Latina,
U.N. Economic Commission for Latin America
(ECLA)

CIAS   Centro de Investigación y Accion Social,
Center for Investigation and Social Action

CIDOC   Centro Intercultural de Documentación,
Intercultural Documentation Center

CLAR   Conferencia Latinoamericano de Religiosos,
Latin American Conference of Religious

CRB   Conferencia de Religiosos de Brasil,
Brazilian Conference of Religious

IPLA   Insituto Pastoral Latinoamericano,
Latin American Pastoral Institute

ISAL   Iglesia y Sociedad en América Latina,
Church and Society in Latin America

MIEC-JECI   Movimiento Internacional de Estudiantes Católicos—
Juventud Estudiantil Católica International,
two international organizations of Catholic students

REB   Revista Eclesiástica Brasileira,
Brazilian Ecclesiastical Review

Foreword

Many religious men and women in Latin America are now living out their commitment to the gospel way of life in solidarity with various segments of the common people. Such a commitment to the oppressed classes raises more than a few tensions and questions in one's personal and community life. Nevertheless these religious feel that their identification with the lives and struggles of the common people is giving new life to their dedication to the Lord and its deeper meaning.

This book proposes to develop the overall perspective that comes to us from the prophetic tradition (Zeph. 2:3) and that finds confirmation in the poor Christ. In him this perspective becomes a key to entering the whole dynamic of the kingdom of God. It is our conviction, based on that perspective, that history is changed and the Christian way of life revitalized insofar as we start from the standpoint of the poor and the oppressed. To join in fellowship with the poor is to become their neighbor. It is amid the poor and oppressed that we can also experience what it means to be a neighbor to those who are not poor but who are summoned to be neighbors.

In these pages I have gathered various reflections that I have shared with religious men and women on different occasions. Of course I do not offer a systematic treatment of the central themes of the religious life. Here I simply elaborate the basic perspective that is under discussion. As is the case with activist exegesis of the Bible, these reflections are subject to further study, closer analysis, and the authority of the magisterium.

The perspective that comes from the poor is primarily a gift from the Lord. It must be a lived experience and an ongoing summons to refurbish our fidelity to his love through the very practice of liberation. Otherwise it will be nothing more than a delusion for us, a betrayal of the people, and a sin against the Spirit.

1

The Poor as a Starting Point

RELIGIOUS AND THE NATIVE INDIANS

The religious life is part of the history of our continent, an integral component of the discovery of the Indies. From the time of conquest and colonization on, religious have been present in the life of the people in one way or another. Most of the early bishops were religious as were those entrusted with teaching Christian doctrine.[1] Tension developed fairly early, of course. Even in the days of Toribio de Mogrovejo we find the religious resisting the idea of giving up their Indian parishes to secular priests, who were growing in number and being proposed for those posts by the bishops.[2] Unfortunately the opposition to this move by religious

---

1. See Enrique Dussel, *Les évêques hispanoaméricains, Défenseurs et évangélisateurs de l'Indien:1504–1620* (Wiesbaden: Steiner, 1970), p. 29, and Appendix I, a critical listing of bishops during the period, pp. 228–49.

2. See Concilium Limense 1538; Francisco Haroldus, *Lima Limata Conciliis* (Rome, 1673). In this collection one can also find the synodal constitutions of Toribio de Mogrovejo. Franciscus A. de Montalvo, *Concilia Limana* (Rome, 1684). Juan Tejada, *Colección de Cánones y de todos los concilios de la Iglesia de España y de América*, 6 vols. (Madrid, 1859). *Apuntes para la historia eclesiástica del Perú hasta el gobierno del VII Arzobispo* (Lima, 1873). *Colección de bulas, breves y otros relativos a la Iglesia de América y Filipinas*, 2 vols. (Brussels, 1879). Lisson Chávez, *Colección de documentos para la historia de la Iglesia en el Perú*, 5 vols. (Seville, 1943–47). Rubén Vargas Ugarte, *Concilios Limenses*, 2 vols. (Lima: Tip. Peruana, 1951–54). "Episcopado de las diócesis del Virreinato del Perú desde los orígenes hasta mediados del Siglo XVII," in *Boletín del Instituto de Investigaciones Históricas* (Buenos Aires) 24 (1940–): 1–31. E. Dussel, *Les évêques hispanoaméricains*, devotes Chapter 3 to a study of the Hispano-American councils and synods.

was not always based on the lofty evangelical interests that they mouthed.

Religious as an institutional body did not play as decisive a role in the social struggle on behalf of the Indians as did the bishops. Exercising their pastoral responsibility, the bishops on the Latin American continent viewed their situation from the standpoint of the native population and acted accordingly.[3] It was the bishops of Spanish America who fleshed out their commitment to the oppressed by trying to defend and protect the native Indians. In practice that amounted to defending the peasants. Their underlying motivation was clearly evangelical and missionary. The native-oriented work of those men was truly historic. It was a concrete sign of their evangelical caliber. Holiness to them meant experiencing God through a commitment to the Indians.[4]

The firmness and generosity of the early bishops in protecting the Indians reveal their grand missionary mystique and their human sensitivity. It also makes up for certain flaws in their vision, such as their inability to see the structural factors involved in the conquest and domination of the Indians. Of course Bartolomé de las Casas and a few other bishops glimpsed the deeper roots of the Indians' terrible plight,[5] but the bishops

---

3. E. Dussel, *Les évêques hispanoaméricains,* presents his working hypothesis in Chapter 3: The essential aim of the episcopal institution was to protect the Indian and in fact it performed that task. He seeks to study the Indian as present in the historical awareness of the bishops of the Indies, with all the ambiguity and unevenness in their approaches to their pastoral mission. See pp. 93f. and pp. 102f.

4. Ibid., p. 227: "The Spanish-American bishops of the sixteenth century fully understood, though they may not have expressly been conscious of the fact, that a catechumenate pedagogy of signs called for a 'struggle for justice' as the first step. Only then could the Indian grasp the sense of evangelization. The bishop was the *protector of the Indians.* He preached the gospel and administered baptism because he first defended the Indian and offered a comprehensible sign *in the realm of civilization.* This is what enabled people to move on to the supernatural plane of the gospel message."

5. Ibid., p. xii: "While the church . . . fought against the injustice and the servitude foisted on the Indian, it did not rise up against the structures causing them. Only the actions of Las Casas and the synods held by Juan del Valle, a stubborn follower of Las Casas, went to the heart of the question and anticipated the whole nativist problem"; see ibid., p. 103. J. B. Lassegue, *La larga marcha de las Casas* (Lima: Ed. CEP, 1974), passim. Las Casas himself viewed the practice of giving Indians as payment as the cause of corruption (see *Historia de las Indias,* Book III, Chap. 90, pp. 103–5). He maintained that the exploitation of the Indians

tended to be more concerned about the ill treatment that resulted from the system of exploitation than about the system itself.

The evangelical and social richness of this option for the Indians did not lead to a theological reformulation of the religious life. Between 1504 and 1620, 66 percent of the bishops were religious, but this was not a central concern for them. However, their desire to serve the Indians did lead them to question the lifestyle of their religious collaborators. In a letter that he wrote near the end of February 1561, Bishop Vasco de Quiroga severely criticized the luxury and the excessive number of covents, and he proposed a reform of the various orders of nuns. In 1594 the bishop of Quito, Luis López Solís, wrote in a similar vein. He had formerly been the Provincial of the Augustinian Fathers in Peru, and he now decided to tackle the evil at its roots. He would embark on a visitation to investigate the lifestyle and habits of religious in order to restore some restraint and force them to live a more disciplined life.[6] Archbishop Lobo Guerrero also stressed the need for reform, pointing out that the religious in his region had increased their property holdings to the point where "they possess more than a third of the land's real estate."[7]

These criticisms do point to real problems, but they should not be generalized.[8] Religious arrived on the continent to risk their lives on

---

by the Spaniards was the basis of accumulation and profit: There was the encomienda system, the allotment of land in more rural areas, and the *mita* (enforced Indian labor) in the mines.

6. Lisson Chávez, *Colección de documentos*, 2:595; 4:117.

7. Ibid., 4:584.

8. In the middle of the sixteenth century the superior of the Mercedarian order in Peru expressed his concern to have religious who strictly observed the rules: "The land is so fit and ready that . . . I need your help in this. When this land was discovered, you asked friars to come from the Franciscan and Dominican orders. Please have them continue to come . . . because the members of those orders always have displayed brotherhood. Today their members seem to maintain the best observance among the mendicant orders, and more good example is needed in these new lands. It seems to me that you should populate the land here with those two orders and prohibit others from coming. Besides not bearing any fruit in the land, the others have no relationships with anyone except as lay people with their own interests and desires for profit. They give bad example and the Indians are scandalized by so much diversity . . ." (in Victor Barriga, *Los Mercedarios en el Perú en el siglo XVI*, Arequipa, 1939, 2:114–15). See also E. Cárdenas, "Vida religiosa y situaciones históricas," *CLAR* 15 (Bogotá, 1974), especially Chap. 3, pp. 81–101.

behalf of the gospel message and the Indians.[9] Rather than following the norms set down in some code, they had inscribed certain precious recommendations in their hearts. "Let them not use any Indian male or female to serve their own necessities."[10] They were to win over the Indians "with humility and demonstrations of love, . . . adapting themselves to the ability of each individual, accepting their ignorance, and working patiently." They were not to accept money payments or stipends from the king or the owners of estates "except what is required to buy a coarse habit and a meager meal.'" All the alms collected in a given day were to be distributed to the poor or handed over to their prelate; they were not to keep one penny for themselves. They were not to accept silver, gold, or any other metal from the Indians. All they could accept from the Indians was vegetables. Their sole concern should be to acquire souls for God, showing the Indians that "religious are not after riches in their land, as are other Spaniards, but rather want to introduce faith and virtue into their souls."[11]

The concrete reality of religious life on the continent of Latin America was one of missionary work and evangelization. Its institutional forms, however, were transported from Europe and left intact, with all their strong points and their limitations. Both in their exterior style and their internal life the monasteries and convents of Latin America were faithful reproductions of their European counterparts. The influence of the viewpoints held by people like Montesinos, Bartolomé de las Casas, and Juan

---

9. E. Dussel, Les évêques hispanoaméricains, pp. 107–8: "In fact religious . . . were the first to raise their voices in defense of the Indians on the basis of evangelical principles." On December 21, 1511, a sermon by Antonio de Montesinos would have a profound impact on Las Casas. It said bluntly that the exploitation of the Indians was a rejection of the gospel message: "A voice crying in the wilderness . . . You all are in mortal sin. You will live and die in it for the cruelty and tyranny you exercise against these innocent victims" (Las Casas, Historia de las Indias, Book III, Chapter 4, I, p. 176).

10. From almost the very start bishops and religious were adamant about not having domestic servants in their houses or convents. See E. Dussel, Les évêques hispanoaméricains, p. 103. The same insistence can be found in the diocesan synods of Toribio de Mogrovejo. Following the same tradition, the Peruvian bishops again brought up the matter of domestic servants in their 1973 document on evangelization (4.3.2).

11. The eight recommendations, reports Calancha, were given to the missionaries. They are reprinted in David Rubio, Los Agustinos en el Perú (Lima, 1912), p. 32.

del Valle is not readily apparent in the religious view of obedience, chastity, and religious consecration. It is somewhat more apparent perhaps in such matters as poverty and the imitation of Christ. These missionaries simply were not preoccupied with the notion of reformulating the religious life in terms of mission.[12] Missionary practice did not automatically lead to a new theological outlook on the religious life itself.

Martin de Porres was a black halfbreed. His life points up both sides of the picture. On the one hand the religious orders were anxious to find native personnel, and that fact indicates a certain degree of openness. On the other hand various restrictions were taken over from canonical legislation, so Martin remained a lay brother. No real attempt was made to rethink the religious life in terms of the cultural and spiritual word of the Indian, the mulatto, and the *cholo*. While bishops and religious institutions struggled to admit the natives to sacred orders and the religious life,[13] their concern for indigenous development was not strong enough to produce a new kind of religious life. It simply represented a way of protecting the Indians and recognizing their dignity.

Close study of the history of chapters, congregations, and assemblies held during the colonial period, when members of various religious orders were working in Latin America, would certainly give us a clearer picture of the contibutions made to practical innovation and spiritual maturation in the religious life by their work among the poor people of Latin America. The historical roots for a theology of the religious life based on Latin American realities must be explored, although I cannot undertake that task here.[14]

Religious communities transplanted from abroad have not been the only ones to flourish in Latin America.[15] Throughout its history many

---

12. E. Dussel, *Les évêques hispanoaméricains*, pp. 80–91. He dedicates this section to religious, focusing on their relationship to the patronate and exemption, the relationship between religious superiors and bishops, and the rights and privileges of religious in the mission field.

13. *Lima Limata Conciliis*, passim.

14. See, for example, Vicentius Maria Fontana, *Constituiones, declarationes et ordinationes Capitulorum Generalium sacri ordinis Fratrum Praedicatorum ab 1220 ad 1650* (Rome, 1872); *Analecta Franciscana sive Chronica aliaque documenta ad historiam Fratrum Minorum spectantia* (Quaracchi, 1885–).

15. In Chap. 8 of the *Apparatus historicus* to *Lima Limata Conciliis*, we find an extensive treatment of the convents of religious men and women and of the works to which they were dedicating themselves. In Lima we find the foundation of St. Clair with 302 professed nuns and novices; the Immaculate Conception order had

native organizations have also appeared, seeking to tackle very precise and often prophetic tasks. They have sought to provide pastoral workers in rural areas without priests or to serve various ethnic groups, for example. In general, however, they were not able to escape the theology of the religious life that underlay their juridical and legal framework. Much charismatic richness can be found in the forms of their mission, but they did not reformulate any of the traditional principles of the theology of the religious life. We find a certain amount of freedom in the fields of their apostolate and even in their organization of community life, but we also note a total dependence on the classical grounding and theological understanding of the religious life.[16] In short, we can rightly say that the generous-hearted presence and activity of religious among the poor of Latin America has not been sufficiently illuminated by an alternative, liberative vision and a corresponding political option.[17]

We religious have been sensitive to personal and community appeals from the lowly and abandoned to lead a simple, austere life. We have even maintained the thrust of the first-generation missionaries to defend native rights and to seek solutions for the injustice that is the plight of the

---

279 nuns; the nuns of St. Catherine of Siena had 220; and so forth. In his diocesan councils and synods Toribio de Mogrovejo tried to make sure that they were truly observing their rules.

16. For the location and kinds of work being done by religious on our continent today see Cecilio de Lora, "Estudio sociográfico de los religiosos y religiosas en América Latina," CLAR, Perspectivas, no. 2 (Bogotá, 1971). For Peru see Boletín, no. 4, of the Conference of Religious, November 1970, which contains a map of the distribution of religious in the country; it remains indicative of the present situation. For a historical approach focusing on the monastic life see M. C. Cymbalista et al., "Le monachisme en Amérique Latine," Chronique in Collectanea Cisterciensia (a review devoted to monastic spirituality), 35, no. 1 (1973):70f.

17. In general we can probably give the same evaluation to religious that E. Dussel (Les évêques hispanoaméricains, p. 103) gives to the bishops who followed Las Casas and to those who simply favored indigenization. José Mariátegui is right when he says: "All theses about the native problem that ignore it as a social and economic problem are sterile theoretical exercises and often purely verbal efforts; they are bound to be completely discredited. Their good faith does not save any of them. In practice all of them have merely served to distort the real nature of the problem. . . . The native question is rooted in our economy, in the system of land ownership" (Siete ensayos de interpretación de la realidad peruana, Havana: Casa de las Américas, p. 23; Eng. trans. Seven Essays on the Interpretation of Peruvian Reality, Austin: University of Texas Press, 1971).

majority. The social apostolate of many of our religious institutions bears witness to all that. But neither the liberation project nor the serious efforts of the poor to break free of their exploited condition has been a part of our institutional commitment to them. Our political awareness has depended largely on the level of political awareness to be found among those to whom we have dedicated our efforts. Even a more clearly political view of our commitment to the oppressed does not guarantee any prompt or automatic reformulation of our theology of the religious life. History shows us that religious were highly politicized at various times, as were their congregations,[18] but this politicized existence did not lead explicitly or in print to a reformulation of the spiritual and religious life as an institution and a topic of theological conceptualization.

The ambiguities and limitations of the commitment of religious to the native population do not invalidate the standpoint from which they sought to be faithful to the gospel message and their religious vocation. Instead they encourage us to go back and pick up the only path that will ensure that the message will be a liberative one. The path of the lowly and the poor is the only one that will ensure the meaningfulness and fruitfulness of religious life for the world.

The magnificent testimony of entire communities of generous, evangelical religious summons us to the challenge of re-creating the religious life on our continent in terms of our mission to evangelize the Indian masses, the common people, and the exploited classes.

New Perspectives

Our aim, then, is not a liberation-oriented restoration of religious life in its classic form. Instead we stand at a new starting point. The novelty lies in the central and perduring fact that we must relate our religious lives to the concrete life and vitality of the gospel message in the church of the common people. The only authentic newness can come from living that message in a church that grows out of the poor, the oppressed, the exploited, and the marginated.

Neither am I talking simply about some new vision of the religious life. There can be no new vision or reconceptualization of the religious life apart from a new historical way of experiencing what it means to be a

---

18. Armando Nieto, "La Iglesia—La acción del clero," in *Colección Documental de la Independencia del Perú* (Lima, 1972), vols. 1–2. It presents many testimonials by priests and religious who took an active part in the struggles for emancipation.

religious. Such an experience must be rooted in the life and death of the poor, in the hopes and struggles of the disinherited, and in the anguish and isolation of those races which have been shunted aside. The spiritual thrust of Christian communities centered around the people is coming to be the locus for a new hermeneutics of the gospel message, for a new understanding of what the church is as the sacrament of universal salvation, and for a new way of making history and doing politics. It is the soil for the prophetic rethinking that we call the theology of liberation.

In this book I should like to share certain thoughts that may help us to rework the central themes of the religious life. They stem from the practice of our brothers and sisters, and their communities, in our land.[19] I do not claim that they exhaust the topic, nor would I propose to universalize these suggestions.[20] They do not represent a full treatise on

---

19. Claude Geffré, *Un nouvel âge de la théologie* (Paris: Ed. du Cerf, 1972), p. 49; Eng. trans., *A New Age in Theology* (New York: Paulist Press, 1974): "Because of the inevitable pluralism of present-day life and experience, there will be various theologies covering scattered and fragmentary aspects of human life. None of these theologies can provide a coherent, complete synthesis of faith. This creates a new situation for the magisterium, which cannot presume to judge a new theological discourse without trying to comprehend its philosophical and cultural presuppositions." See Leonardo Boff, "Vida religiosa en el contexto latinoamericano: oportunidad y desafío," paper delivered at the Second International Conference of Religious in Bogotá, October–November 1974, and reprinted in *Mensaje Iberoamericano* (Madrid), no. 110 (December 1974): 16–20, as well as in *Vida Religiosa*, no. 238 (March 1975). The author attempts to present "the classical themes re-examined and revised from the standpoint of the situation in which God has placed us" (p. 2, section 1.5). His comments are very worthwhile. However, it is not clear in what respect the religious life is reformulated in terms of incarnational practice, and his reflection on religious life is not grounded on liberation practice as a specifically political practice.

20. Claude Geffré, *Un nouvel âge*, p. 13: "However, theology as a science of faith cannot give up its universal scope, its relatedness to every human intelligence be the person a believer or not. . . . A theology that simply justified the practice of a given local church would run the risk of turning into an ideology." I think that every theology is a particular one if it is precise reflection grounded on clearly defined facts and processes. Because it is reflection based on faith, it is a real reformulation of experiences whose dynamism and richness overflow any effort to offer a new synthesis of them. That is what theology is, by the way. It is a synthetic reinterpretation of faith experiences based on the concrete forms they take in the historical praxis of liberation. Theology has a universal perspective not just as a scientific formulation of the faith but also as a dynamics of life and a spiritual experience. It is universal in the sense that no achievement of liberation is

the theology of the religious life. But I am convinced that the outlook of liberation theology can contribute to a reconceptualization of the religious life.[21] This is all the more true because liberation theology has been sparked and nourished by the dynamism of Christian communities made up of the common people in which religious men and women participate throughout the Latin American continent. The theology has emerged only insofar as prophetic practice opened the way for it.[22]

However, religious life in Latin America is not being revitalized solely by the liberative praxis of religious. It is also being revitalized by the historical practice of the populace, by communities broader than our

the property of those who attain it. Every advance is universal because of its underlying collective structure. That holds true for theology as well, for the salvation on which it reflects in its work is collective.

See H. Assmann's description of theology as being provisional and humble in "Reflexión teológica a nivel estratégico-táctico," Encuentro Teológico (meeting held in Bogotá in July 1971), p. 76. J. C. Scannone evaluates the acceptability of Assmann's position in "Teología y política: El actual desafío al lenguaje teológico latinoamericano de liberacíon," in Fe cristiano y cambio social en América Latina, the 1972 El Escorial Convention (Salamanca: Sígueme, 1973), p. 260; see also the section entitled "Visión de síntesis del significado universal de la teología latinoamericana," ibid., pp. 370–71. Faith turns into ideology when it does not start off from the poor. See footnote 26 of E. Dussel's article, "Dominacíon—Liberacíon," Concilium 96 (1974): 347. On the conception and function of theology, its provisional nature and its relation to a given context, see the valuable remarks of G. Gutiérrez, "Teología, Biblia y Misíon indígena," in Estudios Indígenas, CENAPI, 4 (1972): 18–25.

21. I am concerned to stress the point that every overall effort at theological reflection must include a treatment of the religious life. That is what we find in Lumen gentium, for example. The point is stressed by Raphael Schulte, "La vie religieuse comme signe," in L'église de Vatican II, vol. 3, 1966 (Unam Sanctam, 51c); Schulte says: "The religious life is an expression of the essence of the church. If theologians wish to offer a fully valid theological and dogmatic description of the church of Christ, they must also offer a theological examination of the position of the religious state within the church as the people of God and the Mystical Body" (p. 1093). The theological outlook of Schulte is the classic one; he starts off from the Trinity, from the Word. There is not the slightest hint of a vision based on the overall and conflict-ridden reality of history or starting off from there to re-examine the theology of the religious life.

22. See E. Dussel, Historia de La Iglesia en América Latina: Coloniaje y liberación 1492–1972 (Barcelona: Nova Terra, 1974), p. 285: "The realization that theology was part of an oppressed culture did not come at once. First came the prophets, who started the process. Theology follows them later."

formal religious communities, and by movements more extensive than our spiritual families.[23] It is this source that is giving rise to unsuspected perspectives and also tensions. It may also be the standpoint which will make it possible for us to move away from a theology based on a legalistic and canonical conception of the religious life. Such a theology still leaves its imprint on the life of many communities today, though it may be presented in a better way.[24] What we find, then, is a rather monolithic

---

23. By way of example I might mention the convention of basic or grassroots Christian communities in Vitoria, Brazil, in January 1975; see *SEDOC*, vol. 7, May 1975. C. Gerest points out that "spiritual movements are something completely distinct from mere reform of the church. Reforms can be accomplished simply by correcting abuses or revitalizing the 'canons' of thought, law, or practice. A movement seeks to go back and recapture some impulse, not principles or rules. Its opposition to orthodoxy, which is frequently observable, is no mere accident. Concern to keep theological reasoning correct and to focus on the preciseness of formulas may threaten to nullify the desire for renewal in spirit" ("Movimientos espirituales e instituciones eclesiales," in *Concilium* 89, 1973,pp. 340–41).

In our case the movement is one in which political praxis constitutes the new locale of spiritual and hence theological experience. See Raúl Vidales, "La Iglesia latinoamericana y la política después de Medellín," IPLA (Quito), 15–16 (1972); S. Galilea, "El despertar espiritual y los movimientos de liberación en América Latina," *Concilium* 89 (1973): 425–31; Eng. trans.: "Spiritual Awakening and Movements of Liberation in Latin America," *Concilium* 89: 129–38; Rolando Muñoz, *Nueva conciencia de la Iglesia en América Latina* (Santiago, 1973; Salamanca: Sígueme, 1975); "Dos experiencias típicas de las comunidades cristianas latinoamericanas comprometidas en el movimiento de liberación," *Concilium* 96 (1974): 431–39; Eng. trans., "Two Community Experiences in the Latin American Liberation Movement," *Councilium* 96: 137–47; There are two anthologies of statements and viewpoints by such communities: *Signos de renovación* (Lima, 1969); Eng. trans., *Between Honesty and Hope* (Maryknoll, N.Y.: Maryknoll Publications, 1970); *Signos de liberación* (Lima: CEP, 1973).

24. A. Veilleux, "Evolution de la vie religieuse dans son contexte historico-spirituel," in *Collectanea Cisterciensia*, 32, no. 2 (1970): 129–54. This synthesis is valuable because it is very clear and because it stresses the richest strands of development. The author maintains that history shows clearly that renewal of the religious life comes from the grassroots level, from the activity and holiness of the Spirit operating there, not from canonical, bureaucratic, or institutional reform. Reform of the religious life based primarily on institutional reform proves to be a failure (p. 138). The same held true for Pius V and the Council of Trent because the reform was juridical and institutional (p. 147). However, see the criticisms of A. de Vogue in *Revue d'Histoire Ecclesiastique* no. 2, 69 (1974): 45–53. De Vogue maintains that Veilleux's work is based on a systematic error and reveals a "theological

theology of the religious life in communities such as these.[25]

Throughout the history of the church we find movements growing up alongside the religious life that was officially recognized as such by the church. They paved the way for new forms of the religious life that eventually saw the light of day.[26] In church history the religious life is both a concrete experience and a perduring fact. When I talk about the theology of the religious life here, I am talking about this experience as it is reflected upon from the standpoint of faith. Only when the phenomenon of the religious life becomes a large-scale experience based on the project and praxis of liberation will we be able to gain a new understanding of its theological import and its spiritual content. It is in that experience that we find the nucleus for the further development of the religious life.[27]

However good practice may be, on the other hand, it does not automatically lead to a good theory. There is a need for serious efforts on the theoretical level to rework concepts and themes. We must recall the organic unity between practice and theory as well as their formal and methodological differences. Each has its own rationality and set of proper instruments.[28]

One conception of theology equates it with theory, making it synonymous with something abstract and idealistic. It is thus set in contrast to concrete experience and practice.[29] Insofar as the theology of

stance already taken." For the influence of scholastic thinking on the theology of the religious life see the remarks of Luis Artigas, "Sobre la oración del religioso apostólico," in CONFER (Madrid) 12, no. 45 (1973): 603–4.

25. Alvaro Restrepo, "De la 'vida religiosa' a la 'vida consagrada,' una evolución teológica," 3 vols., a doctoral thesis written at the Gregorianum in Rome, 1974. This excellent work by a Colombian Jesuit deals with theological reflection on the religious life in the twenty-five years that preceded Vatican II. On page 644 the author reminds us that "if the law really wants to foster 'life,' it must respect and incarnate the spirit of each institute."

26. See Veilleux, "Evolution de la vie religieuse," p. 152.

27. J. Kampschreur, "El nucleo de la evolución de la vida religiosa," Concilium 97 (1974): 143–47, adopts a personalist perspective in which politics and the common people have no place.

28. G. Gutiérrez, course notes on "Teoría y Práctica en K. Marx," 1973.

29. I share the keen observations of D. Chenu in "Expérience chrétienne et théologie," Spiritus, no. 49 (1972): "I think that the shift, not only in theory but also in practice, from a deductive theology to an inductive one is a phenomenon that does not hold good solely for new churches or mission experiences. It is the whole body of the church that is changing its behavior, its ways of governing, and its way of understanding the faith" (pp. 131–32). Further on he says: "I think that

the religious life is concerned, some feel that it cannot be expected to contribute to renewal. That view is correct if we regard theology simply as theoretical reflection which does not start out from, or end up with, historical practice.[30] One of the great contributions of liberation theology has been its highlighting of the relationship between theology and practice, and its insistence that the practice in question is the liberation practice of the exploited classes.[31] The changed method of doing theology in Latin America is the embodiment of an ideological and political change in the conception of history and the struggles for liberation as well as a valuation of ethnic and cultural factors.[32]

---

the locale for understanding human and Christian values is praxis, not primarily abstract principles. In other words, it is the *veritas vitae* of St. John: truth embodied in life. Truth is not some abstract thing which I bring to a concrete situation. The concrete situation itself is the locale for understanding the faith. . . . The witness of God's word can be discerned only in praxis, in an involvement with the world" (pp. 138–39).

30. Though his remarks operate on a very general level, there is much to be said for what C. Geffré brings up (*Un nouvel âge*, p. 12): The fact is that "praxis" has other elements that define it more precisely. It is not a matter of some Christian praxis in general but of the liberation praxis of the poor and the exploited. "Theology cannot rest content with being a justification of the magisterium's teaching or the transmission of some already established knowledge. As the actualization of God's word, theology is not faithful to its commitment if the life of the church in a given situation does not constitute its privileged locale, and if its interpretation of Christianity does not lead to renewal in the praxis of Christians."

31. In that sense it is not a matter of some risk but a perspective for which one has opted. See C. Bravo, "Notas marginales a la teología de la liberación," in *Ecclesiástica Xaveriana* 25, no. 1 (1974):49: "Liberation runs the risk of becoming a classist theology."

32. Raúl Vidales, "Cuestiones en torno al método en teología de la liberacíon," MIEC-JECI, Document 9, Lima, 1974; translated in the anthology *Frontiers of Theology in Latin America*, ed. Rosino Gibellini (Maryknoll, N.Y.: Orbis Books, 1979). Idem, "Logros y tareas de la teología latinoamericana," *Concilium* 96 (1974): 423–30; Eng. trans., "Some Recent Publications in Latin America on the Theology of Liberation," *Concilium* 96: 127–36; J. C. Scannone, "El actual desafío planteado al lenguaje teológico latinoamericano," *CIAS* (Buenos Aires), 211 (1972): 5–20. Scannone rejects any dialectical identification between faith and politics, whether it be Hegelian or Marxist. He advocates the historico-salvific unity of faith and politics. See J. C. Scannone, "El lenguaje teológico de la liberación,"*Víspera* 30 (1973): 41; idem, "Teología política: el actual desafío planteado al lenguaje latinoamericano de liberación," *Fe cristiana y cambio social*, pp. 247–65; idem, "Necesidad y posibilidades de una teología socio-culturalmente

This new perspective in doing theology offers the possibility for theological creativity,[33] for challenging the erudite obtuseness that sometimes seems to mark theological reflection. Yet the latter sometimes accuses liberation theology of being very uncritical and lacking in rigor, or of being a "rhetorical theology" which is too "Christian" and too spiritual.[34]

---

latinoamericana," ibid pp. 353–72. Juan Luis Segundo, "La teología: problema latinoamericano," IDOC 14 (1968); idem, "Instrumentos de la teología latinoamericana," paper at a theological convention in July 1971: "The fact is that the interaction between social praxis and theology is the most decisive methodological fact for present and future Latin American theology. This comes down to saying that no authentic theology will exist here without the methodological contribution of sociology" (p. 41). Luis N. Pagon, "Teología y praxis de liberación," ibid. Carlos Welsch, "¿Puede el proletariado hacer teología?" *Pastoral Popular* 21, 126 (1971): 45–48. Pedro Negre Rigol, "La significación de los cambios metodológicos de las ciencias sociales para la interpretación teológica," Convention on liberation theology, IDOC, 71-181-012, reprinted in *Fe y política*, ISAL, 1974. Symposium on "Liberación Latinoamericana" in *Stromata*, January–July 1972, pp. 3–194. E. Javier Alonso Hernández, "Reconceptualización de la teología en America Latina," *Revista de Ciencias Morales Pentecostés* 28 (1972): 25–38. Carlos Bravo, "Notas marginales a la teología de la liberación," in *Ecclesiastica Xaveriana* (Bogotá) 24, no. 1 (1974): 40–50. See G. Gutiérrez, *A Theology of Liberation*, Eng. trans. (Maryknoll, N.Y.: Orbis Books, 1973), Chap. 2, pp. 25–36; J. L. Segundo, "Teología y ciencias sociales," in El Escorial anthology *Fe cristiana y cambio social*, pp. 285–95.

33. C. Geffré has caught this methodological angle and expressed it lucidly: "This approach obviously represents a revolution when compared with a type of theology that reflects primarily on Christianity as a body of doctrines rather than as a line of action." See C. Geffré, "La conmoción de una teología profética," *Concilium* 96 (1974), pp. 304–7; Eng. trans., "Editorial: A Prophetic Theology," *Concilium* 96: 7–16; see G. Gutiérrez, "Teología, biblia y misión indígena," in *Estudios Indígenas*, CENAPI (Mexico, D.F.), 4 (1972): 17–36.

34. Such in my opinion are the belligerent and often contradictory remarks of A. Fierro in his work *The Militant Gospel*, Eng. trans. (Maryknoll, N.Y.: Orbis Books, 1977). Appealing to the demands of scientific and critical rigor, he finds liberation theology to be too rhetorical and unreflective as theology. He feels it is more homiletics than theology in a strict, critical sense (see pp. 323–29). But I think that theology must stay in touch with real practice if it is not to turn into mere ideology. Only in that way can it face up to the challenges posed by the mystery of the risen Christ. And this is very much in line with patristic tradition. I prefer the view that holds if you really pray, you are a theologian. It brings out the spiritual and contemplative dimension of theology. We do not do theology to know things in a more scholarly way but to become truly familiar with God and to love God.

All theology, including the theology of the religious life, finds new possibilities for progress and contributions from within the organic totality of the people's liberation process and Christian experience. For that reason we do not share such a view as that offered by Comblin:

The most obvious conclusion to be drawn from these theological essays is that the fundamental problem is of a practical nature rather than a theological nature. As we saw, it was relatively easy to reach agreement about the basic tenets of a theology of the religious life. Meanwhile confusion and obscurity remain when it comes to defining the practical orientation of renewal. At the very least theological renewal did not shed the hoped-for light on practical issues. By now theologians have made whatever contribution they possibly could. No more revelations can be expected from theology itself whereas the problem remains unsolved.[35]

Starting from precisely the opposite viewpoint, some expect to see a revitalization of the theology of the religious life through a theoretical revitalization of its doctrinal principles.[36] Rather than starting off from the new experiences in Christian living that are found in the struggle for liberation, these people begin with an exegesis of the New Testament in which the political and cultural sphere does not serve as a vital mediating

---

Eastern tradition sees the monk in the same terms. The monk is "a theologian who knows how to pray." By dint of purification he becomes a practicing adept of God. See R. F. Esposito, "Monachesimo orientale e communità religiose nelle chiese della riforma," in the anthology *Per una presenza dei religiosi nella chiesa e nel mondo* (Turin, 1970), pp. 57–111; Peter Damian, Opus XV, 5, *P.L.* 145, col. 339. Damian points up the eminently pastoral function of the theologian when he says: "As the special role of the priest is to give himself totally to the offering of the divine sacrifice, so that of the theologian is to preach." Note the comment of J. A. Ubillus: "This spiritual dimension of theology is a permanent one. It must be rediscovered and put into practice once again. We must envision and elaborate a theology whose very elaboration will be simultaneously a spiritual activity" ("Dirección espiritual y concientización en América Latina," doctoral thesis for the Gregorianum, Rome, 1973, pp. 184–85).

35. J. Comblin, "A vida religiosa na sociedade actual," in the periodical *Perspectiva Teológica*, no. 5 (July–December 1971): 214; published by the theology department of Cristo Rei, São Leopoldo (Brazil).

36. One representative of this approach is Jules Cambier, "Théologie de la vie religieuse aujourd'hui," *Etudes Religieuses* (Brussels: CEP, n.d.) Cambier moves within the concept of *Perfectae caritatis*. His fine exegetical training led one to expect that he would probe more deeply into the biblical foundation of the religious life; and his personal experiences in Africa led one to expect a treatment based on the reality of the Third World (see pp. 13–15).

factor and then move on to a hot-house reformulation of dogmas.[37]

My attempt here is to offer reflections that begin by elaborating the overall perspective of our mission and the religious life.

RELIGIOUS COMMITTED TO THE POPULACE

A commitment to be with the poor and the common people and to be poor both as individuals and as communities in the religious life breaks down and replaces any concern to find religious identity in essentialist definitions. Instead we enter the dynamism of an ongoing process through which we seek to incorporate ourselves into the life and living conditions of those who are poorest.[38]

This is the missionary concern expressed by Paul when he reminds the Philippians about Christ. Jesus chose to immerse himself as a poor brother in the dynamism of human history so that people might be able to believe his message. He thought that was more important than any of his prerogatives as the Son of God.[39]

That is our perspective here in trying to deal with the themes and experiences of the religious life.

We must frankly admit that the world of the exploited classes is a reality that is culturally and racially remote from the experience of most religious. The age-old struggle of these classes for justice and their deeper aspirations[40] constitute a cultural experience and a historical project that calls for a commitment to the poor on our part and makes that commitment clearly political. It is in terms of this world that the religious life should be redefined. It is in terms of this world that religious can be

---

37. G. Barauna, notes for a course on the religious life given in Medellín (Colombia), 1972, to a group of Latin American Franciscans; see p. 13 of this text.

38. G. Gutiérrez, "Praxis de liberación, teología y anuncio," *Concilium* 96 (1974): 372–74; Eng. trans., "Liberation Theology and Proclamation," *Concilium* 96, pp. 57–77; E. Dussel, "Dominación–liberación, un discurso teológico distinto," ibid., pp. 337,342,349; Eng. trans., "Domination–Liberation: A New Approach," *Concilium* 96: 34–56.

39. L. Cerfaux, *Le Christ dans la théologie de S. Paul* (Paris: Ed. du Cerf, 1954): 283–97; Eng. trans., *Christ in the Theology of St. Paul* (New York: Herder & Herder, 1959).

40. See Rolando Mellafe, *Breve historia de la esclavitud en América Latina* (Mexico, D.F.: Ed. Sepsetentas, 1973). He deals with black slavery. There is a fine bibliography at the end of the book.

something meaningful for the others.[41] Any effort at renewal which bypasses such political and cultural mediation distorts the criteria laid down by Vatican II for sound renewal and is doomed to sterility.[42] For that reason I believe that general statements advocating orthopraxis[43] are correct, but inadequate in themselves. We must spell out the popular orientation and the class perspective involved in such orthopraxis.

Theological reflection on the religious life based on commitment to the poor requires the support of an interdisciplinary approach. Today theology is very open to the support of the human sciences and to interdisciplinary effort. But the combined assistance of new disciplines does not in itself guarantee that we will start from, or arrive at, a truly new and liberative perspective. We can be more scientific and rational in formulating a point of view that is ultimately conservative. We can fashion a theology that is wiser and more erudite, one that is more pastoral insofar as it is comprehensible to an enlightened public because it is framed in biblical and patristic terms. We can do all these things while still retaining the same political and ideological posture.

For that reason interdisciplinary dialogue in theology has real limitations if it does not imply a political commitment to liberation from the standpoint of the poor and exploited classes. Herein lies the real matrix and rationale for scholarly and theological work. Scholarly science and theology find their justification in being bound up with this historical task.[44] To start off from the exploited classes is also to encounter a cultural

---

41. See Antonio Fragoso, "Profetismo y compromiso concreto con la liberación de la clase trabajadora y campesina," *Pastoral Popular* 19 (1969): 11–16.

42. *Perfectae caritatis* points to a return to the gospel, to the founding charisms of an order, and to the signs of the times as the criteria for a satisfactory renewal of the religious life. I shall come back to this later. P. Raffin, "Resurgimientos espirituales y renovación de la vida religiosa," *Concilium* 89 (1973); Eng. trans., "Spiritual Revival and Renewal of the Religious Life," *Concilium* 89:139–48), insists that renewal in the Spirit is the key to renewal of the religious life. But how does this renewal in the Spirit operate? Which "stirrings in the world" are bearers of liberation? Raffin notes that the theology of the religious life is not neutral but he does not spell out in what sense they are not. He offers no people-centered perspective as the mediating political element for renewal.

43. See C. Dumont, "Les trois dimensions retrouvées en théologie: eschatologie, orthopraxie, herméneutique," *Nouvelle Revue Théologique* 92 (1970): 561–91.

44. G. Gutiérrez, section on "the practice of liberation" in "Praxis de liberación," *Concilium* 96, pp. 354–60; E. Dussel, Part II of "Dominación–Liberación," ibid., pp. 342f.

and racial perspective that leaves its peculiar mark on the political realm and that opens up new horizons in trying to outline the liberation struggle and the creation of the new human.[45] Theology born of liberation praxis must also be culturally and racially marked by the Christian communities composed of our dominated peoples.[46] It is not enough for theology to be the work of the community more than the work of individuals. It must also be the experience of Christian communities that are clearly class-based.[47]

---

45. See Ramiro Reynaga, "Lutte de classes et lutte des races in Amérique Latine," *Frères du Monde* 74 (1971): 80–85. He presents the history of Latin America as one of racial oppression. He points out how colonialism has seeped into revolutionary thinking and how class struggle might sometimes evade the whole tragedy of the native Indian. He also suggests that the avante-garde wing of the white revolution is seeking contact with the Indian masses. This work may help people not to lose sight of cultural and anthropological factors in the liberation project. His concern for the Indian, however, might cause him to neglect the political picture. Reynaga has also written a book entitled *Guerrillas blancas en las masas indias.*

46. See the theological symposium on "Théologies noires et sud-américaines de libération" organized by the "renewal" group of the W.C.C. in Geneva, May 1–4, 1973; *Lumière et Vie,* no. 120. (1975): *Théologie de la libération: les noirs ont la parole.* In it see the contributions of James H. Cone, "Prise de conscience des noirs et église noire"; idem, "Le Christ dans la théologie noire"; Joseph R. Washington, Jr., "La mission du peuple noir: 'peuple élu' et serviteur souffrant." CERIT sponsored a discussion of liberation theologies in Latin America at the University of Strasbourg; the proceedings were published as *Théologies de la libération en Amérique Latine* (Paris: Ed. Beauchesne, 1974). Y. Congar reviewed the debate ("Libération et salut") in *Revue des Sciences Philosophiques et Theologiques* 58, no. 4 (October 1974): 664–65. Insofar as the contribution of E. Ibarra is concerned, the judgment of H. de Lavalette is more correct: "A very tendentious exposition. He tends to turn liberation theology into the latest of the passing fads. He sees Medellín as a sop thrown to aroused Christians. What he really fears is politicization." See the "Bulletin de théologie politique" in *Recherches de Science Religieuse,* no. 4 (October–December 1974): 605–30. G. Gutiérrez, "Teología, Biblia y misión indígena," *Estudios Indígenas,* pp. 32–34.

47. That is why we must fill out the remark that Luis del Valle has offered on this subject in "El papel de la teología en América Latina" (reprinted in *Liberación en América Latina,* Bogotá: Ed. America Latina, 1971, pp. 17–33). He says that "the thinking subject who does the theological reflection cannot be simply the professional theologian or the teacher. The subject must be every level of 'the community' . . ." (p. 28). I agree with the conclusion of Marcel Xhaufflaire: "The

A commitment to the political project of the exploited classes raises serious doubts about the individualistic perspective that continues to characterize the spiritual life and the various forms of the religious life. Viewed from the standpoint of the common people, the political realm reveals and challenges the limitations of a perspective that served as a cover for the individualistic orientation of our methods of training and many of the values and virtues inculcated. A populist political standpoint offers us a perspective that is collective, communitarian, and universal.

A political commitment to the oppressed does more than challenge the prevailing individualistic view of the religious life. It also uncovers a highly intramural perspective which prevails both in the church and among religious congregations. This perspective is evident in the work of religious and in many efforts for renewal of the spiritual life on both the individual and the community level. The realm of politics and the realm of the common people as inseparable categories require us to reconsider the mission of the church and ecclesial communities. We must not only open up to the world in general terms; we must do it from a platform both more concrete and more specific, more conflict-ridden even though more fraught with hope.

For many committed Christians in the religious life here in Latin America, this new point of departure provides them a new perspective in trying to pinpoint and comprehend the tensions involved in renewal efforts. It is an asset in trying to explore the basic charisms of their congregation. Liberation theology is a new point of departure in any effort to reinterpret the central problems of the Christian experience. The popular classes struggling for their human liberation constitute this starting point rooted in history. They are not only the motivating factor and the takeoff point but also the point of arrival. In them the message becomes once again a transforming force, the community becomes an agent of liberation, and theology becomes a spiritual experience.[48]

---

most correct way of theology to involve itself as theology in the area of revolutionary political struggle is to find its articulation in the counter-institutional practice of 'grassroots groups.' . . . It is there that this theology will be revitalized" ("Paradigme de la théologie politique et problèmes institutionnels ecclésiaux," in *La théologie positive,* Paris: Ed. du Cerf, 1972). See R. Muñoz, "Dos experiencias típicas de las comunidades cristianas latinoamericanas compremetidas en el movimiento de liberación," *Concilium* 96 (1974): 431–39.

48. G. Gutiérrez, "Praxis de liberación," *Concilium* 96, pp. 372–74.

Thanks to the ground broken by liberation theology,[49] we hope that we will soon be able to reconsider and reformulate the central experiences and elements associated with a theology of Latin American religious life. Such reflection is urgently needed by those of us who work on this continent. And we are bold enough to think that it could also enrich the theological reflection being done on the religious life on other continents.[50] But here again we do not propose to standardize everything, falsely to universalize reflections and experiences. One cannot maintain that there is only one possible theology of the religious life.[51]

The perspective we would like to see worked out seriously in Latin America is the one raised by Tillard when he talks about "faith and mission." Unfortunately he leaves it aside in his brilliant reworking of previous essays that was published in a recent volume.[52] Basically we must move to a new conception of charity. Instead of regarding charity as "aid due to one's neighbor" we must view it as work "performed on behalf of justice, peace, and freedom for others." So it is not simply a matter of opening up to the complex and conflict-ridden realm of politics as the mediation of the religious life. As Tillard rightly senses, we are talking about the very level at which the necessary reformulation of the religious life must be undertaken.[53]

---

49. There is a point to C. Duquoc's preference for talking about a theology of the *acts* of liberation. It might be even better to talk about a theology of the liberation *process*. This would suggest the idea of continuity, progress, and maturation in liberation through the various actions that embody it. See *Cahiers Evangile*, "Libération des hommes et salut en Jésus-Christ, une étude biblique" (2nd part) 7, pp. 11–13.

50. *Concilium* 97 (1974) is concerned with the topic of the religious life. It is exclusively European in its composition. Thus it embodies some of the theological reflection now going on, but it also displays complete ignorance of religious life on other continents.

51. G. Barauna, notes for a course on the religious life given in Medellín, p. 8; A. Restrepo, *De la vida religiosa*, p. 868.

52. J.M.R. Tillard, *Devant Dieu et pour le monde. Le projet des religieux* (Paris: Ed. du Cerf, 1974), is a collection of reworked studies that is serious, erudite, capable of shedding light on many questions and stimulating further search.

53. Ibid., pp. 47–48. It is not the professed life that will serve as the best perspective for understanding faith and mission. My point of departure is the praxis of liberation and an option for the exploited classes. This is the irreplaceable historical mediation of any attempt to reconsider the religious life as a project. Tillard operates from a different perspective. It would have been enriched, if not altered, if he had taken some account of the more worthwhile points of European

In Latin America we are experiencing the anguish that comes from hearing the cries of oppressed peoples and cultures. As religious we glimpse the inconsistencies and betrayals that have marked the history of many of our communities here. They have been disloyal to the demands of the living gospel summons embodied in the poor of our continent. Yet the poor are a source of hope as well as of reproach, for they also help us to open up and invite us to share their hopes. The conversion and renewal of religious in Latin America must operate through the mystery of Jesus as it is revealed in the poor on our continent and lived amid their struggles.

Here in Latin America, however, we do not possess any finished future model.[54] What confronts us is the challenge of a continent that invites us to give new life to the gospel message by giving new life to people's deepest aspirations. There is no automatic mechanism for the renewal of our religious life.[55] Concrete experience reveals our ability to incorporate the novel historical reality of the liberation struggle into our old schemas and motivations dealing with the religious life. To believe and dare in the Spirit is to assert that we can overcome the existing situation, and then courageously to accept the consequences of such an assumption.

In all its various manifestations the religious life in Latin America must become one of the unsuspected embodiments of Christians committed to the liberation praxis of the oppressed. Otherwise it will lose the prophetic character that highlights its public structure. Religious life in Latin America is not anonymous. It moves in the realm of the explicit even though it may not chance to make explicit or to summon. Yet that is its horizon.[56] It is supposed to live in Jesus Christ, to proclaim and make explicit and summon in the effort of liberation praxis.

---

political theology. See the anthology *La pratique de la théologie politique* (Paris: Casterman, 1974).

54. M. Xhaufflaire, "Cristianismo crítico y vida religiosa," in Supplement to *La Vie Spirituelle* 23 (1970); also in *Selecciones de teología*, 40, 10 (1971); A. Durand, "Recherches sur le sens de la vie religieuse," *Lumière et Vie* 96 (1970): 54–90. Besides being open enough not to decide the forms of the religious life in advance, we must link it with the "agents" of a new creation (i.e., the poor) and their approach (i.e., the project of liberation). This point also applies to the article by H. Loeffen, "Entre el pasado y el futuro," *Concilium* 97 (1974): 138–42.

55. See B. Deleplanque, "La rénovation de la vie religieuse dans l'Eglise et le monde moderne," in Supplement to *La Vie Spirituelle* 78 (1966): 339–64; P. R. Regamey, "La vie religieuse dans la mutation du monde et de l'homme," Supplement to *La Vie Spirituelle* 88 (1969): 132–43, whose tone is rather polemical.

56. This seems to be equally valid for secular institutes. Their members do not make public their involvement with an institute, but their personal life and activity in the world is the same. They seek to have human beings recognize, live out, and proclaim the Father's love.

2

Approaches to the Religious Life

The richness of the religious life has found expression throughout history in a surprising variety of approaches and concrete experiences. At the risk of oversimplifying, I want to present some of the main approaches and outlooks here. To present a complete historical picture of the development of the religious life in eastern and western Christianity would be to go far beyond the bounds of this volume; and it would be rash to attempt a theological synthesis of the religious life at this point in time.

After considering some of the basic approaches to the religious life in this chapter, I shall proceed in the next chapter to consider some current Latin American approaches to the same issue.

A rapid survey of the voluminous literature on the religious life would enable us to discover the ideological, political, cultural, and theological presuppositions underlying reflection on the religious life. Worthy of particular attention would be a comparative study of the various descriptions of the so-called "crisis" in the religious life and of the factors that account for its development. Herein lies the starting point for any attempt to reinterpret the theology of the religious life.

However, we do not always find a direct relationship between analysis of society, interpretation of the causes for crises in the religious life, and one's theological focus. Take Vatican II's decree on the appropriate renewal of the religious life *(Perfectae caritatis)*, for example. It completely avoids offering any diagnosis of social and ecclesial realities that might serve as the framework for discussing religious renewal. It does not even touch the general level in which *Gaudium et spes* moves when it talks about the signs of the times.[1]

---

1. Vatican II, *Gaudium et spes*, Pastoral Constitution on the Church in the Modern World, Introductory Statement, nos. 4–10; all citations of Vatican II documents are from *The Documents of Vatican II* (New York: Guild-America-Association, 1966).

Closer to home, the Medellín document on religious also fails to relate to social and ecclesial realities. It does not incorporate into its outlook the perspectives mentioned in its message to the people of Latin America, its Introduction, and its document on peace. In these documents we find a discussion of the chief characteristics that mark Latin American life today: marginality, shocking inequalities between social classes, growing frustrations, ruling minorities and oppressed majorities, unjust exercise of power by a minority and growing awareness of their oppressed situation by the majority, international tensions, neocolonialism, nationalism, and so forth.[2] What is more, the Medellín document on the religious life does not even follow the format of the other Medellín documents. It does not start off with a diagnosis and it does not offer any doctrinal synthesis.

As is the case with some groups and communities, some authors of theological works on the religious life feel a growing need to analyze and interpret the central features of current changes and of present-day political, economic, social, and cultural realities. For it is in this context that the life of the church and of religious institutions moves. In these various efforts at description and interpretation we find much diversity and varying levels of understanding insofar as the social and scientific grasp of reality is concerned.[3] But on the whole I would say that critics of

---

2. Reference is to the documents of the Second General Conference of Latin American Bishops, which was held in Medellín, Colombia, in 1968. Citations will be from the official English edition edited by Louis M. Colonnese and published by the Latin American Division of the United States Catholic Conference, Washington, D.C., 2 vols. *The Church in the Present-Day Transformation of Latin America in the Light of the Council:* Vol. I, *Position Papers;* Vol. II, *Conclusions.*

3. Several presentations are cited here by way of example. E. Schillebeeckx, "Het nieuwe mens en Godsbeeld in conflict met het religieuze leven," *Tijdschfift voor Theologie* 7 (1969): 1–27; secularization challenges the orders and the religious life itself. See Alain Durand's illuminating article "Recherches sur le sens de la vie religieuse," *Lumière et Vie* 96 (January-February 1970): 51f; he sees cultural and anthropological change creating a crisis for the theological signification of the signs of the religious life. M. Llamera, "Crisis y reorientación de la vida religiosa," in *Teología Espiritual* 17 (1973): 7–70. Tillard devotes forty-five pages to a diagnosis of the crisis in the religious life in Chapter I of *Devant Dieu et pour le monde* (see note 52 of Chap. 1 in this volume). He, too, does not offer a socio-political vision of reality. His horizon is that of the nonbeliever and his world: secularization, crisis of faith, changing outlooks, and so forth. This is also the impression one gets from the Dutch Pastoral Council on Religious: Spanish edition, *Religiosos en una nueva sociedad* (Salamanca: Sígueme, 1971). See also: Candido Pozo, "La discussione sulla vita religiosa al Concilio pastorale olandese," in *Civiltà cattolica,*

the literature on the religious life have not devoted enough space to evaluating political and cultural presuppositions or the various features that characterize descriptions and interpretations of the crisis in the religious life.[4]

My intention here is to offer a brief summary of the main features to be found in certain approaches to describing and understanding the religious life. I shall try to pinpoint the most valid features and intentions to be found in each point of view.

Here I do not intend to get into the whole debate about the religious life as a consecrated way of life specifically. That debate can be fruitful, of course. But the use of language lends itself to confusion when we take the religious life to mean the form of Christian living that is officially recognized as such by the church. Moreover, the notion of a "consecrated life" often tends to suggest the less positive connotations of separation and escape. As A. Restrepo points out,

the theology of the consecrated life does not exclude the basic and important elements of the evangelical life that have been formulated by the theology of the

---

June 1970, pp. 540–54; the anthology *Presencia de los religiosos en la nueva sociedad* (Madrid: Instituto Teológico de Vida Religiosa, 1973); Canadian Religious Conference, *Les religieux et l'évangélisation du monde,* collection *Donum Dei,* no. 21, 1974. There is a quick overview of the crisis in "La vida según el Espíritu en las comunidades religiosas en América Latina," *CLAR,* no. 4, 1969. The same holds true for the theological reflection in "Vida religiosa en América Latina, sus grandes líneas de búsqueda," *CLAR,* no. 4, 1973. However, its focus is not as fruitful as some earlier documents, such as "Pobreza y vida religiosa en América Latina," *CLAR,* no. 20, 1974. The 1972 draft document of CLAR, "Vida religiosa y situación sociopolítica en América Latina," is an effort to reconsider certain features of the religious life from a more structural view of the continent. A pioneering effort to re-examine the theology of the religious life in terms of Latin American theological reflection is Luis Pérez Aguirre, *Teología latinoamericana pàra la crisis de la vida religiosa* (Buenos Aires: Ed. Guadalupe, 1973).

4. See P. Jacquemont, "La vie religieuse à l'heure de Vatican II" (Bulletin de Théologie), *Revue des Sciences Philosophiques et Théologiques* 52, no. 3 (1968); Vianney Delalande, "La théologie de la vie religieuse, états des recherches," in *Vocation* 249 (1970): 101–18; J. Beyer, "Premier bilan des châpitres de renouveau," *Nouvelle Revue Théologique* 95 (1973): 60–86; L. Renwart, "Théologie de la vie religieuse. Bulletin bibliographique," *Vie Consacrêe* 46 (1974): 104–16; Alvaro Restrepo's excellent work *(De la vida religiosa,* see note 25 of Chap. 1 in this volume) on the preconciliar literature focuses only on the relationship between Catholic Action and the clergy and the dispute between diocesan and religious priests as factors affecting the crisis of identity for religious.

religious life. But insofar as it stresses the typological and charismatic elements, it avoids any levelling that would have an adverse effect on the authenticity of the original heritage, and hence on the way that it should be lived and embodied in the Church.[5]

FOCUS ON BIBLICAL ORIGIN AND ROOTS

Monastic tradition has frequently presented the life of the monk as a continuation of the life of the early Christian community. A kind of apostolic succession is evident in that monks continue the way of life that the primitive community apparently followed.

John Cassian, a monk himself, talked about a real historical continuity between the apostolic community of the book of Acts and monasticism. The way of life described in Acts was common to all Christians. With the passage of time the majority of believers gave up the demands of the period immediately after Pentecost. It was then that monks began to withdraw from the common people and the cities to isolated areas in order to live lives of poverty, austerity, and prayerfulness.[6] Thus the term "monk," *jahid*, means beloved, preferred, well-beloved, solitary, isolated, and unique. For Pachomius it also means celibate. Monks are those who have dedicated themselves to the ideal of evangelical virginity out of a desire to follow Christ and the Apostles.[7]

It is not surprising that up to the twelfth century the religious life was synonymous with the apostolic way of life. The profession of the religious was seen to be prefigured in the profession of the original apostles voiced by Peter (Matt. 19:27). The monastic tradition was often referred to as the

5. A. Restrepo, ibid., "Conclusion," p. 868. See A. Severino, *Vida consagrada, sintesis teológica* (Madrid: Instituto Teológico sobre Vida Religiosa, 1973); Roger van Allen, "Religious Life and Christian Vocation," *Cross Currents* 22 (1972): 179–80.

6. M. H. Vicaire, *L'imitation des Apôtres* (Paris, 1963), pp. 19–20, 36–37, passim.

7. F. E. Morard, "Monachos, moine. Histoire du terme grec jusqu'au IV siècle. Influences bibliques et gnostiques," reprint from the *Freiburger Zeitschrift für Philosophie und Theologie* 20 (1973): 329–45. See the presentation of C. Kannengiesser, "Théologie Patristique" (Bulletins Critiques), *Recherches de Science Religieuse* 62 (1974): 3; A. Veilleux, "La théologie du l'abbatiat cénobitique et ses implications liturgiques," in Supplement to *La Vie Spirituelle*, no. 86 (1968): 351–94. This serious and instructive article on the cenobitic life in the East, its origin and development, enables us to appreciate the contribution of monasticism to the experience of common living *(koinonia)* of which Pachomius is regarded as the founder.

professio apostolica. In the twelfth century St. Bernard described the monastic profession as "renunciation of the world," and the "apostolic profession."[8]

Other currents of spiritual reflection saw monks as people who had reached a higher level of perfection by virtue of their ascetic efforts at purification and their service of praise to God. Indeed some saw them as angels on earth, and the monastic life as an "angelic life." To their flight from earth was added their flight into heaven. To some it would be seen as a flight to the paradise humankind had lost.

Thus there gradually developed what might be called a "monastic ideology." It pictured the life of monks as a life in the Absolute, a flight from the world, an angelic way of life in a paradise outside time and this world. Stressing the purely contemplative life, it did not focus on the correlative aspects of presence, responsibility, and mediation that would restore the totality of the Christian experience to the religious life.[9] Although it is clearly a fact that monasticism did adopt some platonic and pythagorean ideas, not all the deviations to be found in the religious life more recently can be charged to their account.[10]

We know that in the monasticism of the Qumran Essenes separation from the world was an important feature of the quest for holiness. Such separation did signify a participation in the life of the angels. Christianity proposed a different conception of holiness based on love for the world, service to fellow human beings, and a kind of presence that transformed our relationship with God, human beings, and the world. Congar has

---

8. See M. D. Chenu, "Moines, clercs, laics au carrefour de la vie évangélique (XII siècle)," in *Revue d'Histoire Ecclesiastique* 49 (1959): 59–89; I. E. Lozano, "De vita apostolica apud Patres et Scriptores monasticos," in *Commentarium pro religiosis et missionariis* (1971): 97–120; "De vita religiosa ut vita apostolica," ibid., 53 (1972): 3–23, 124–36; Manuel Garrido Bonaño, "La vida monástica en la contienda religiosa del siglo XII," in *CONFER* (Madrid) 2, no. 39 (April-June 1972).

9. See L. J. Bataillon and J. P. Jossua, "Le mépris du monde," *Revue des Sciences Philosophiques et Théologiques* 51 (1967): 27.

10. See L. Bouyer, *Le sens de la vie monastique* (Paris, 1970); J. Leclercq, *La vie parfaite, points de vue sur l'essence de l'état religieux* (Paris, 1958); idem, *Le message des moines à notre temps* (Paris, 1958); M. M. van Molle, "Aux origines de la vie communautaire chrétienne, quelques équivoques déterminantes pour l'avenir," in Supplement to *La Vie Spirituelle*, no. 88 (February 1969), pp. 101–21. The last cited article is the third and last of a series; the first two articles were published in the February 1968 issue (pp. 108–27) and the September 1968 issue (pp. 394–424).

good reason to ask whether the angelic is in the last analysis evangelical.[11]

The monastic life was not just an apostolic life. It prefigured and anticipated here on earth the form of our future life. The eschatological import of the religious life was concretely embodied in the way of life shaped by chastity, obedience, poverty, permanent contemplation, prayerful praise, availability to God, and life in common. Thus the religious life would serve as an anticipation of beatified life.[12] Underlying such a view, however, is a refusal to devote serious attention to terrestrial affairs and a radical relativization of history in the name of the other life.[13]

It is to the extent that the religious life incarnates evangelical values today that it continues to serve as a sign of the kingdom. Only a literal interpretation and direct application of the biblical verse, "You will be like the angels in heaven," could justify the notion that we religious are a preview of what our future life will be like.[14] But we religious definitely

---

11. Y. Congar, "La vie religieuse dans l'Eglise selon Vatican II," in *Vie Consacrée* 43, no. 2 (1971): 69f. See J. C. Didier, "Angélisme ou perspectives eschatologiques?" in *Mélanges de Science Religieuse* 11 (1954): 25–53.

12. R. Carpentier: "Being of a social order, the religious life establishes on earth a 'city' that seeks to correspond with the supernatural vocation. For its universal laws it chooses love, submission, total subjection to God the Father, and mutual charity. It is an order wholly oriented toward heavenly beatitude. At the very center of the militant church on earth we find an anticipation of the heavenly Jerusalem" (*Iniciación a la vida religiosa. Testigos de la ciudad de Dios*, p. 94).

13. See J. Daniélou, "Puesto de los religiosos en la estructura de la Iglesia," in the anthology edited by G. Barauna that contains studies on Vatican II's constitution on the church (*Lumen gentium*): *La Iglesia del Vaticano II* (Barcelona: Juan Flores, 1966). According to Daniélou, "by virtue of its detachment from riches, worldly pleasures, and ambitions, the religious life reminds us that earthly goods are not the ultimate ones. It directs our gaze toward the goods above" (p. 1129).

14. See for example G. M. Gozzelino, "La vita religiosa come segno e testimonianza," in the anthology *Per una presenza viva*, pp. 349–90 (see note 34 of chap. 1 in this volume). Gozzelino rejects a series of views on the specific nature of the religious life and manages to frame the problem well. However, he also tries to justify Vatican II's view of religious life as a "higher level or degree of charity." Granting that there is an abysmal distance between life on earth and life in celestial glory, he maintains that the religious life is the form of earthly ecclesial life that comes closest to the immediate relationship with God in heaven (see p. 374). At bottom, then, the religious life is the sign most capable of pointing to the future kingdom that is already present in the world. Thus he sticks close to the

are not previews or samples of the future life. Through our lifestyle we seek to serve as signs evoking the historical exigencies involved in the presence of the kingdom and its coming; and for that very reason we seek to incarnate those exigencies.

The important thing is not that other people should get some idea of what their own life will be in the future world when they look at us. Rather, in their own yearnings and struggles to transform the world they should be able to experience the love that is giving liberative content and a human face to our lives. Only in this way can we be signs of a very different sort of life rather than of the other life.[15]

The monastic life was also compared with a flight to paradise, and this notion has left its mark on some features of the spiritual life of religious.[16] The analogy of paradise suggested two things. On the one hand it evoked the state of life in which humans were originally created by God and his love. On the other hand it suggested the state of life that is perpetuated forever in paradise.[17]

---

thinking of Vatican II, regarding the religious life as a sign of the kingdom because it is closest to what the future life will be like. But what do we really know about the shape of this "future life"?

15. M. Rondet, "Signification ecclésiologique de la vie religieuse," in *Lumière et Vie* 19, no. 96 (1970): 150. Another view is that the religious life is the visible manifestation of God's gratuitous *gift*. See F. M. Genuyt, "Approche philosophique de la vie religieuse," in *Lumière et Vie* 19, no. 96 (1970): 107–8. He maintains that "religious somehow anticipate the coming of this *gift* through a lifestyle that tries to embody in advance the 'effects' which will be produced by this gift in its plenitude."

16. J. Leclercq, "Le cloitre, est-il un paradis?" in *Le message des moines à notre temps* (Paris, 1958), p. 141f; idem, *Etudes sur le vocabulaire monastique du moyen âge*, Studia Anselmiana 48 (Rome, 1961). Also see the remarks of R. Bultot in "Anthropologie et Spiritualité," *Revue des Sciences Philosophiques et Théologiques* 51, no. 1 (1967): 5, n. 7. Bultot feels that Leclercq does not point up the negative features of certain concepts.

17. G. M. Colombas, *Paraíso y vida angélica. Sentido escatológico de la vocación cristiana* (Monserrat, 1958), p. 246: "While a return to paradise does constitute one of the major monastic themes, it does not entail any simple regression to the state of the first human being. Rather than being a return to Eden, it signifies entry into the supraterrestrial kingdom of Christ. There all things are restored to their pristine being, including the order destroyed by the first sin. Here again the first paradise is used as an image of the eschatological paradise. Terms like *paradisus claustri* signify that future realities are already present somehow in monasteries, hermitages, and the huts of anchorites. There people are already living according

It is not suprising, then, that throughout Christian tradition some have attributed a divine origin to the religious life. To stress this divine origin is not necessarily to claim any superiority for religious. Rather, this view highlights the mediational character of the religious life and its role as a sacrament of salvation for others:

To dissociate the religious life from redemption is not only to demean it but to do something much worse. Such dissociation vitiates the redemption brought by Jesus Christ, the only redemption there is, the only one that saves human beings. As a part of redemption, the religious life is something that affects all the faithful and even all human beings. For even though not all are called to practice it, no one can be saved except by virtue of the one gospel that God revealed and the one redemption that God sent to human beings, from which the religious life is inseparable.[18]

Thus every theological approach must consider the theme of the divine vocation to which the religious life is one response. If theology does not do this, then it does not correspond with the gospel message, which proposes a particular way of following Christ; that way is fleshed out in the religious life.[19]

We can conclude this section with a few brief considerations on the role of Scripture in theological reflection on the religious life. This will permit us to examine a few basic theological principles stemming from doctrine and the thought of several authors.

The use of Scripture in theology is a central fact in the history of theology, and particularly in the history of dogma. Systematic theology

---

to the pattern of the angels." There is a French edition of this work also: *Paradis et vie angélique, Le sens eschatologique de la vie chrétienne* (Paris, 1963).

18. A. Bandera, "A ejemplo y en representación de Jesucristo, la consagración religiosa según 'Evangelica Testificatio,' " in *CONFER* (Madrid) 11, no. 39 (1972): 202. This is in line with the thought of Gilberto Crispin in the twelfth century: "Thus no one can be saved who does not adopt the life of the monk as far as he possibly can" (cited by Tillard, *Devant Dieu et pour le monde*, p. 101).

19. A. Bandera, "¿Radicalismo evangélico o pluralismo de la santidad?" in *CONFER* 11, no. 38 (January-March 1972): 22–33. The author presents an orthodox rehearsal of conciliar and magisterial doctrine, challenging the approach of evangelical radicalism and posing a series of objections to it. He seems to focus on the hermeneutic problem of Matthew 19. He also thinks that in the last analysis the approach of evangelical radicalism is based on an a priori sociological theory that reduces the people of God to the laity. See Severino M. Alonso, "Origen divino-cristológico de la vida religiosa," in *Vida Religiosa*, June 1971, pp. 501–3.

used exegesis to provide it with corroborative passages that proved its assertions. This methodological process embodies a specific conception of Scripture, not only with reference to the work of theology in the strict sense, but also with reference to the spiritual life and pastoral activity. But it also clearly embodies a particular stage in the scientific development and growth of exegesis itself.

Reducing Scripture to a series of passages that support theological formulations has resulted in the destruction of the scriptural text itself and the undermining of theological affirmations.[20] The presence of scriptural texts in this sort of theology, pastoral activity, and liturgy did not necessarily guarantee any biblical content. This holds true for the theology of the religious life as well, particularly since it has always been grounded on dogmatic theology. We might well adopt the complaint voiced by R. Ware about one particular use of Scripture as the norm for theology: while we find a superabundance of textual references, there is a complete absence of any real biblical sense.[21]

Theological reflection on the religious life has been called into serious question by the exigencies of modern exegesis, but it has also been thoroughly enriched. If we consciously accept the questions posed to us by scholarly exegesis, this will affect not only our theoretical framework for understanding the religious life but also our aspirations, our way of behaving, and the way in which we interiorize certain values. That is to say, it will affect the way in which certain human experiences, actions, and symbols speak to our intelligence. More serious exegesis of this type is necessary,[22] however rough its purifying effect may be. It will help us to

---

20. See C. Duquoc, *Christologie* (Paris: Ed. du Cerf, 1973), 1:19–10.

21. R. Ware, "La escritura en la teología actual," in *Concilium* 70 (1971): 563–65; Eng. trans., "The Use of Scripture in Current Theology," *Concilium* 70:115–28: "Paul VI's encyclical on priestly celibacy contains 110 biblical citations. But there is no biblical reflection as such in it, and no hint of exegetical evaluation. If those citations were not in the text, they would not be missed at all. Contrary to the view of Vatican II's *Dei verbum* (n. 12), all the citations are accorded the same speculative and dogmatic value. Yet they prove insufficient to establish the necessity of celibacy, or even to give it a post-factum biblical basis and sense."

22. See Luis Alonso Schoekel, "¿Es necesaria la exégesis?" in *Concilium* 70 (1971); Eng. trans., "Is Exegesis Necessary?" *Concilium* 70:30–38. He criticizes scientific exegesis for being too western, Germanic, and Saxon and thus complicating the reading of the faithful (pp. 470–71). But exegesis also has made real contributions: "Today scientific exegesis has the function of criticizing the many and varied traditions that have grown up in an unruly way and without ever rendering an account of themselves. We cannot simply appeal to tradition today

overcome decadent allegorizing, a strain of biblical fundamentalism, excessive subjectivism, and exaggerated pietism in the interpretation of Scripture. That in turn should lead to better theological reflection on the religious life.[23]

We fully realize how people have had recourse to certain biblical passages throughout the history of the religious life. The summary passages in Acts that describe the life of the primitive Christian community have been used to legitimate discipleship and communal living. But they have also been regarded as a historical description of the life of the Jerusalem community, and the religious life has been presented as a historical continuation of that community's life.[24]

Relying on a particular interpretation of Matthew 19:10–12 and 1 Corinthians 7:25–32, some have tried to view celibacy as the essential and constitutive element of the religious state. More recent scriptural studies give us a better picture of the literal meaning and the historical context of these passages. They certainly are not alluding explicitly to what we today call consecrated virginity based on love for God's kingdom. Recent studies also question our belief that one can use New Testament texts to set up two categories of people among the people of God, the more perfect and the less perfect, with the celibate life and the evangelical counsels being part of the lifestyle of the former. Among recent authors E. Schillebeeckx, T. Matura, and R. Schulte maintain that consecrated chas-

---

when we are trying to understand Scripture because we are then simply appealing to human traditions or routines" (p. 475).

23. R. Marlé, *Herméneutique et catéchèse* (Paris: ISPC, 1970), p. 101: "The danger of manipulation is all the greater insofar as one confronts a symbolic language whose terms are 'overdetermined.' This is eminently the case with the Bible." See L. Alonso Schoekel, "¿Es necesaria la exégesis?" p. 471.

24. For the relationship between exegesis and theology of the religious life, some of the decisive works have been: S. Legasse, *L'appel du riche, contribution à l'étude des fondements scripturaires de l'état religieux* (Paris, 1966); idem, "Les fondements évangéliques de la pauvreté religieuse," in *Vie Consacrée* 42, no. 5 (1970): 282–83. See also J. Cambier, "Théologie de la vie religieuse aujourd'hui," see note 36, chap. 1 in this volume; I. E. Lozano, "De vita apostolica apud Patres," passim (see note 8 of this chapter); idem, "De vita apostolica apud canonicos regulares," in *Commentarium pro religiosis et missionariis* 52 (1971): 193–220; idem, "De vita apostolica apud ordines mendicantes," ibid., pp. 301–13; I. Hausherr, "Vocation chrétienne et vocation monastique chez les Pères," in C. Colombo et al., *Laics et vie chrétienne parfaite* (Rome, 1963), 1:35–115. For a critical evaluation of the current use of Scripture in the theology of the religious life, see the superb comments in chaps. III and IV of Tillard, *Devant Dieu*.

tity is the axis of the religious life and that it is the only counsel that can be recognized with certainty in Scripture.[25]

Interpretations of New Testament passages that seek to establish a distinction between counsels and precepts, and that then proceed to set up two corresponding states in life (one more perfect than the other), can no longer justify any sort of double morality. One cannot possibly attribute to Jesus the intention of establishing two categories of Christians: the popular masses on the one hand and an elite on the other. Discipleship does not establish a twofold ethics within the people of God.[26] The basic requirements for participating in the kingdom are the same for all. All are called to be perfect, holy, consecrated, and good.[27]

---

25. See E. Schillebeeckx, *La mission de l'Eglise* (Brussels: Ed. du CEP, 1969), pp. 289–90; idem, *Autour du célibat du prêtre* (Paris, 1967); T. Matura, *Célibat et communauté* (Paris, 1967); R. Schulte, "La vida religiosa como signo," in G. Baraúna, *La Iglesia del Vaticano II*, 2:1113–14; Sabine Villatte, "Redonner sens au célibat religieux? in *Vie Consacrée*, no. 3 (May-June 1971): 145; Bandera, "¿Radicalismo evangélico o pluralismo de la santidad?" p. 23.

For a directly opposite stance see: J.M.R. Tillard, "Le fondement évangélique de la vie religieuse," in *Nouvelle Revue Théologique* (1969): 916–955; A. Durand, "Recherche sur le sens de la vie religieuse," p. 65; F. Sebastian Aguilar, "Origen de la vida religiosa," in *CONFER* 10, no. 35 (1971): 321; compare that with his article "Valoración teológica de los consejos evangélicos," in *CONFER*, no. 7 (1965): 353–75, where he sought to use Scripture, tradition, and the thought of Thomas Aquinas to prove that there is both a perfect and an imperfect way to fulfill the precept of charity. Idem, *La vida de perfección en la Iglesia, sus líneas esenciales* (Madrid, 1963). In his *Kirchliche Dogmatik* (III/4–IV/2) K. Barth admits that on the basis of the Bible one can justify a threefold situation akin to the three vows: flight from the world, celibacy, and obedience.

26. While not going so far as to establish a double moral code, some authors focus on the existence of a restricted group of "disciples" summoned by Jesus to his mission and to certain demands not shared by all believers. They regard this as a historic fact that cannot be called into doubt. See B. Rigaux, "Die Zwölf in Geschichte und Kerygma," in *Der historische Jesu und kerygmatische Christus* (Berlin, 1961), pp. 468–86.

27. Besides the citations in note 24, see the following works of differing value: E. Gambari, "Principi evangelici e teologici della vita religiosa," in *Via, Verità et Vita*, no. 16 (1967): 6–17; J. M. R. Tillard, "Le projet de la 'vita religiosa' dans l'ensemble du fait évangélique,'" manuscript notes only (Brussels 1969); G. Turbessi, "Prefigurazioni bibliche e fondamenti evangelici della vita religiosa," in the anthology *Per una presenza viva*, pp. 182–228; J. L. Espinel, "Fundamentos bíblicos de la vida religiosa," in *Ciencia Tomista* 99 (1972): 11–71; E. Vallauri, "Lo stato religioso secondo il Nuovo Testamento," in *Laurentianum* 13 (1972): 265–93; J. M.

Today, then, we cannot focus on some particular biblical passage as the explicit basis for the religious life. Thanks to the work of historical and textual criticism, we have lost the security blanket once provided by isolated texts. On the other hand we now possess a better picture of the overall experience that is only partially transmitted in these biblical passages. Moving on from biblical fudamentalism, we have learned that the intuition embodied in the religious life is rooted in the overall dynamism of the Christ happening and its mysterious nature. Far from erasing the charismatic and prophetic inspiration of the religious life, present-day exegesis is revitalizing it in terms of the grace of the Spirit which both inhabits Scripture and overflows it. As an experience of the Spirit, the religious life is rooted in the biblical message, is permanently oriented toward that message, and is also its epiphany here and now. The only way to take the New Testament seriously as a norm for theology and the spiritual life is to take it in its totality; only thus is it truly the evangelical foundation.

Throughout the centuries the New Testament has always been regarded as the wellspring of the most salient features in the lifestyle of religious. The traditions embodied in spiritual authors and the founders of religious orders bear witness to an interpretation and spiritual exegesis of Scripture that has stressed the radical and total nature of the Christian and religious vocation. Once again Scripture and tradition is the problem that must be clarified at each new stage of history and of the theology of the religious life.

The indefectible truth of the Bible lies far beyond any literalist explanation or historical specification, though one must engage in these efforts to arrive at it. The indefectible truth of Scripture lies at the level of the *totality* of the scriptural testimony, particularly its total fulfillment in Jesus Christ.[28] The totality of Scripture puts us right in the heart of Christology. To say that the religious life finds its evangelical grounding in the totality of the scriptural message is to affirm its roots in Christology.[29]

Finally, I should like to enumerate some of the theological principles that have helped to ground the theology of the religious life. I do not

---

Van Cangh, "Fondement évangélique de la vie religieuse," in *Nouvelle Revue Théologique* 95 (1973): 635–47.

28. See R. Marlé, *Herméneutique et Catéchèse*, p. 74, where he makes reference to Norbert Lohfink, *L'Ancien Testament. Bible du Chrétien aujourd'hui* (Paris: Centurion, 1969), pp. 37–70.

29. Thus I do not share the criticism of Tillard's focus that was expressed by P. Galot in *Gregorianum* 56, no. 2 (1975): 387–88.

propose to offer a historical presentation of their growth and development. I simply want to present some of the basic points involved in any
theological explanation of the religious life.[30]

The distinction between "counsels" and "precepts" in Scripture was
supported and reinforced by a theology of the religious life that persists
right up to today among some authors and that was not clearly excluded
even by Vatican II.[31] The separation between the two is often very strict
and rigid, and it is bound up with the whole theological and canon-law
debate over the religious life as a state of life markedly distinct from the
lay state and the priestly state.[32]

The theme of the religious life as a state in life evokes not only the
stability demanded by this option[33] but also the theological import and

---

30. See A. Restrepo, *De la vida religiosa,* who devotes a section of his valuable
study to what he calls the theological phase: "An attempt is made to arrive at the
very nature of the evangelical life and to define its ecclesial mission. Essentially
the religious is a gift and a participation in the life of the Trinity. It is a participation
in the mystery of saving love that the Father communicates and reveals through
the incarnate Word and his Spirit, first to the Mystical Body and then to the world.
Thanks to the priesthood of the faithful, the baptized share in the divine life and
are able to respond to the vocation to which they have been summoned: to the
perfection of charity. When this has been interiorized in the members of the
Mystical Body, it can then become visible and find expression in a variety of
evangelical attitudes. This means, first of all, that the religious life is basically
Christian life. But it also means that within the universal vocation to holiness it
possesses its own physiognomy. It is the fruit of a grace that is not granted to all,
and that is made manifest through concrete evangelical attitudes. The latter are all
the more clear and effective when they are lived in a well defined sociological state
of life as a public ecclesial reality. Two consequences follow. First and foremost, it
is impossible to theologize about the religious life in and of itself, apart from the
other states of life in the Church" (pp. 860–61).

31. See J.M.R. Tillard, *Devant Dieu,* pp. 95–96, n. 71.

32. See J.M.R. Tillard, manuscript "La 'vita religiosa' comme 'etat' dans
l'Eglise" (Brussels, 1972); R. Schulte ("La vida religiosa como signo," *Per una
presenza viva,* p. 1101) sees the fact of being a believer as the basis. The tasks taken
on in the body of Christ form one's state in life. Every state in life is special,
something in addition to merely being a believer. Thus the lay person is not
simply a believer. There are three states: lay person, priest, and religious.

33. Thomas Aquinas: "Thus people are said to be in a state of perfection, not
because they already possess the state of perfect charity, but because they obligate
themselves permanently and with some solemnity to the things that bespeak a
relationship to perfection" (*Summa Theologica,* II, 2, cf. 184, 4–5). The element of

scope of the consecration involved in the profession of religious vows.[34]
In time people arrived at a monolithic conception of the religious state, as
a moralistic view of it. More and more the three vows were associated
with the counsels of poverty, chastity, and obedience.[35] The theology of

---

"permanence" should not be associated too closely with state in life as a static
condition. Instead it should be associated with an ongoing experience of fidelity
that expresses not only stability but also initiative and creativity. See J.M.R.
Tillard, *Devant Dieu*, pp. 60–61.

34. On the theme of consecration see A. Restrepo, *De la vida religiosa*, chap. IV.
Also see P. R. Regamey, "La consécration religieuse, aujourd'hui contestée," in
Supplement to *La Vie Spirituelle*, no. 75 (November 1965): 385f. His article is a brief
commentary on Vatican II's teaching about baptismal and religious consecration,
stressing the phrase "et divino obsequio *intimius* consecratur" (pp. 387–91). In the
second part of his article he disputes those who reject the notion of the *religious
state* or who regard such notions as silence and the cloister as arbitrary (pp.
392–413). See A. M. Triacca, "La vita di consacrazione nelle sue origini sacramen-
tarie," in the anthology *Per una presenza*, pp. 283–348, a well documented study
with a fine bibliography on the theme of baptismal and religious consecration (p.
289). A. Boni, "La vita religiosa nel suo contenuto teologale," in *Vita Consacrata* 7
(1971): 265–76; idem, "Note storico-giuridiche sul concetto di consacrazione nella
professione religiosa," ibid., 8 (1972): 665–82. A. Bandera, "A ejemplo y en
representación de Jesucristo, la consagración religiosa según 'Evangelica
Testificatio,' " in *CONFER* 11, no. 39 (1972): 179–204. Y. Beyer, "El nuevo derecho
de los religiosos, un proyecto original y abierto," in *Concilium* 97: 102.

35. See Tillard, *Devant Dieu*, chap. V., pp. 353–97. Canon 487 embodies a
theological conception of the religious life as a state in life, an option for the
evangelical counsels, and an obligation under vows to practice poverty, chastity,
and obedience. A. Gemelli reacted against this view in his ground-breaking work
Le associazioni di laice consacrati a Dio nel mondo. He pointed out that Scripture and
tradition put the accent on the *totality of consecration*, questioning the view that it
should be restricted to the specific elements of poverty, chastity, and obedience.
His view gradually began to make headway. See C. Koser, "Mensaje del P.
General a los Franciscanos de Méjico," 1969: "In the gospels we do not find just
three counsels. We find a large number that could serve for a religious life very
similar to what we call the religious life. For example, we find an invitation to be
peace-loving, meek, and forgiving. An institute basing its spirituality on such
counsels would be incredibly relevant today and could be enormously attractive."

But the number of counsels is not the main question either. The main question
is the total self-giving that is realized through the counsels individually and
collectively. So suggests O. Rousseau, "Le caractère totalitaire de la réponse à
l'appel évangélique dans la vie religieuse," in the anthology *La liberté évangélique*
(Paris, 1965), pp. 13–28; E. Ranwez, "Tres consejos evangélicos," in *Concilium*

the religious life came to be a theology of the states of perfection. For F. Suárez it entailed an obligation to "something better and more distinctive," to "works of perfection and supererogation."[36] The teaching of Pius XII would fortify this theology of the states of perfection.[37] Vatican II would later attempt to avoid setting up differences in the summons to sanctity, but it did not manage to eliminate contradictory viewpoints in various passages and conciliar documents. Thus in *Lumen gentium* (nos. 44 and 45) it asserts that religious do something more than other Christians and that they are summoned to a higher perfection.

At the same time, however, Vatican II put particular emphasis on the relationship of religious consecration to baptismal consecration. It stressed that the former was not an additional or superior kind of consecration, thus moving out to meet a whole medieval and patristic tradition that had elaborated a theology of second baptism for religious in connection with the profession of monastic vows.[38]

Moreover, the ecclesiology of the Council constitutes an important nucleus for the theology of the religious life. The notions of the church as the people of God, as a sign of salvation, and as a body called to serve the world breaks new ground for reworking the whole experience of the religious life. The eschatological, charismatic, prophetic, and paschal dimensions of the church are other theological elements offering us a new chance to rework the spiritual and pastoral focus of the religious life.

Until Vatican II explanations of the religious life and its meaning were frequently based on certain dogmatic principles. The dogma of the Trinity, for example, occupies a central place in the work of R. Carpentier.[39] Through adoptive sonship in Christ one participates in this mystery. Perfection consists in living this sonship ever more intimately. The Trinity is also the starting point for J. Beyer.[40] Clearly enough the mystery of

---

9 (1965): 74–81; Eng. trans., "The Three Evangelical Counsels, *Concilium* 9:71–80; E. Pousset, "L'existence humaine et les voeux de religion," in *Vie Consacrée* 41 (1969): 66–72; J. M. Hennaux, "Voeu et promesse, supprimer les voeux temporaires?" in *Vie Consacrée* 44 (1972): 3–33.

36. See F. Suarez, *De Religione*, Tr. VII, in *Opera Omnia*, XV (Paris, 1859).

37. See D. Bertetto, *La vita religiosa nel magisterio di Pio XII* (Alba, 1960).

38. Y. Congar, "La vie religieuse dans l'Eglise selon Vatican II," pp. 80–81.

39. See R. Carpentier, *Témoins de la Cité de Dieu* (Paris, 1958); the author has deepened and enriched his views in his postconciliar writings.

40. See J. Beyer, "Premier bilan des châpitres de renouveau": "The essential thing in every consecrated life is the consecration of one's life to God and human

Christ and the demands of discipleship have served as a guiding thread in theological tradition about the religious life. An ecclesiology focusing on charisms will tend to give a certain prominence to the theme of the Holy Spirit and his gifts. This is evident in more recent theological studies on pneumatology, which attempt to understand the mystery of Christ and the Trinity on the basis of the life and activity of the Spirit in the world, in human history, and in the community of believers.

In trying to explain the meaning of unconditional surrender to God, some doctrinal starting points have prompted even more recent theological reflection to stress the dimensions of renunciation, abnegation, and ascesis implied in religious consecration and the profession of the evangelical counsels. Cotel, for example, has stressed that renunciation is inseparable from the gift of self to God.[41]

In the history of the religious life more than one person has tended to view renunciation and asceticism as the very nature of consecration to God and the essence of the counsels.[42] Rahner sought to offer a theological interpretation of abnegation as the essence of the evangelical counsels but not as something merely negative. Renouncing material goods, the goods of the body, and the free disposal of oneself is not simply an act of omission. By the very fact that one has to "make" or "perform" these renunciations, it is clear that the act of renunciation is also positive. Moreover, the vacuum created by these renunciations rightly and inevitably creates other attitudes which represent an objectification of faith

---

beings in union with the eucharistic oblation of Christ to his Father for the salvation of the world." For him the trinitarian foundation of the apostolic life is complemented by a vivid sense of action and prayer and an ongoing effort to adapt it to the current needs of the world and the church. This calls for a plurality of charisms.

41. See P. Cotel, *Catéchisme des voeux;* also Cotel and Jombart, *Les principes de la vie religieuse.* Stress is placed on the ascetic character of the vows as an instrument of perfection and as a condition for self-surrender to God.

42. M. M. van Molle, "Aux origines de la vie communautaire chrétienne," pp. 105–21. The third mistake in the community of Pachomius would be its interpretation of the Pauline antithesis between flesh and spirit in terms of the Platonic antithesis between body and soul. Asceticism would proceed to kill the body so that the soul might triumph. When the New Testament talks about fasts, vigils, and mortification, it is talking about the consequences of apostolic labor, not about liberative practices. See A. M. Denis, "Ascèse et vie chrétienne, éléments concernant la vie religieuse dans le N.T.," in *Revue des Sciences Philosophiques et Théologiques* (1963): 606–18.

operating through love. That is why one opts for abnegation. In positive terms, then, the counsels are an objectification and a manifestation of faith in the grace of God that transcends the world, and these manifestations are not given as such in any other way. Though it seems to me that Rahner's reflections center more around renunciation than around the following of Christ,[43] he does rediscover two theological perspectives that will be central to future reflection on the religious life: the church as a sign and the eschatological structure of the love that constitutes its message and its inner life.[44]

To sum up, then, we can say that the effort to ground the religious life on Scripture and dogmatic theology is based on the vital insight that it is a life oriented to the demands of the Lord in the gospel message and nurtured by the mysteries of our faith. Advances in exegesis and theology may change the picture, to be sure. But the fact remains that any new understanding of the religious life can be authentic only insofar as it helps us to center our lives on the whole gospel message, on Jesus. It must also make sure that our lives are inspired by the central truths of our faith, experienced not as frozen dogmatic formulas but as the concrete reality of those who believe in the Lord and are struggling accordingly.

Emphasis on the state of perfection brings out two main concerns that summon us imperiously and call for our creative effort. We must be loyal to our self-surrender to God and never turn back. We must also fulfill our vocation to be saints. Therein lies our support and our effectiveness today, even as it did yesterday.

---

43. K. Rahner, "Sobre los consejos evangélicos," in Escritos de Teología (Madrid, 1969), 8:458, note 28; German original; the same series of volumes is translated into English as Theological Investigations, published by Helicon and later Herder & Herder. Idem, "Sobre la teología de la abnegación," originally written in 1953, ibid., 1961, 3:61–71. Rahner points out that the ultimate meaning of abnegation must be determined by love. Renunciation of a positive value would be absurd if it were done for its own sake because that would be ontologically impossible and ethically perverse in intent. Along the same lines see A. Colorado, "Los consejos evangélicos a la luz de la teología actual," doctoral thesis in Lux Mundi (Salamanca), 13 (1968). Hans Urs von Balthasar, 'Une vie livrée à Dieu," in Vie Consacrée, no. 1 (1971): 5–23, makes total availability the key to a reinterpretation of a life based on the counsels. For one who does not make renunciation the essence of the counsels see Y. Congar, "La vie religieuse dans l'Eglise selon Vatican II," p. 74.

44. Rahner, "Sobre la teología de la abnegación," p. 69.

Focus on the Absolute: Evangelical Radicalism
and Secular Relativization

Here we consider the approach that seeks to give full weight to God as the Absolute in the project of the religious life. The category of the Absolute applied to God takes on such import that every other reality cannot help being viewed as merely relative. Stress is placed on the eschatological, transhistorical horizon of faith and our acceptance of God in our lives. This means that absolute value will be attributed to those things that bespeak a more direct or vertical relationship with God; by the same token, those things that have to do with historical and social activity will be viewed as merely relative. Thus people will "radicalize" those attitudes, things, and acts that more readily bring out the absolute aspect of our faith (i.e., God) and the absolute feature of our life project (i.e., the Lord). Sometimes this may also lead to a contrasting picture of all that is relative. Seen vis-à-vis the Absolute, what is relative may be viewed in pejorative terms. Rather than being something "in relation to" the Absolute, it becomes something stripped of all solidity and worthwhile content.

Such a schema seems to me to be akin to that which distinguishes between the exterior and the interior life. It sounds like another version of the distinction of planes.[45] We would certainly not want to deny the absolute character of the love of the Father; it is the fundamental and ultimate thing which gives meaning to our life always. But neither would we want to deny the decisive character of the historical mediations through which this love is realized and human beings live in the Absolute.[46] This is the problem that I see in the eschatological theology of hope and its related political theology. Insofar as they stress the need to maintain a critical reservation so that social processes are not built up into absolutes, they also tend to support and reinforce the distinction between the absolute and the relative. They tend to imply that we must radicalize and concentrate only on that which links us directly with the Absolute.

In reflection on the religious life we find a new way of talking about the

---

45. See J. Comblin, "Libertad y liberación," in *Concilium* 96 (1974): 394; Eng. trans., "Freedom and Liberation as Theological Concepts," *Concilium* 96:92–104.

46. See J. L. Segundo, "Capitalismo—Socialismo," *Concilium* 96:405,408–9; Eng. trans., "Capitalism—Socialism: A Theological Crux," *Concilium* 96: 105–23.

following of Christ when the latter is defined as a radically evangelical life or a radically baptismal life, or when the following of Christ, as a commitment of faith, is regarded as a life exclusively oriented toward the Absolute.

The religious man or woman is one who has a passion for the Absolute.[47] Religious are specialists with regard to God and religious affairs.[48] In this view the essential aspect of the religious life lies in its orientation and dedication to "the cause of God."[49] The centrality of faith in the life of the Christian and the religious is the basis for the radical way in which they propose to live their baptismal vocation in some absolute way.[50] Religious will live their lives centered on the absolute reality of the kingdom so that those with other concerns will not forget or diminish the kingdom's presence among human beings.[51] With very good reason Tillard proposes that we ask ourselves this question: Is the religious life one that is meaningful in terms of faith?[52] To talk about such concern for the Absolute and for a radical life is to turn the faith into the central axis of any effort to understand what the religious life is.

The notion of evangelical radicalism as a standpoint for situating the religious life has produced reactions that may help us to situate it more clearly.[53] As I see it, evangelical radicalism seeks to overcome any rigid dividing line between counsels and precepts,[54] and thus to rehabilitate

---

47. See, for example, F. M. Genuyt, "Approche philosophique de la vie religieuse," p. 105: "Religious know better than anyone that they can make no claim to moral superiority or special perfection. They simply are . . . passionate devotees of the Absolute. Exclusively attached to transcendence, they have the function of manifesting the religious dimension inscribed in the hearts of human beings."

48. Many religious no longer favor the view of their vocation that would make them professionals and initiates in the things of God. See Roger van Allen, "Religious Life and Christian Vocation," Cross Currents 22 (1972): 177.

49. See Tillard, Devant Dieu, pp. 68–69.

50. Thus Tillard (in "Le fondement évangelique de la vie religieuse," Nouvelle Revue Théologique 91 [1969]: 916–55) seems to stress what he calls "the summons to radicalism implied in the experience of faith strictly as such." Then he adds that there is "an absolute form of living the common vocation."

51. See P. Jacquemont, "La vie religieuse à l'heure de Vatican II," p. 564.

52. Tillard, Devant Dieu, p. 53.

53. See A. Bandera, "¿Radicalismo evangélico o pluralismo de la santidad?" p. 34. He feels that this view can hardly be reconciled with solid sociological advances already achieved.

54. See Galot, "Le fondement évangélique du voeu religieux de pauvreté," in Gregorianum 56, no. 3 (1975): 441–46. Though I do not get a clear picture of his way

other important features of the gospel message. In any case it serves to ground the specific nature of the religious life within the summons to radicalize our life in accordance with the gospel's demands.

There are two features in this radicalism. First of all, it concerns something that cannot equally be generalized and applied to all. Second, it does not rule except in limit situations vis-à-vis salvation. In the religious life one is enrolled among those who feel, by virtue of a special gift, that they are summoned to fulfill more radical demands. That which would ordinarily be an occasional or extraordinary project becomes the ordinary day-to-day project of a certain group of people. The result is a response which other people would regard as the most total and absolute one possible.[55]

This radicalization based on the Absolute, however, seems automatically to imply a relativization of other aspects. Focusing on the imminence of the kingdom, people have all too often "relativized" its historical demands. The tendency to stress eschatology in tradition has often emptied the message of its social and historical content. And the consequences of this conception of the kingdom are still present in the theology of the religious life: flight from the world as evasion of social responsibilities, apoliticism, asceticism, and so forth. To relativize all reality for the sake of the values of the kingdom is to deprive creation and the work of transforming history of their roles as the mediation and initial locale for the realization of those values.[56]

To sum up, the focus on the Absolute seeks to remind us that the Lord and his love is the ultimate reason underlying every moment of our life and every effort to follow Christ. Evangelical radicalism stresses the

---

of viewing the difference between counsels and precepts, the author does react against any attempt to turn radicalism into something belonging to religious exclusively and rejects the idea that the same demands be placed on the laity as on religious.

55. See Y. Congar, "La vie religieuse dans l'Eglise selon Vatican II," pp. 66, 79, 81.

56. There is a more conciliar perspective in J. Aubry, *Teologia della vita religiosa* (Turin, 1969). He thinks that consecration gives religious a relationship with God that is direct and related to the service of his kingdom, not indirect and mediated through the profane (p. 31). Religious withdraw from the ordinary living circumstances of their fellows (p. 17) and give up the idea of participating directly in economic development or exercising any political initiative; and they do all this out of love for the kingdom. See also P. Raffin, "Resurgimientos espirituales y renovación de la vida religiosa," *Concilium* 89, p. 438.

demands of the kingdom as they are lived out in what we now call the religious life. But it should not cause us to forget that the radical feature of the good news lies in proclaiming that the kingdom is in our midst because the poor, the oppressed, and the captive are liberated. When bound up with this radical option, evangelical radicalism avoids a certain kind of "spiritualism" and qualitative elitism. The radical demand is to make every effort to see the kingdom grow among human beings and to make sure that the new heavens and the new earth are its concrete embodiment in history. As I see it, this perspective is not present in the theologians who advocate evangelical radicalism or in their opponents. In arguing with each other, they do not seem to alter the perspective which they share in common.[57]

This preoccupation to make sure that the religious life is an experience centered in God and an existential proclamation of him may well correspond with the nonbelieving and atheistic context of the affluent societies. We on this continent feel that any such reference to the Absolute must take account of the real-life conditions of the dispossessed masses and try to transform them. Otherwise evangelical radicalism will be little more than an asceticism that can have little appeal to the people caught in the throes of dire needs.

Focus on the Religious Life as a Project

Initial concern to define the essential and distinctive elements of the religious life has paved the way for a different focus, one that is less centered on rigorous definitions and more open to describing the religious life in functional terms. Vatican II tends to operate in terms of the latter focus, perhaps influenced here by European brands of existential theology. At the same time, however, its overall way of looking at the question tends to maintain the rigid distinction between being and acting that continues to prevail in the spiritual and religious life.[58]

Some rightly see the danger of talking about the "nature" of the

---

57. See Tillard, *Devant Dieu*, passim; F. Sebastian Aguilar, "Origen de la vida religiosa," pp. 327–28. On the other side see A. Bandera, "¿Radicalismo evangélico o pluralismo de la santidad?" passim; J. Galot, "Le fondement évangélique du voeu religieux de pauvreté," passim.

58. See, for example, S. Galilea, "A los pobres se les anuncia el evangelio," *IPLA*, no. 11, p. 84. Efforts to present consecration as mission tend to mitigate the ultimately dualistic thrust of a relationship that is viewed too rigidly.

religious life when this life is basically a historical happening.[59] Others, such as Tillard, rightly feel that the time for seeking some element specific to the religious life has passed. There is no such thing as the religious life as such. What we find instead is a project that is quite broad in scope, that is open to all sorts of concrete expression, and that is inspired by the Spirit in Christians who desire to be faithful to the gospel message.[60]

To talk about a "project" is to talk about something that is not finished and ready-made. Rather, it is an effort to flesh out something that one is trying to do. I like this particular way of focusing on the religious life, of seeing it as a project. For it takes in both the dynamism of the Spirit in action and the creative responsibility of those who accept his gift.

Tillard is the one who has developed this focus most recently, and here I should like to make some comments about his work. I find valuable contributions in his work and I share his central concern: i.e. How are we to be witnesses of the Father's unfathomable love for all the human beings of our world? But in the light of the perspective I have chosen here, certain aspects of Tillard's approach are objectionable.

His initial social diagnosis, it seems to me, remains external to the project itself. In any case our relationship to the world is not presented as the historical and social mediation of our commitment to God. Though he states that the two poles of reference are inseparable,[61] he does not clarify the relationship between them.

I think he is correct to insist that we must turn our flight from the world into an involvement in the world. However, his vision of history is not dialectical, and his analysis of society is not a structural one. Thus the relationship to the world which he rightly insists upon tends to remain a vague generality without any political import. This seriously affects his presentation of the religious life as a prophetic sign and strips it of

---

59. See V. Ayel, "La exigencia evangelizadora de la vida religiosa 'en acto'," in Usig, *Evangelio y vida religiosa* (Rome, 1974), pp. 7, 33: "I favor talking about the nature of the religious life so long as it is understood to be an activity, not an abstract idea. This does not mean that we need encourage 'subjectivism' in our definition of the religious life, for in the latter we find an objectivity of an existential order. It is the mystery of Christ as a fact, and the history of the religious life as a fact." A. Durand, "Recherche sur le sens de la vie religieuse," p. 65, insists that rediscovering the deeper meaning of the religious life is more important than offering definitions.

60. Tillard, *Devant Dieu*, pp. 12–13 and 61–62.

61. Ibid., p. 444.

historical content. The religious life as a project carried out "before God" ceases to be very credible to human beings.

Tillard does not question the basic historical framework of his reference to the world. He wants the religious life to be a response to contemporary human beings and their quest for meaning, but he offers no viable response. In my opinion there is no response at the collective or universal level unless we realize the meaninglessness of the established order of society from which the author writes and try to construct a historical alternative. The visage of the religious life must be that of the poor and hungry in this world, whose presence denounces the irrationality of worldwide exploitation and injustice.[62]

If the religious project and its reference to God is to be meaningful for our people today, then it must be lived and expressed within the liberation project of the poor. For it is there that our relationship to the world as religious will find real historical roots.

To sum up once again, this chapter offers a brief overview of some of the basic approaches to the religious life. Thanks to Vatican II, there has been progress in trying to turn religious renewal into an effort to respond to the world and contemporary human beings; but there have been difficulties too. Even in the most advanced approaches, I feel, the world horizon envisioned is not that of the alienated and the oppressed. It is only from the perspective of the latter that our efforts to be prophetic signs of the kingdom can be meaningful. Only in this way can we proclaim the good news to the world with our lives.

This radical change in perspective opens us up to a different theological focus and a different outlook on the spiritual life. It is from this new perspective that we must rework the theology of the religious life on our continent.

---

62. Ibid., p. 416f, 445: "Today's religious should be free from the attractions of a world through which they freely pass." But what if that world is one of injustice and exploitation? Can religious still pass it by?

3
Latin American Reflection
on the Religious Life

Here I wish to deal specifically with the postconciliar reflection on the religious life that has been taking place in Latin America. The Medellín era has borne rich fruit in the life of the Latin American church and in its efforts at theological reflection. More than a few religious have contributed to all this.[1] But it is particularly the whole process of Christian living, spiritual experiences, and liberative activity embodied in the thrust of Medellín that has left its impression on the lives and thoughts of Latin American religious.

Religious have always been a vital part of the history of our church in Latin America. Both in the past and the present religious men and women have represented a high percentage of the active efforts of the Latin American Christian community.[2]

I should like to offer a brief outline of the main concerns and topics of theological reflection on the religious life here on our continent. The theology of the religious life forms one whole. It is a partial expression of the searching and the activity of countless groups, grassroots communities and segments within the church. An ever-increasing number of religious men and women are taking part in that activity, redefining their options, and thus giving historical embodiment to their commitment to the Lord.

Back in 1965 the Latin American Conference of Religious (CLAR) in-

---

1. In *A Theology of Liberation* (Maryknoll, N.Y.: Orbis, 1973), chap. 7, Gustavo Gutiérrez discusses the presence of religious and others in the church's involvement in the liberation process. See also note 14 in that chapter.

2. Cecilio de Lora, "Estudio sociográfico de los religiosos y religiosas en América Latina," CLAR, *Perspectivas*, no. 2, Bogotá, 1971.

itiated an in-depth study of the religious life in Latin America in the light of Vatican II and the pastoral conditions of our nations. At the end of 1966 its board of directors approved a document on the "renovation and adaptation of the religious life in Latin America and its apostolic implementation."[3] It was the first of a series of very valuable works on the life and activity of Latin American religious.

On the eve of the Medellín Conference many religious congregations, prompted by the spirit of Vatican II, held continental meetings to evaluate their religious life and presence and to redefine their contribution in the light of our continent's needs.[4] In all these meetings we detect a concern to respond to the demands imposed by Latin American realities. This meant, of course, that religious would have to get to know the realities so that they could review their existing efforts and try to align them more closely with their own particular charisms.[5] In this way they could revitalize their fidelity to the Lord.

Of course the conclusions of the Medellín Conference offered new elements to the picture. With greater clarity it stressed the option for liberation and for the oppressed than the documents of the aforementioned meetings had done. Earlier texts had not been so explicit.[6] How-

------

3. *CLAR*, no. 1, Mexico City, December 1966; 3rd edition, Bogotá, 1969, pp. 32–39.

4. So we have the proceedings and conclusions from a variety of meetings held by religious groups: the first meeting of South American Dominican provincials and vicars, Buenos Aires, July 1968; the first meeting of Latin American Franciscans, Bogotá, August 1968; the third Latin American conference of the provincials of the Brothers of the Christian Schools, Bogotá, August 1968; the letter of the Jesuit provincials in Latin America, Rio de Janeiro, May 1968; and the conclusions of the first Latin American meeting of Salesian superintendents, Caracas, May 1969. These documents, with the exception of those produced by the Dominican provincials mentioned above, can be found in *CLAR*, no. 8, Bogotá, 1969. It also contains the conclusions reached by Dominican provincials at their meeting in La Paz in July 1969.

5. For example, the Salesians and the Brothers of the Christian Schools stress youth work, popular action, and pedagogical activities. See ibid., pp. 47–52, 96–98.

6. See the letter of the Jesuit provincials in Latin America, May 1968, in *CLAR*, no. 8, p. 70f: "The social problem of Latin America is the problem of humanity itself. The era through which we are living in Latin America is a moment of salvation history. For that reason we propose to give this problem absolute priority in our apostolic strategy. What is more, we wish to view the totality of our apostolate in terms of this problem. . . . In all our activities our goal must be the

ever, here is one such document which does breathe the spirit of Medellín and bring out the desire of religious to serve our people with generosity, human warmth, and open availability:

A no less necessary thing is that our lives be rooted in the life and history of the people of America, as has been true since the early period of discovery. The Franciscan cord has bound the children of St. Francis to the destiny and development of this continent in an intimate way. We cannot escape the duty of carrying on our service in an effective and up-to-date way. We must keep adapting to the distinctive nature of its peoples and to their concrete conditions today. We must share their fate, suffering the same vicissitudes, nurturing their hopes for progress, and collaborating in the human and Christian construction of their future with all the means and energy at our disposal.[7]

THE RELIGIOUS LIFE AND THE MEDELLIN CONFERENCE

The results of the Second General Conference of the Latin American Episcopate at Medellín were the fruit of long years of quiet searching and effort, of successes and failures, by many Christians who were sincerely committed to our continent and who were vitally aware of their faith in Jesus Christ and their membership in the church.[8] The Medellín Conference did not suddenly descend from the skies. The conscience of the Christian community gradually matured against the backdrop of Vatican II and the revolutionary struggles of our people against an inhuman reality marked by injustice and its concomitant violence.[9]

---

liberation of human beings from every sort of servitude that oppresses them. . . . We propose, first of all, to shift some of our apostolic efforts towards the large and growing mass of abandoned people."

7. *Primer Encuentro Franciscano de América Latina*, Bogotá, 1968, published in 1969, pp. 15–16; reprinted in *CLAR*, no. 8, p. 23.

8. G. Gutiérrez, *A Theology of Liberation*, chap. 7; H. Parada, "Hace cinco años," in *Medellín: cinco años después sigue el desafío*, ISAL, Cuadernos de Estudio, no. 5, Santiago, 1973. This is an eight-page summary of a 200-page study. S. Silva, "La Iglesia Latinoamericana entre la tecnocracia y la liberación. Su opción política de Mar del Plata a Medellín," ibid.; Liberio Lopez, "Medellín, nueva imagen de la Iglesia Latinoamericana," doctoral thesis (Paris, 1973), mimeographed, with complete documentation.

9. G. Gutiérrez, "Introduction" to *Signos de Renovación* (Eng. trans., *Between Honesty and Hope*, Maryknoll, N.Y.: Maryknoll Publications, 1969) offers an excellent summary and interpretation of the process through which the Latin American church is living. *Páginas para una accion solidaria* (henceforth *Paginas*), nos.

Three main ideas, the embodiment of lived experiences, form the central preoccupations of the Medellín Conference: justice, the evangelization of the people, and poverty.[10] These three themes provide the outlines of a unique reality. Those who suffer most from the ravages of a dependent and dominated society are the poor, who constitute the majority of our people. Our people, who suffer from the stigmas of poverty in all its forms, are believers for the most part. It is impossible to proclaim the gospel message while turning one's back on this situation of exploitation. The church cannot be in solidarity with the poor unless it has a real commitment to erase injustice. Thus Christians reaffirm their conviction that the proclamation of a liberative gospel, based on a commitment to the poor, is their way of helping to construct a just and fraternal society. Here we have the heart of the Medellín Conference. Here is the wellspring of the more concrete historical demands required for the spiritual renewal of the community.

The Medellín Conference did not just express a vague or general concern about our continent. It also made an effort to analyze and interpret Latin American reality. It inaugurated a new style of theological reflection that openly incorporated the findings of the social sciences. Even in the preparatory drafts we find that to the diagnosis of reality is added a theological exploration of such themes as salvation and the mission of the church.[11] The life of our Christian communities since the

---

34–35 (Lima: CEP, 1973), pp. 1–27, commemorates the five years since the Medellín Conference. E. Dussel, "Sentido teológico de lo acontecido desde 1962 en América Latina," in *Nuevo Mundo* 1, no. 2 (1971): 187–204, states that he has gone beyond the interpretation he had arrived at years before. See also the somewhat disorganized article of R. Avila, "La teología de la liberación y los cristianos revolucionarios de América Latina," in ISAL, *Cuadernos de Estudio*, no. 5, Santiago, 1973; he sketches some of the antecedents of this movement.

10. G. Gutiérrez, "De la Iglesia colonial a Medellín," in *Vispera* 16 (1970): pp. 3–8. The Peruvian episcopate has devoted three successive assemblies to studying these topics: January 1969, see "Closing Statement of the Thirty-Sixth Peruvian Episcopal Conference," in *Between Honesty and Hope*, pp. 228–34; August 1971, see "Justicia en el Mundo," in *Signos de Liberación* (Lima: CEP, 1973), pp. 178–85; January 1973, "Evangelización" (Lima: Ed. Paulinas). On the latter document see G. Schmitz, *En torno al documento "Evangelización": algunas líneas pastorales de la Conferencia Episcopal Peruana* (Lima, 1973); *Evangelización, commentarios y notas* (Lima: Ed. CEP, 1973); J. C. Scannone, *Situación de la problemática fe-política entre nosotros* (Buenos Aires: Ed. Guadalupe, 1973), especially pp. 28–46.

11. "The Working Draft of the Medellín Conference," in *Between Honesty and Hope*, pp. 171–92.

Medellín Conference has enabled us to get a better picture of the strengths and weaknesses of its social analysis and its theological perspective. The practice of truly committed Christians is the concrete exegesis of the Medellín Conference and the locus of continuity and progress.[12]

For us the Medellín Conference was an effort to rethink Vatican II in terms of the reality of our own continent, and to situate ourselves with the help of conciliar perspectives. The "Message to the People of Latin America" and the "Introduction to the Final Documents" point up the basic features of the present day and our contribution as a church. The document on peace presents the Latin American situation in more specific terms: different forms of marginality, extreme inequality among social classes, growing frustrations, growing awareness of the oppressed sectors, international tensions, external neocolonialism, exacerbated nationalism, and so forth.

Unfortunately the document on religious does not do its reflection from the same standpoint. There is no social diagnosis or doctrinal synthesis in it. In short, it does not follow the methodological approach of the other documents. Instead it recalls the principles of Vatican II and then tries to examine those aspects of the religious life that are directly related to development and joint pastoral work in Latin America.[13] Instead of rethinking the religious life as a whole insofar as it relates to our continent, the document simply adapts certain aspects of the religious life to our cultural, social, and economic conditions.[14] It does not start off from the dominated classes mentioned in the document on peace, and a concern for the socially marginal classes takes fifth place in its set of recommendations.[15] The document on religious talks about the religious life and the process of humanization. But commitment to this process is viewed as the locale for sign and testimony, not as the focal point from

---

12. See R. Vidales, "Cuestiones en torno al método en teología de la liberación," MIEC-JECI, Document 9, Lima, 1974; translated in the anthology *Frontiers of Theology in Latin America* (Maryknoll, N.Y.: Orbis Books, 1979). "Iglesia y realidad social latinoamericana en Medellín," *Paginas*, nos. 34–35, pp. 8,11,26–27. J. Comblin, "Medellín, problema de interpretación," ISAL, *Cuadernos de Estudio*, no. 5, Santiago, 1973. Jorge Mejía, "Valor de los documentos de Medellín, in *Teología* 7 (1969): 15–16, 182–88.

13. Medellín Conference, concluding document on religious, no. 6; see note 2 of chapter 2 in this volume.

14. Ibid., no. 8.

15. Ibid., no. 13.

which we must rethink the content and demands of sign and testimony.[16]
This Medellín document stresses consecrated chastity as that which serves as the principal expression of our personal identification with Christ that began with baptism, and charity in the life of the community as the preview of the perfect union in the future kingdom.[17] Separation from the world does not signify scorn for the world; it is simply meant to remind people of the world's transitory and relative nature.[18]

The same criticisms can be levelled at this document that one might level at Vatican II's document on religious (Perfectae caritatis). It lacks theological substance, evangelical inspiration, and boldness. But like its conciliar counterpart it has the merit of pointing us toward the realm of practice.[19] The problem is that the Medellín document on religious is more faithful to Perfectae caritatis than to the outlook and approach of the other Medellín documents, even though its aim is to offer a response to Latin American realities.[20] It does not even measure up to the aforementioned document issued by CLAR in 1966.

In the years immediately preceding and following the Medellín Conference people may well have been primarily concerned with gaining a better understanding of what Vatican II had to say about the religious life.[21] But it was not the document on religious that would pave the way

---

16. Ibid., no. 10.

17. Ibid., no. 4.

18. Ibid., no. 3.

19. José Aldunate, "A los cinco años de Perfectae caritatis," in Teología y Vida 11, nos. 3–4 (1970): 177.

20. See S. Galilea, "Teología de la liberación y nuevas exigencias cristianas," in Medellín 1 (March 1975): 36. As he points out, the major thing is to accept and involve oneself in our people's liberation process. This requires an analysis of reality, a Christian and theological interpretation of it as a "state of sin" and as "institutionalized violence," and solidarity with the poor and oppressed.

21. Such was the orientation of some Latin Americans and foreign religious working in Latin America. See the three articles of E. Vigano, "La naturaleza de la vida religosa y su aspecto eclesiológico," "Renovación en la Iglesia y consiguientes cambios de perspectiva en la vida religiosa," "Los religiosos en la pastoral de conjunto," in La vida religiosa a la luz del Concilio Vaticano II, Permanent Secretariat of the Federación de Institutos Religiosos de Chile, 1966, pp. 91–150. B. Kloppenburg, "A doutrina do Vaticano II sobre a natureza da vida religiosa," Revista Eclesiástica Brasileira 30 (1967): 59–70. G. Barauna edited the anthology of commentaries on Vatican II, La Iglesia del Vaticano II (Barcelona: Juan Flores). The same perspective can be found in the earlier writings of J. M. Guerrero, P. Beguin,

for renewal. It was a more vital and concrete understanding of the Latin American church's commitment to the oppressed and their liberation that would revitalize religious communities and theological reflection on the religious way of life.

THEOLOGY ABOUT THE RELIGIOUS LIFE

Here I propose to engage in theological reflection on the religious life in terms of a few central themes. This will help us to visualize the standpoint and main concerns of Latin American reflection. Taken together, these themes reflect both the strong and weak points of the Latin American contribution.

The situation of religious in Latin America is brought out well in the demands voiced by a group of religious superiors in 1974. They wanted to see a deeper theological grounding of the religious life. They wanted to know how religious are to harmonize contemplation and action, how they are to shoulder the socio-political dimension of the religious life, how they are to become an integral part of the world of the poor, and how they can find ways to make the religious life respond better to the demands imposed by Latin American realities.[22]

---

and J. Comblin (who is neither a Latin American nor a religious). See, e.g., "Os fondamentos teológicos da vida religiosa," in *Revista Eclesiástica Brasileira* 49 (1969): 308–52; "Os religiosos e o mundo," ibid., pp. 550–79. Beltrán Villegas, "La visión renovada de la Iglesia como marco de la vida religiosa," in *CLAR*, 2 (1969): 11–21. R. Muñoz, "Los religiosos en la Iglesia y para el mundo," ibid., pp. 23–37. Houtart, De Lora, and Poblete, "La vida religiosa en América Latina: consideración sociológica," ibid., pp. 41–50. Simão Vigot, "A vida religiosa como carisma," in *Grande Sinal*, 1969, p. 71f. At the end of 1969 CLAR approved two documents: "Pobreza y vida religiosa en América Latina," *CLAR*, no. 4, and "Formación para la vida religiosa en América Latina," *CLAR*, nos. 3–1, 3–2. They were a real effort to think out things along the overall lines of the Medellín Conference. Back in July 1968 the Brazilian Religious Conference had produced a valuable document, "A vida religiosa no Brasil de hoje," reprinted in *CLAR*, no. 6. That issue, devoted to the religious life and Latin American development, embodies a serious effort to reconsider the conciliar and social teaching of the church.

22. See CLAR, "Seminario Latinoamericano de Superiores Mayores," April–May 1974 (Lima: D1-G1). Among the fears discussed by these religious superiors were uncertainty about the future of the religious life and varying reactions to changes occurring.

The Religious Life as an Experience of Faith

Vatican II made it clear that the religious life can be viewed and understood only as an expression of the life of faith. It is a life of discipleship in the mystery of Christ. The concrete experience of religious lies in making their experience of God the central, motivating core of their lives. God is the central project of the lives, and relationship with God becomes the guiding pole of all the other dimensions in their lives.[23] As one statement puts it: "The religious life is a mystery of faith. Faith is not simply a point of departure. It is also an ideal to be realized throughout one's life. It must be stressed that in the last analysis it is faith that justifies and explains our consecration."[24]

The centrality of faith in the religious life directly points up the christological character of this lifestyle. From a theological standpoint it shows that the religious life goes beyond any juridical conception of it. And faith also brings out the peculiarly Christian understanding of the religious experience, which itself is a worldwide phenomenon.[25]

Leonardo Boff maintains that it is the motivation, not the forms, of religious life that differentiates the Christian religious life from that of other creeds. Some of the motivating factors mentioned by Boff are the eschatological horizon, the principle of hope, the primacy of *agape*, the body of Christ, and the following or imitation of Christ.[26] Faith, then, is

---

23. See *CLAR*, no. 14: "La vida según el Espíritu," pp. 23 and 39.

24. See *CLAR*, no. 3–2: "Formación para la vida religiosa renovada en América Latina," p. 58.

25. The draft document of "La vida según el Espíritu" pointed out that in strict theological terms "religious" were all those who sought to live the evangelical life under the impulse of the spirit. This point was not retained in the final version of the document. See E. Cornelis, "Phénomène universel de la vie religieuse," in *Lumière et Vie*, no 96 (1970): 4–24. L. Boff says: "In this light the universal phenomenon of the religious life presents itself as a sacrament of human destiny. It signals the transcendent dimension of human life and bears witness to the existence of a higher reality, God. God is present within man and at the same time totally other, and it is worth sacrificing all the goods of this present life for him. On this universal level the religious life is already the symbol of God's love for human beings in the future world" (*O destino do homen e do mundo*, Petrópolis: Ed. Vozes, 1973, p. 152).

26. L. Boff, *O destino*, p. 143: "The essence of the religious life does not reside

the axis that makes this option comprehensible: "Speaking in Christian terms we can say that the religious life is also a matter of faith. . . . It is a phenomenon that can find its reason for being only in faith."[27] Precisely because the religious life finds its meaning in faith, it finds its verification in real life. It must be fleshed out in deeds if it is not to be a dead faith. Thus it is on the existential level that religious must look for the distinctive import of their way of life.[28]

The Religious Life as the Following of Christ

The following of Christ is a primordial value in the religious life.[29] It is the supreme rule of any religious community.[30] One cannot talk about the religious life without reference to the following of Christ.[31]

The Brazilian Conference of Religious (CRB) points out various elements involved in the following of Christ. Identification with Christ means sharing his anguish over the plight of human beings and being ready to give one's life for them. But there is also a concrete locale in history where the following of Christ appears in its full and authentic force. Following Christ does not mean simply living a life of faith and imitating his attitude toward universal values. Even more importantly, it means "recognizing him in those who are poor and those who are suffering."[32] A commitment to the poor is an essential part of the following of Christ.[33]

---

in virginity or any other vow, though they can be the expression of something far more profound and fundamental: the experiencing of God. As such, the religious life reveals a vast anthropological dimension that has found different articulations in the various civilizations and religions of the world.

27. R. Muñoz, "Los religiosos en la Iglesia y para el mundo," in *CLAR*, no. 2 (1969):25. He offers highly suggestive reflections for a revitalized theology of the religious life.

28. *CLAR*, no. 14, p. 64: "Religious, urged on by their own faith, must involve themselves in the history of our continent. Complex and ambiguous though the latter may be, it is the history of God with humanity. See J. M. Guerrero, "Religiosos de América Latina frente al desafío de un tiempo nuevo," in *Vida Religiosa Hoy*, the bulletin of CONFER, Arequipa, April 1974, mimeographed. On page 11 he quotes exactly what R. Muñoz said on page 34 of the article cited in 27.

29. *CLAR*, no. 1 (1967): 9.

30. R. Muñoz, "Los religiosos en la Iglesia y para el mundo," p. 34.

31. CRB, "Vida religiosa y desarrollo latinoamericano," in *CLAR*, no. 2, p. 19.

32. Ibid.

33. See L. Boff, "La vita religiosa nel processo di liberazione," in *Noticeial*, CEIAL, no. 2 (April 1973): 1–11, especially page 4.

Thus there are two elements involved in the religious life. First, one must assume the lifestyle that Christ led. Second, one must assume responsibility for some specific area of missionary activity.[34] The second element, which was part of Christ's own concrete lifestyle, brings out the priority of mission in the very conception of the religious life and in the effective fulfillment of discipleship. Hence the theme of following Christ is intimately bound up with evangelization and involvement in the liberation process: "Following Christ in their lives, religious cannot evade the aspects of commitment contained in his message and his own attitudes. Here on our continent they constitute a direct challenge for our faith."[35]

The following of Christ renews and synthesizes the relationship of sonship between people and God, the relationship of brotherhood between people and people, and the relationship of lordship between people and nature, people and history.[36]

When people view the religious life as an effort to follow Christ the poor person, the person sent to proclaim the good news to the poor, they find themselves in an active, dynamic, missionary perspective. That is why the charismatic and prophetic structure of the religious life is much in evidence in the reflection and searching of our Latin American communities.[37] The Spirit gave the charism of prophecy to the religious

---

34. CRB, "Vida religiosa y desarrollo latinoamericano," p. 20. *CLAR*, no. 31, insists that "the religious life establishes in this world a lifestyle that is as close as possible to that of the blessed" (p. 12).

35. *CLAR*, no. 14, p. 64.

36. Ibid., p. 32.

37. The theology of the religious life has benefited from the stress that exegesis and ecclesiology have put on the prophetic character of the chosen people and the Christian community. Latin American realities have caused Christians to feel the need for evangelical proclamation and denunciation. Gustavo Gutiérrez rightly talks about a prophetic pastoral activity in *La pastoral de la Iglesia en América Latina,* Serv. Documentación, Montevideo, 1968. The theme of liberative evangelization is another way to represent the church's prophetic vocation. Finally, what is called "militant exegesis" is nothing else but a prophetic reading of God's word in the present hour of liberation.

See A. Fragoso, "Profetismo y compromiso concreto con la liberación de la clase trabajadora y campesina," in *Pastoral Popular* 19, nos. 110–11 (1969): 11–16. R. Concatti, "Profetismo y política," in *Nuevo Mundo* 2, no. 1 (1972): 90–108. G. Gutiérrez, "El fenómeno de la contestación en América Latina," in *Concilium* 68 (1971): 41–53; Eng. trans., "Contestation in Latin America," *Concilium* 68: 40–52. R. Cabello, "El sentido auténtico del profeta y del profetismo," in *Christus* (Mexico City) 36, no. 428 (1971): 50–53; S. Galilea, "El profeta: garantía de la pastoral en

life.[38] In Latin America revitalizing our basic institutional charisms means more than going back to our origins in the past. It means more than trying to fulfill our earlier promise clearly and explicitly in the present-day history of our continent. The charism of a bygone day is revitalized insofar as it operates prophetically in the liberation process of today. Insofar as prophecy is religious and evangelical, it has a political import and must be fleshed out politically today. This is inescapable, as we shall see further on.[39]

The following and imitation of Christ are typical ways of expressing the fact that the religious life is a lifestyle based on the radical nature of the gospel message. As Panqueva puts it: "Religious turn this evangelical radicalism into the basic norm governing their lifestyle and structuring the dimensions of their life: love, work, family, freedom, personal relations, and so forth."[40]

This radicalism is understood in two senses. On the one hand it signifies the total and unconditional surrender of religious to the Father and his salvation plan through a public commitment in the church.[41] On the

---

América Latina," in *Misiones Extranjeras* 1 (1971): 13–20.

On the religious life see the following among others: S. Vigot, "A vida religiosa como carisma," in *Grande Sinal,* 1969, p. 71f. A. Barreiro, "A vida religiosa á luz do misterio da graça," in *Convergência* 75 (1954): 1173–80. J. Batista, "Vida religiosa y testimonio público," in *CLAR,* no. 19, Bogotá, 1974. G. Pennock, "Vida religiosa y vocación bautismal," in *CLAR,* no. 17, Bogotá, 1974; see especially chap. 1, pp. 13–24, "Inserción en Cristo profeta." C. Palmes, "Teología bautismal y vida religiosa," in *CLAR,* no. 16, Bogotá, 1974; especially chap. 3, "La vida religiosa, signo profético," pp. 81–128. "Vida según el Espíritu," *CLAR,* no. 14, pp. 43–45, 65–66.

38. Alvara Panqueva, "La consagración religiosa," a commentary on *CLAR,* no. 14 in *Vinculum* 117 (1973): 45. See N. Zevallos, "Nuevas formas de vida religiosa y de comunidades religiosas in América Latina—I," in the El Escorial anthology *Fe cristiana y cambio social en América Latina* (Salamanca: Sígueme, 1973), p. 374; Edwards and Agudelo, "Nuevas formas de vida religiosa y de comunidades religiosas en América Latina—II," ibid., p. 379.

39. N. Zevallos, "Nuevas formas de vida religiosa," p. 375. J. Batista, "Vida religiosa y testimonio público," p. 99.

40. A. Panqueva, "La consagración religiosa," p. 47. Ibid: "Religious are not to be defined as a sign but as people seeking to follow Christ in a radical way. Posing as a sign is not enough. Public consecration is an effective sign to the extent that religious truly live it in a radical way" (p. 49).

41. See CLAR, "Seminario Latinoamericano de Superiores Mayores," Lima, 1974, mimeographed: "The radicalism lies in making the experience of God in Christ the fundamental project and central nuculeus of my own life" (D2, D3).

other hand it is meant to remind the world of the most important and basic demands of the gospel message.[42] If people live in a radical way, then they cannot be halfway human beings. They become people trying to make God tangible in a world fraught with contradictions.[43]

Fidelity in following the Lord is an inherent feature of such radicalism. Here we find the obligation to keep on creating continuity in a novel way. Rather than presenting itself as a state of perfection, the following of Christ presents itself as an uninterrupted process of straining toward the Lord. Fidelity, besides being a process itself, requires that we be faithful to the rhythm of the process entailed in following the Lord.[44]

The Religious Life as Mission

Two central notes of the church were brought out clearly in the ecclesiology of Vatican II: i.e., its sacramental nature and its community structure. These two dimensions both point up and flesh out the experience of the kingdom here and now. Without exaggeration we can say that this has prompted people to rethink the theology of the religious life as a

---

42. *CLAR*, no. 20: "Vida religiosa en América Latina, sus grandes líneas de búsqueda," written by CLAR's team of theologians. They say: "We live in a world where God and his presence are recalled and made explicit less and less. In such a world we, with our lives of prayer and fraternity, must restore to human beings the certainty that God is love, that he is at work in history as the liberator, and that salvation is not solely something for the future. Salvation becomes history in movements and human beings that seek brotherhood, justice, and the creation of a more human world" (p. 17).

43. *CLAR*, no. 14, p. 23.

44. See R. Muñoz, "Los religiosos en la Iglesia y para el mundo," especially the section subtitled "Una explicación superada: el estado de perfección," pp. 28–29. C. Palmes, "Teología bautismal y vida religiosa," pp. 131–32: "It is not a state but a process. Here is another characteristic of the vows viewed in terms of the inner attitude they presuppose. They do not create some acquired state; instead they inititate a dynamic process that actualizes consecration from day to day."

Other writers, following the lines of Vatican II, have dealt with the religious life as a state. See J. Hortal, "Estado da vida consagrada—estado secular. Ensaio de caracterização canônico-teológica," in *Perspectiva Teológica* 5 (1971). P. Beguin has a suggestive approach to analyzing and interpreting the position of Vatican II with regard to the lay, priestly, and religious states. He suggests that the only states are the laity and the religious life, while the condition of the clergy is an intermediate state: see "La vida religiosa franciscana," in *Cefepal* 5 (1972); idem, "La vocación de la orden hoy," ibid., 20 (1972): 221.

maximum expression of the sacramental nature of the church.[45] It has led them to stress the sign character of the religious life and its functional role in the mystery of the church and the proclamation of the good news.

The real situation of Latin America and its people, however, forces us to put the stress on mission, commitment, liberative action, and transforming presence.[46] It is on the basis of this practice that people derive the need to reconsider the concrete forms of the religious life and its theological interpretation.

Mission is thus becoming the basic principle and experience of conversion,[47] holiness, and theological work. Without this clear-cut option for mission as the locale for spiritual and theological renewal, all theological reflection on the religious life is in danger of becoming abstract and sterile.[48]

The import of consecration, then, must be reinterpreted from the standpoint of mission:

Suppose we assume that consecration to God is consecration to all that which God loves and for which Christ laid down his life. That leads us to a clear conclusion on religious consecration as such. It must be a consecration to humanity, inextricably linking the consecrated person with everything human and everything that somehow relates to the life of human beings. And the link follows from the nature of religious consecration itself, not in spite of it.[49]

In the thinking of CLAR we find two sides. On the one hand we see an effort to maintain Vatican II's stress on the thrust of baptismal consecration.[50] On the other hand we also see it beginning to stress

---

45. Beltrán Villegas, "La visión renovada de la Iglesia como marco de la vida religiosa," pp. 18–19,22.

46. See L. Boff, "La vita religiosa nel processo di liberazioni," p. 5 (2.11).

47. C. Palmes, "Teología bautismal y vida religiosa," p. 65: "Converting to Christ is adopting his existence, and the life of Christ is his mission." C. Caliman, "Missão, gratuidade divina e esforço humano," in Convergência 57 (1973): 201–11.

48. G. Pennock, "Missão e tarefas prioritarias," in Convergência 59–60 (1973): 343f: "The more we reflect on the import of the religious life, the more we come to the conclusion that it is mission first and foremost." See also J. Sansão, "Teologia da missão," ibid., 53 (1973): 9–17; H. Baggio, "Missão e comunidade," ibid., 55 (1973): 73f; C. Perani, "Missão: proclamação do reino ou promoção humana," ibid., 58 (1973): 265–73.

49. E. Delaney "Reflexiones teológicas," in Vida en Fraternidad 12 (1973): 11.

50. CLAR, no. 3–1, pp. 11–12; C. Palmes, "Teología bautismal y vida religiosa," chap. II, p. 41–79.

mission as the dialectical pole of the reserve implicit in consecration.[51]

If consecration is fundamentally mission,[52] then flight from the world is not just a deviation, as it always was. Insofar as it suggests scorn for the world, lack of historical responsibility, apoliticism, or neutrality, then in Latin America it would be a sin against the Holy Spirit. For it would be a sin against the liberation awaited by a people subject to injustice, exploitation, and racial discrimination. If following Christ really means setting out in his footsteps, then his journey means plunging more and more into the world, as Paul reminds us (Phil 2:6–11). His passion and death are the culmination of his involvement in history, of his unconditional self-surrender to human beings. In Christ mission is a flight to the world where he loses himself as the Son of God and finds himself specifically as the liberator. For religious on our continent, then, the old *fuga mundi* is presenting itself more and more as solidarity with the plight of the marginalized majorities and as a rejection of the political options and the basic system that has generated these exploited masses.[53]

It is through this sort of presence in the life of our people that evangelization, as the most explicit embodiment of mission, constitutes the center of the life led by religious. The religious life becomes comprehensible and effective when it is imbedded in the work of evangelization and the holiness of the people, when it is an effort to turn all into a people, a people of God.[54]

---

51. *CLAR,* no. 14, pp. 39–45. See the commentary of A. Panqueva, "La consagración religiosa," p. 42f. See also J. Comblin, "A vida religiosa como consagração," in *Grande Sinal* 24 (1970): 21–30.

52. L. Boff, "Vida religiosa y secularización," in *CLAR,* no. 18, p. 14: "Consecration and exclusive attachment to God do not mean that God needs human beings for himself. That would be a pagan conception of consecration. God needs instruments to act in the world, to make the promises of the kingdom present and visible among human beings. Hence consecration basically signifies mission." Idem, "La vita religiosa nel processo di liberazione," pp. 4–5 (2.9). The Brazilian Conference of Religious makes mission an essential element of the religious life. See *CLAR,* no. 6.

53. See *CLAR,* no. 1, pp. 16–17. Also see the Medellín Conference's final document on religious: "If it is true that the religious removes himself from the events of the present world, he does so not because he despises the world, but because of his awareness of its transitory and relative character" (no. 3). Notice that this suggests an approach that has not managed to reformulate the more positive and creative import of flight from the world. In a more historical vein see E. Delaney, "Reflexiones teológicas," p. 12; and L. Boff, "Vida religiosa y secularización," pp. 34–35.

54. *CLAR,* no. 3–II, p. 13; *CLAR,* no. 13, p. 33.

The growing centrality of mission as a theological principle and as the locale of religious experience is our way of translating the important role given to apostolic work by Vatican II. *Perfectae caritatis* pointed out that apostolic activity is part of the very nature of the religious life.[55] It is the understanding of mission today in Latin America that is producing the renewal and the tension, the conflict and the maturing process, in the life of various religious communities.[56] So it is in terms of mission that we must ponder religious formation and the structures of the religious life.[57] When we talk about mission in the practice of our communities, we mean something more than catechesis and cultic worship. We are referring to the presence and activity of the church in the process of transforming Latin America. We are referring to the church's committed involvement in the liberation of our people. Latin America presents itself as the theological locale of mission,[58] which means we must recognize the historical, social, political, and conflict-laden factors that will serve as the basis for our reconsideration of what that mission entails.

Two major preoccupations stand out in the reflection of religious on the nature of their mission. One has to do with their involvement in diocesan pastoral activity and other phases of joint pastoral effort.[59] The other

---

55. Vatican II, *Perfectae caritatis*, no. 8. In that case it does not seem quite right to talk about the apostolate as a projection of the religious life. See *CLAR*, no. 1, p. 21.

56. *CLAR*, no. 1, p. 20: "The integration of the apostolic life in all its forms into the life of religious congregations is taking on the character of a dramatic problem in Latin America. This is particularly true in the case of young people, who have been sensitized by the conditions surrounding the humanization process on our continent." See J. Hernández Pico, "Renovación de la vida religiosa en América Latina," a report to the national convention of Guatemalan Religious (1973), in *Vida en Fraternidad* 20 (1974): 41–48, and in CLAR's Bulletin, January 1974.

57. *CLAR*, no. 3–1, p. 57: "The evangelization of human beings and of human society is the criterion that must govern the outside activities of religious congregations." See the comments of the third Latin American conference of the Provincials of the Brothers of the Christian Schools in *CLAR*, no. 8, p. 55: "The apostolic aim of the congregation should shape the entire training of brothers in order that we may avoid a dichotomy between the spiritual life and the apostolic life. The potential danger of such a dichotomy was pointed out by our holy founder: "Do not create differences between the works of your industry and the business of your perfection and salvation.' "

58. E. Cardenas, "Vida religiosa y situaciones históricas," in *CLAR*, no. 15, pp. 96–98; see Luis Pérez Aguirre, *Teología latinoamericana para la crisis de la vida religiosa* (Buenos Aires: Ed. Guadalupe, 1973), pp. 127–39.

59. See *CLAR*, no. 1, pp. 19, 49–50; *CLAR*, no. 4, p. 63; *CLAR*, no. 20, pp. 35–36.

preoccupation, which touches very closely on our past training, has to do with the relationship between action and contemplation.[60] Put in more complex terms, it has to do with the role and sense and purpose of contemplative congregations vis-à-vis the historical challenges on our continent. CLAR does not hesitate to grant them a major role, provided that they are grounded historically on the reality of Latin America,[61] but it does not go further. The sign embodied by contemplatives and their witness cannot easily be grasped or accepted by people such as our own, who are being driven to act and to fight. Yet we do find much esteem and even admiration for the "little sisters of the cloister" among certain segments of the common people. In all likelihood this is due to the fact that they see them as realizing the values of asceticism, renunciation, mortification, privation, sacrifice, suffering, and penance that left such a profound imprint on their own traditional spiritual life.

The Religious Life as a Commitment to Liberation

It is in committed involvement with Latin America that we will give historical expression to our option for Christ, for discipleship, and for his proclamation to human beings. On our continent today commitment must have a certain quality in the case of Christians. It must be liberative commitment. It must unfold in the concrete struggles to liberate our people from exploitation and injustice and to create a just, fraternal, socialist society. This sums up the political option and the revolutionary task.

We religious have been coming to realize that this obligation is not an addendum to our vocation but rather something that is part of the very nature of the religious life. *Perfectae caritatis* (no. 8) indicated that good works, along with apostolic activities, are part of the very nature of the religious life. Given the present history of our people, we can say that "good works" mean liberation. Liberation is a grave and urgent good work.

CLAR puts the matter very clearly:

The hour striking in Latin America lends particular urgency to this solidarity and openness and imposes a very specific way of living it. In that sense the need of

---

60. See N. Zevallos, *Contemplación y política* (Lima: CEP, 1975). S. Galilea, "Contemplación y apostolado," in *IPLA* (Bogotá) 17 (1973), and in *Espiritualidad de la vida* (ISPAJ, 1973), pp. 13–32 ("Contemplación y compromiso").

61. See *CLAR*, no. 1, p. 23 ("Institutos contemplativos"), and *CLAR*, no. 14, p. 46.

Latin America is the norm determining how we should live our community life. It is not simply one feature that our community life must have. Instead we must live a community life that corresponds with the demands of Christ in Latin America.[62]

We cannot escape the risks, the confusions, and the oversimplifications that can be found in many Christians. That is the price we must pay if we wish to keep our gifts alive. But now we find that our awareness is growing clearer and that we can begin to express the thrust of our experience more precisely. We are coming to see that salvation works out by way of historical liberation, that evangelization takes the same route, and that it is in liberation that the religious life will find its meaning and efficacy if it has any at all. As one group of Franciscans put it:

We now know that concrete experience of God is given in the concrete historicization of the life of the people, not just on some merely spiritual or private level. We will have to get involved in that dimension where human destiny is now being decided in Latin America: i.e., politics. By politics here we are referring to our obligation to participate as much as we can in a praxis aimed at defending human rights, promoting the full person, and working for the cause of peace and justice in ways that are in conformity with the gospel message.[63]

Even earlier the Medellín Conference had pointed out that change was the most basic aspiration of our people, and that it could not be effected without breaking the existing situation of dependence and domination. Thus the social and political struggle for liberation is nothing else but a creative and hope-laden response to the existing situation of institutionalized violence. This is the reality that cries out to the religious life. The crisis we face now is not necessarily the crisis of the generation gap. It is not necessarily a conflict between an older generation and a younger one. It is basically a crisis of clarifying and defining the religious life vis-à-vis the struggle for the liberation of our continent. It is that struggle that is raising questions about our faith, our identity, our charisms, and our works.

There has rightfully been much insistence that we religious must become better acquainted with the reality of our continent.[64] The crisis,

---

62. *CLAR*, no. 31, p. 47 (n. 42b).

63. Letter from the third Latin American meeting of Franciscan Major Superiors to Franciscans throughout the continent (Mexico City, October 1972), in *Nuevo Mundo* 2 (1972): 453–54. They candidly admit that it was not possible to arrive at conclusions because of the differences in cultural horizons and outlooks.

64. See *CLAR*, no. 1, p. 17; *CLAR*, no. 31, p. 47, n. 43; *CLAR*, no. 20, p. 30.

however, is not just on the level of information about reality. It also has to do with our interpretation and our option: "Our way of getting to know reality is conditioned by our frame of reference and the people around us."[65]

There is a whole set of factors that explain the crisis in the religious life. The key factor is the situation of underdevelopment, poverty, marginality, and discrimination that exists both as a structural reality and as a mass phenomenon affecting the majority of people.[66] This basic factor explains the huge effort of the people to shore up the liberation movement, the slow growth and articulation of a leftist front which is organically linked to the proletariat and the peasant masses, and the creation and implementation of an alternative historical project rooted in the popular classes. When religious are invited to involve themselves in the liberation movement, all that is involved.[67] Today on our continent it also involves clandestine activities, repression, torture, exile, and perhaps even death.[68] Much of our anxiety and searching is due to that, and to our desire to be a prophetic sign in this context of group or class confrontation and struggle.[69]

Only within this overall, concrete political perspective is it permissible for us to go on to talk about cultural changes, secularization, a new scale of values, and a new type of human being as components of the current crisis in the religious life.[70] The phenomenon of secularization has oc-

---

65. *CLAR*, no. 4, p. 62, n. 110.

66. See the excellent theological observations on the gospel of the poor in the face of Latin American underdevelopment in *CLAR*, no. 4, pp. 46–50, nos. 81–89. *CLAR*, no. 31, pp. 13–15, offers a very general description of the world situation and points to oppression and poverty as the two great problems on our continent. A more technological point of view, devoid of a more political vision, can be found in Houtart, De Lora, and Poblete, "La vida religiosa en América Latina: consideración sociológica," in *CLAR*, no. 2, pp. 47–50.

67. See L. Patiño, "Problemi, compiti e prospettive," in *L'apporto dei religiosi italiani nella chiesa dell'America Latina*, documents and proceedings of a meeting held in Rome, 1972, p. 172.

68. Countless religious men and women find themselves in this situation. I need only mention the Brazilian Dominicans who have been tortured, the Chilean Salesian (Poblete) who died under torture, and those who are now living in exile.

69. See J. M. Guerrero, "El religioso y la política," in *Vida Religiosa Hoy*, the bulletin of CONFER, Arequipa, October 1974, mimeographed, p. 5.

70. That is why I find the diagnostic remarks of J. M. R. Tillard to be insufficiently political, though they are good. See his *Devant Dieu et pour le monde* (Paris: Ed. du Cerf, 1974), pp. 15–58. The same holds true for the fine remarks of A.

cupied a central place in the re-examination of the religious life.[71] It has been examined with more or less originality in Latin America also.[72] The process of growing politicization and theological maturation based on political praxis has led to a distinctively Latin American understanding. It might be summed up in the following terms: The secular realm demanded by faith itself is to be discovered in political practice. It is one dimension of the historical project of liberation. This prevents secularization from ultimately becoming a new way to maintain the status quo of an affluent society, to stay ensconced in the system, and to neutralize the prophetic message of the gospel by making faith and the church purely private matters.[73]

More than the secular realm in general, it is the political realm that serves as the basic category covering the process of maturation now being undergone by our people.[74] To be more specific, it is the category of liberation, which points more clearly to the import and content of the political realm. It makes it evident that the vocation and historical task of our people is liberation as praxis, process, and project. It reveals that the most vital aspect of the liberation effort here is to transform a nonhuman world into a truly human one. In other areas of the world the major concern may well be to face up to a nonreligious, nonbelieving world.[75]

Durand, "Recherche sur le sens de la vie religieuse," in *Lumière et Vie*, 96, pp. 55–61.

71. I refer the reader to the bulletins of the Institute "Fe y Secularidad" in Madrid; see "Secularización," 1970, Bulletin no. 1, especially p. 76. Also see the anthology, "Fe y secularización en América Latina," IPLA, 12, Bogotá, 1972.

72. See. J. M. Guerrero, "Vida religiosa en un mundo secularizado," in *CLAR*, nos. 9–10. L. Boff offers enlightening remarks in "Vida religiosa y secularización," in *CLAR*, no. 18.

73. See G. Gutiérrez, *A Theology of Liberation*, Part III. S. Galilea, "La fe como principio crítico de promoción de la religiosidad popular," in *Fe cristiana y cambio social en América Latina*, pp. 154–55. R. Poblete, "Formas específicas del proceso latinoamericano de secularización," pp. 159–77. J. C. Scannone, "Necesidad y posibilidades de una teología socio-culturalmente latinoamericana," ibid., pp. 353–72, especially pp. 357–59.

74. Here I mean "political realm" in the sense brought out so well in CLAR's working draft, "Vida religiosa y situación socio-económica en América Latina," chap. I, pp. 8–9.

75. G. Gutiérrez: "Liberation theology's first question cannot be the same one that progressivist theology has asked since Bonhoeffer. The question is not how we are to talk about God in a world come of age, but how we are to tell people who are scarcely human that God is love and that God's love makes us one family. The

A second focal point for various pastoral and theological factors is the historical position of the institutional church amid the reality of our continent. Taking cognizance of the situation of injustice and exploitation, we have discovered the allies and accomplices who are participants in it. Sad to say, it is not just isolated, individual Christians who are involved. All too often the ecclesiastical institution itself has been on the side of the powerful who control the lives of the majority of our people. CLAR, for example, acknowledges that the ongoing renewal of the religious life is real enough. But it asks: "Is it deep and broad enough to erase the traditional image of the church as an ally of the powerful and an opponent of social changes?" Even the Medellín Conference admitted that there was much evidence to substantiate the complaints that "the hierarchy, the clergy, the religious are rich and allied with the rich."[76]

These historical facts, which still persist today, are having a profound impact on many religious. We have been rudely awakened from our sleep. We have come to see that we were mistaken when we thought that

---

interlocutors of liberation theology are the nonpersons, the humans who are not considered human by the dominant social order—the poor, the exploited classes, the marginalized races, all the despised cultures. Liberation theology categorizes people not as believers or unbelievers but as oppressors or oppressed. . . The interlocutors of liberation theology "share" the same faith as their oppressors, but they do not share the same economic, social, or political life ("Two Theological Perspectives: Liberation Theology and Progressivist Theology," in Sergio Torres and Virginia Fabella, M.M., *The Emergent Gospel,* Maryknoll, N.Y.: Orbis Books, 1978, p. 241).

Gutiérrez would then proceed to ask how we can proclaim God as Father in an inhuman world, how we can convince nonhumans that they are children of God. This is the focus of those doing theology in Latin America. They do not avoid the theological problem of justifying their faith, nor do they naively think that the liberation of the poor will automatically be the resurrection of God or the reformulation of our expressions of faith. They have not given themselves up wholly to human liberation alone and abandoned theology as A. Fierro claims. According to Fierro (*The Militant Gospel,* Eng. trans., Maryknoll, N.Y.: Orbis Books, 1977, pp. 356–60) the sole purpose of theology is to prevent the world, society, and history from closing in upon themselves and saying no to transcendence; it does this by expressing things symbolically. But that still leaves us with the problem of the concrete, historical mediation of this world, this society, and these particular symbols today. See E. Dussel, "Dominación—liberación," in *Concilium* 96 (1974): 328–52.

76. *CLAR,* no. 4, pp. 24–26, nos. 33,36. Medellín document on poverty, no. 2.

our service to the people had to take the form of dedicating ourselves to the ruling classes.[77] For in the end the latter always managed to impose their outlook and interests on the church and its religious communities. This realization has stirred up broad and profound human questions on both the personal and collective level. Theological revisions, changes in ecclesiology, and changes in our understanding of the church have then followed to shed some further light or further complicate the picture.[78]

We can readily see why many religious and even whole communities have difficulty in trying to gain a more historical understanding of the country and the local church in the light of interpretations about their commitment made in Rome, Madrid, or Paris. The problem does not just confront foreigners or European decision-making centers for communities working in Latin America. It also affects members of Latin American generalates and foreigners who have spent a brief spell in Latin America. It is getting harder and harder for them to grasp what is going on in our countries and our grassroots churches.[79]

The problem is not just one of discipline. It is not simply of a juridical nature. Obedience is mediated through politics and ideology on the one hand and through theology and pastoral work on the other. Herein lies one of the reasons for the "departure" of religious men and women, though it may not be the main reason.

There can be no doubt that the new awareness of religious owes much to the conciliar emphasis on a poor church. Committed involvement with

---

77. A key text for the renewal of the religious life on our continent is in *CLAR*, no. 4, p. 56, n. 103: "Here we encounter a twofold mistake. First of all there is a sociological mistake, because the elites who could lead the process of development are increasingly people from the ranks of the common people rather than the rich. Second there is a theological mistake, because the 'economy' of the kingdom's expansion normally starts off with the poor and then moves on to invite the rich to conversion."

78. *CLAR*, no. 1, p. 40 points to the new ecclesiology and developments in the theology of marriage, the lay state, and authority as causes of the crisis in the religious life. Also see *CLAR*, no. 3–II, p. 49, nos. 24–28, which adds anthropocentrism, secularization, and the absence of a theology of obedience. For the notion that theological renewal follows afterward see J. L. Segundo, "Liberación de la teología," *Cuadernos L. A.* (Buenos Aires) 17 (1975): 88–104; in Eng. see Segundo's *The Liberation of Theology* (Maryknoll, N.Y.: Orbis Books, 1976).

79. Since 1967 CLAR has been stressing the importance of decentralizing our decision-making centers, particularly because we must train young religious for participation in the socio-political evolution of Latin America (*CLAR*, no. 1, pp. 45–51, especially p. 17).

the poor clearly occupies a key role in the new realization that the religious life is to be viewed as a commitment to liberation for Latin America. This is the theological outlook of the Medellín Conference in attempting to reformulate the presence and activity of the church in the process of continental change.

Thus stress is placed on the need for "integration" and "incarnation" into the world of the poor. As CLAR put it in 1967, there must be a clear-cut personal definition vis-à-vis the poor as they exist in the economic society of today. Religious must choose to focus their attention on the poor, "establishing solidarity with the poor, their problems, their struggles, and their commitments. They will do this in line with papal and episcopal norms, seeking the evangelical import of authentic justice as it relates to the kingdom. Only in such a way can religious be truly present in the world of the poor, assimilate the values of the poor, and thus adapt their lifestyle to that of the poor. Religious must 'incarnate themselves' in the world of the poor."[80]

There can be no integration in the world of the poor without an option for them. Voluntary adoption of the lifestyle of the poor is the result and embodiment of an option for the historical project and the interests of the poor. Herein also lies the real sense of solidarity with the poor. Sharing the living conditions of the poor is not worth much if we do not also share the import and concrete historical embodiment of their struggles and their concerns. Unfortunately our communities have often failed to realize this. While they may live with the poor and share their lifestyle, they do not share the thrust and concrete incarnation of their struggles and their interests. Religious women brought this out clearly at their 1971 meeting in Mexico: "We must identify ourselves with the real plight of the Latin American people, recover their values (which are basically Christian), and actively accompany them in all their historical projects."[81]

There is solid theological motivation and clear-cut socio-political objectivity in this option for the poor.[82] It is theologically sound because the

---

80. *CLAR*, no. 1, p. 34.

81. This brings out the inadequacy of a distinction between personal poverty and a collective situation of non-poverty, between poverty of spirit and a society that produces poor people. See *CLAR*, no. 6, p. 41; *CLAR*, no. 13, "La religiosa hoy en América Latina," pp. 27, 41–42. Also see *CLAR*, no. 4, p. 55, n. 100: "Religious are really living signs of evangelical poverty, but they cannot lose sight of the goal of integral human development that will enable the poor to be active participants in their own liberation."

82. *CLAR*, no. 4, pp. 41–53, n. 98 and n. 103.

"economy" of the kingdom's growth normally starts off with the poor. It moves on from there to invite the rich to conversion, as CLAR reminds us. We reread the gospel message from the standpoint of the poor. An exegesis based on the experiential struggles of our people does not merely enable us to discover the gospel of Jesus Christ; it is also necessary if we wish to reconsider the meaning and function of the religious life today. The most burning questions confronting many religious can find a response only there.[83] The good news of the kingdom is addressed to the poor. The kingdom implies that the poor are liberated from their poverty. So we simply must interpret the gospel message from the standpoint of the poor and the present juncture in history.[84]

What is more, a commitment to the poor is not optional. It is an obligation based on the summons to be perfect and to practice evangelical poverty.[85] Christians and Christian religious communities can live out their lives and their eschatological mission only if they are really immersed in the life of the people.[86] With sound evangelical sensitivity CLAR reminds us that our grasp of the signs of the time will depend on our understanding of the world of the poor.[87]

Clearly then, a commitment to the poor is the center and starting point for our understanding of the gospel message and history. An option for the poor is the "qualitative leap" required for the revitalization of the religious life as a prophetic charism and a contribution to liberation on our continent.[88] It is in such a commitment that the Lord seeks to revitalize the holiness of his people, the spiritual life of those who dedicated themselves to him and chose to follow him in the religious life. For us religious this option for the poor is a spiritual experience with tremendous historical implications.

---

83. *CLAR*, no. 20, pp. 29–30.

84. There is an excellent example of interpreting the gospel message in terms of our continent's conditions and vocation in *CLAR*, no. 4, pp. 44–50, nn. 75–89.

85. Ibid., p. 39, n. 65, and p. 53, n. 95.

86. Ibid., p. 52, n. 93. See C. Palmes, "Una vida religiosa más auténtica," in *Vida en Fraternidad* 18 (1974): 43. His article offers many worthwhile observations. The third section, however, contains views that might well be re-examined. He is somewhat anti-Marxist, he tends to justify any type of work with any social class, and his emphasis is more theological and spiritual when it comes to the sociopolitical option.

87. *CLAR*, no. 4, p. 9, n. 2.

88. Edwards and Agudelo, "Nuevas formas de vida religiosa y de comunidades religiosas in América Latina—II," *Fe cristiana y cambio social*, p. 379.

We have not just taken cognizance of the evangelical richness of this commitment; we have also noted its socio-political implications. With serene boldness CLAR spoke out in 1967 on this matter. It admitted that polarizing our lives around one particular social class, in this case the poor, could cause us to forget the more universal perspective of the people of God. But it then went on to say: "Given the peculiar circumstance of Latin America, those whose human development and acceptance of the saving message is impeded by poverty, dire need, ignorance, or illness cry out for special attention."[89]

It is our work with peasants and laborers, our tasks of training their people and accompanying them, that puts us right into the heart of political action. Work with the poor requires that we undergo a conversion to evangelical poverty and rational political activity.[90] Direct contact with the social problems of oppressed groups does give us an awareness of Latin American realities, but it does not spare us further effort. We must interpret those realities in the light of the social and political sciences, and we must constantly re-examine the thrust and aims of our option for the common people. This is all the more true because this option brings us face to face with a collective reality and a structural situation.[91] In 1973 a group of people involved in the training of religious had this to say:

We believe that our mandatory summons to universal brotherhood and filiation entails a political stand against any and every unjust structure. . . . Political and socio-economic commitment concretely means a commitment to liberation in

---

89. *CLAR*, no. 3–II, p. 62.

90. Ibid., p. 29, n. 4: "The betterment of peasants and laborers, participation in youth groups, and consciousness-raising are activities well suited to the formation of evangelical poverty. We must remain cognizant of the political dimension that we often confront. Working calmly and objectively and taking due account of concrete circumstances, we must work toward a mature position through trust and dialogue. Such a position would include commitment and responsibility." The same point was made in CLAR's working draft, "Vida religiosa y situación socio-política en América Latina," p. 13, n. 56: "The conversion of religious to evangelical poverty and service to the oppressed is a political act with wide-ranging implications."

91. *CLAR*, no. 4, p. 48, n. 86: "If the gospel simply asked us to attend to isolated individuals insofar as our 'private' action could do so, that would mean today that the gospel was not the least bit concerned whether the activity of Christians on behalf of the poor was efficacious."

which we join hands with the oppressed people. It means identifying our lives and interests with the oppressed in order to attain justice, freedom, and fraternity. This is salvation as well.[92]

In the face of specific situations, however, the picture becomes much more complicated. "There are no clear guidelines or even clues where the destiny of our people is concerned."[93] Involvement with labor organizations and various forms of more direct political involvement bespeak an ability to respond, to make our service effective and flexible, to maintain fidelity to the gospel message and the prophetic charism of the religious life.[94]

This particular point, a commitment to direct political action on our continent, is both central and delicate.[95] To say it once again, clarification will come from mature and creative practice, from serious and serene evaluation of concrete experiences. The past history of our nations and our churches may shed some light on our quest,[96] but the fact remains

---

92. CLAR, First Latin American Seminar on training for the religious life, Lima, 1973; in *Vida en Fraternidad* 20 (1974): 22.

93. Letter of the Franciscan Major Superiors, Mexico City, 1972; in *Nuevo Mundo*, no. 2 (1972): 453–54.

94. In 1967 CLAR stated: "In general the structures for involvement in the world should grow out of the professional character of the work done by religious. To put it more concretely, they will be embodied in representative associations that bring together people of the same profession."

95. For a more reserved point of view see J. Cifuentes, "La religiosa y la política," in *Testimonio* 17 (1972), CONFER, Chile. He gives fifteen reasons why religious women should not participate in politics. See P. Bigo, "Vida religiosa y liberación," in *Mensaje* 226 (1974): 21f. He stresses the liberative dimension of the religious life but insists that it does not derive from a political option or ideology. Rather, he says, it derives from the spirit of the gospel message (p. 27). The liberative work of Jesus was neither political nor apolitical (p. 22). In another article he pointedly reminds us that Jesus' message is not political because it does not propose any ideology or any strategy (Bigo, "Jesús y la política de su tiempo," in *Medellín* 1 (1975): 51. For some bold but uneven proposals see J. M. Guerrero, "El religioso y la política," in *Vida religiosa hoy* (CONFER, Arequipa), October 1974, pp. 2–15, mimeographed.

96. See CLAR's working draft, "Vida religiosa y stiuación socio-política en América Latina," chap. II, p. 15, nos. 60–75 and chap. III, p. 20, nos. 81–84,117: "The situation often leads people to take on options where it is hard to see how far one can go. Every day religious find themselves in extremely difficult and varied situations. Factory work leads to membership in labor unions or political par-

that Latin America is going through processes which are unheard-of in many other areas of the world. We are called upon to show prudence and the boldness of the Spirit.

The situation is all the more ticklish because political activity is not necessarily derived from, or sustained by, theological principles. It has its own rationale. Moreover, such options are expressions of personal charisms that may not be normative for the rest of the religious community. Even when they are more collective and communitarian on one level, they may not necessarily apply to the religious congregation throughout a larger region or the world.

Thus the concrete political expressions of our evangelical option for the oppressed are not the hallmark of devilish people who are trying to divide our communities and empty our religious houses. The political picture that is challenging and upsetting our communities is also opening up many to a better understanding of the universal solidarity of the people of God and enabling them to give it historical embodiment among the poor and the oppressed:

Today religious communities are suffering from the tensions existing between members with different ideological options. At the same time there is arising a new sense of solidarity between religious who think the same way even though they may belong to different congregations. The same bond of harmony is being forged between people with similiar views in country after country. It seems desirable that all religious display an awareness that Latin America as a whole is their true homeland, united by its state of dependence and its common yearning for liberation. Religious should serve to give cohesion and impetus to the task of transforming this continent.[97]

The challenges involved here are not confined to the question of how

---

ties. They get involved in strikes, protest marches, and street fights. They sign letters and petitions protesting injustices or promoting a particular point of view. All these problems must be handled with the help of the community. The community must stand by those involved, offering criticism or enlightened support that takes due account of all the circumstances of the case." For a serious study of the activity of Franciscans and their socio-political conflicts see L. Gomez Canedo, "Evangelización y promoción social, algunos antecedentes históricos," in Nuevo Mundo, no. 2 (1972): 322–62.

97. CLAR's working draft, "Vida religiosa y situación socio-política en América Latina," p. 26, nos. 118–19. See also the conclusions reached at the meeting of the Maryknoll Sisters held in Peru (1971) in Contacto 8, 1 (1971): 95–97.

we are to provide religious with socio-political training.[98] There is also the problem of deciding how we can start from the political realm to give new and deeper meaning to the following of Christ, prayer life, the sense of *koinonia*, and the fraternal way of life.

Finally, the experience of those who have embraced the cause of the oppressed is one of passion and death. The cross is an inherent part of the liberation of the poor. The clear-eyed generosity of truly committed Christians and religious is contributing to the liberation that is growing out of the cross carried by the people. Martyrdom has always provided an image for those in the religious life. Today the serene and discreet self-surrender of religious men and women to the cause of the poor often means experiencing the martyrdom that the poor suffer. Here we can indeed reinterpret the image that tradition used to typify the religious life.

The authenticity of this religious renewal is real in qualitative terms, though it may not yet be affecting the majority. As CLAR points out, "its authenticity is proved by the criticism and persecution that is being suffered unjustly by priests and religious who have made this commitment to the poor."[99] As a commitment to liberation, the religious life accentuates the following and imitation of Christ from the standpoint of the poor. It highlights the historical exigencies of the kingdom, of God's love. Only from the standpoint of the poor and their hopes does the religious life serve as a sign of eschatological hope.[100]

---

98. See *CLAR*, no. 1. p. 17. See the third Latin American conference of the provincials of the Brothers of the Christian Schools, 1968, in *CLAR*, no. 8, p. 59: "The postulant is to offer proof of a genuine concern for the social problem in Latin America." On the specific problem of women see Pérez, "La religiosa y la promoción de la mujer," in *Testimonio* 9 (1970): 26f; M. A. Natoli, "La visión de la religiosa de hoy como contribución a la liberación de la mujer de mañana," ibid., p. 32f; and *CLAR*, no. 13, pp. 17–18, 29–33.

99. *CLAR*, no. 4, p. 24, n. 32. Also see *CLAR*, no. 8, pp. 70–71; J. Isaac, "La cruz, esencia de la vida religiosa," in *Cuadernos Monásticos* 8 (1973): 25–40.

100. J. Hernández Pico, "Renovación de la vida religiosa en América Latina," in *Vida en Fraternidad* 20 (1974): 46: "Justice is deteriorating more and more in our world. But there is only one thing that will signify our Christian radicalism and our hope against hope: being with the poor and alienated and accepting the risks of that stance." Also see L. Boff, "Vida religiosa en el contexto latinoamericano: oportunidad y desafío," Second Conference of Latin American Religious in Bogota, 1974, in *Vida Religiosa* 38, no. 283 (1975); E. Moureaux, "A vida religiosa entre os pobres," in *Convergência* 44 (1972): 31–40.

The Religious Life as Life According to the Spirit

Chapter V of Vatican II's *Lumen gentium*, which deals with the summons of the whole church to holiness, does two things. On the one hand it officially eliminates any exclusive expropriation of the vocation to holiness by those who have made a solemn religious profession and vowed to seek perfection. On the other hand it opens us up to a new understanding of Christian love as the core of the life to which the Lord is calling all of us.[101]

In the last analysis holiness is nothing else but charity: love for God and love for one's fellows. Holiness is the effort to bring together brotherhood and sonship.[102]

On our continent brotherhood between human beings must go by way of liberation from everything that produces inhuman situations and attitudes. Charity calls for justice as its point of verification. The Brazilian Conference of Religious (CRB) is quite correct when it sees an indissoluble link between holiness and the development of the Latin American continent: "Holiness is also a participation in the very holiness of God, i.e., in his power at the service of his goodness. So true is this that we can say that for us holiness would be integral development in the service of love."[103] If charity operates by way of liberation, then the motive and goal of liberation can be only to fashion love and bring it to maturity.[104]

To conceive love in such terms is to spell out its point of verification and its two essential dimensions. First of all, love has a collective, integral dimension. Second, its nature is to transform the existing social order.

We can readily imagine the subversive character of any holiness that is viewed in those terms. We can also appreciate the difficulties involved in trying to rethink what the older manuals of spirituality referred to as "the means leading to holiness." Holiness somehow expresses the transformation of our continent and of its people, of their awareness and orientation to the gratuitous love of the Father in Christ through the Spirit. It is in terms of this perspective that we are now looking for a spirituality of

---

101. See B. Kloppenburg, "Normas del Vaticano II para una vida santa," in *Cuadernos Monásticos* 8 (1973): 7–24.

102. See *CLAR*, no. 1, p. 9f: holiness is charity.

103. Brazilian Conference of Religious, 1968, in *CLAR*, no. 2, p. 22.

104. G. Gutiérrez, "Praxis de liberación, teología y anuncio," in *Concilium* 96, pp. 359–60.

development.[105] CLAR has chosen to dedicate one of its best efforts at study and reflection to the whole issue of life according to the Spirit as it is embodied in the religious communities of Latin America, though CLAR's perspective goes beyond the sphere of formal religious life as such.

Concern for the spiritual life and for the growth of love in our lives and the world has found solid support in biblical and liturgical renewal and in further theological reflection on the activity of the Holy Spirit.[106]

The spiritual life is the initiative and work of the Spirit of Jesus Christ.[107] The spirituality which most of us Latin American religious operate with somewhat uneasily is a difficult way of living our faith, but a way that is also quite novel. It entails fortifying our hope and sharing love from within the anxieties and struggles of our people. Our experience of God must come through our revolutionary experience. There it finds nourishment and support.

Theological reflection on liberation spirituality is growing richer and more extensive. It is reflection on a praxis that has been turned into prayer, poetry, and art. On all those levels we are expressing our understanding of the Father's gratuitous love, the militant love of his son, Jesus, and the creative love of the Spirit. In choosing to display our baptismal fidelity in the trammels of continental liberation, we religious are going through a vast spiritual experience. It should help us to clarify our own personal and communitarian experiences.[108]

---

105. First meeting of Latin American Franciscans, 1968, in *CLAR*, no. 8, p. 34: "We must combine correct knowledge of our people's socio-cultural situation with a deep knowledge of Catholic theology and Franciscan thought in order to create an authentic spirituality of development. At the same meeting a paper was delivered by E. Franco, "Pastoral franciscana en América Latina," in the volume published by the organizers of that meeting, Bogotá, 1969, p. 111. However, Franco seems to think that the problem of underdevelopment will be solved by a social spirituality designed to promote development.

106. See C. Henrique de Lima Vaz, "El Espíritu y el mundo," in *Grande Sinal* 1 (1972): 5–22; also in *Panorama de la teología latinoamericana*, Seladoc (Salamanca: Sígueme, 1975), pp. 71–90. See L. Boff, "La era del Espíritu," *Grande Sinal* 10 (1972): 723–33; reprinted in *Panorama de la teología latinoamericana*, pp. 91–192.

107. *CLAR*, no. 14, pp. 25–29. See Darío Restrepo, "Espíritu Santo y vida religiosa," in *Vinculum* 117 (1973): 24–28. On the whole relationship between experience of God, conversion, the activity of the Spirit, contemplation, and religious experience and knowledge see B. Kloppenburg, "As razões do coração," *REB*, 34 (1974): 343–51; also in *Vinculum* 120 (1974): 12–19.

108. Here is a brief bibliography. G. Gutiérrez, the section subtitled "A Spirituality of Liberation," in chap. 10 of *A Theology of Liberation*. Idem, "Espirtualidad

There are three central concerns in the characteristic dimensions of our liberation spirituality: commitment to the poor, a praxis that will transform history on the basis of the reality and the criteria of the poor, and the celebration of God's word in the light of this practice. Thus the experience of God is historical, communitarian, and cultic.[109] Experience of the Spirit becomes real, concrete experience only when it becomes history, when it becomes a people, when it becomes poor, when it becomes confidence, fortitude, fidelity, boldness, and lucidity in the struggles for liberation.[110] It is then that the life of prayer takes on full meaning as an experience that sums up our option for liberation and our decision to acknowledge, thank, and proclaim Jesus Christ in the struggle for liberation.

The life of prayer is inextricably bound up with real life, service to our fellows, and communion with them.[111] That is why "it is necessary to

---

liberadora," mimeographed copy of a 1973 lecture, Lima. Idem, "Praxis de liberación," *Concilium* 96, pp. 362–63. Idem, "Introduction" to *Signos de liberación*, pp. 13–36. S. Galilea, "A los pobres se les anuncia el evangelio," *IPLA*, no. 11, passim. Idem, "Espiritualidad liberadora," anthology of articles, ISPAJ, 1973. Idem, "Contemplación y apostolado," in *IPLA*, 17, Bogotá, 1973. Idem, "Liberación como encuentro de la política y de la contemplación," in *Concilium* 96 (1974): 313–27. Idem, "Espiritualidad liberadora de S. Juan de la Cruz," in *Testimonio* 78 (1975): 13–17. The organization of priests, ONIS, "Espiritualidad liberadora," working draft no. 3, Lima, 1974, mimeographed. Discalced Carmelites, "La espiritualidad para un continente en cambio: teología y espiritualidad de la liberación," Third Latin American meeting on spirituality, Quito, 1974, in *Vida Espiritual*, 47/49, 1975, pp. 3–269.

109. These are the same dimensions that the Peruvian bishops have stressed with regard to evangelization. See their document on Evangelization, 4, 1f. See J. Hortal, "Experiencia de Deus: seu lugar na teología actual," in *Perspectiva Teológica* 6 (1972): 59–71. *CLAR*, no. 14, p. 19f.

110. P. Fontaine, "Vida religiosa y experiencia de Dios," in *Testimonio* 28 (1975): 5–7. The author presents an excellent consideration of the historical, communitarian, and personal experience of God, correctly identifying the historical experience of God as stemming from concrete experience with the poor. C. Cheisie, "Hacia una espiritualidad carismática latinoamericana," in *Testimonio* 28 (1975): 8–12, is in a more critical vein. He makes some sharp observations on the charismatic movement. He says that its spirituality is ahistorical and apolitical, that it is culturally dependent on the big Catholic pentecostal centers of the United States and Europe, and that it has no impact on the poor or more highly politicized young people. Put more positively, the question is how we are to present the Holy Spirit in Latin America. What cultural categories are we to use: metaphysical, existential, personalist, mystical, or political?

111. *CLAR*, no. 3-II, pp. 43–44, n. 28–29.

bring what we live to prayer and to turn every action into a prayer. Prayer loses force insofar as it is removed from what happens every day. Real life and prayer begin to move on parallel lines. . . . In other words, the reality of our lives is not just the stimulus for prayer but also its content."[112] When we adopt this outlook, then our personal relationship with the Lord does not lose the mediation of history; it is enriched and given content by the latter. Our personal relationship with the Lord gains in meaningfulness and confers meaning on our real-life commitments.[113]

For us religious, an option for the poor and oppressed goes only half way if it does not become an attitude and a lived experience of evangelical poverty and simplicity of spirit. Thus our prayer life, which both assumes and creates an attitude of spiritual childlikeness, must express our option for the exploited and our openness to him from whom all gifts come.

Here we must stress the necessity of giving fraternal prayer a social dimension. Standing before our Father, we must address our prayer on behalf of the poor and needy of this continent. Today, more than ever before, they need to have their problems . . . become a vital part of the prayer life of religious. Fraternal prayer will lead religious to review and revise their commitment to the poor.[114]

Situating prayer life in this framework does not mean that we have solved the problems that many religious face today. More and more religious feel that CLAR is talking about them when it talks about religious whose prayer life is more an attitude toward life than a special moment in time or a set of formulas and prescribed practices. Their prayer is the prayer of the mystics, prayer as a basic attitude.[115]

---

112. Ibid., p. 17, no. 37. See CLAR, no. 6, p. 46: "Prayer is not an escape from real life . . . and the tasks devolving on the individual or groups; it is an activity belonging to the faith of the person who lives in communion with the real world. If it is not to be a meaningless escape, prayer must arise from the same human depths that faith does. In short, it must well up from the human spirit, a spirit aware of its responsibility for its own personal destiny and that of the community."

113. Ibid., pp. 14–16, nos. 28–35.

114. Ibid., p. 19, nos. 42,52: "Prayer must be the channel for the Latin American yearning for social action, development, and liberation. Far from being an obstacle to concrete commitment, it must serve as a permanent impetus to such commitment and be regarded as the necessary expression of it."

115. CLAR, no. 14, pp. 46–47. There the point is rightly made that a preoccupation and concern for others already establishes an encounter with God in the case of those who look to the Lord as the fundamental project of their lives. Also see

This is not to minimize personal prayer or special times for prayer. But a concern for liberative commitment and for prayer as a basic attitude in life sets up other criteria and other focal points that are not the special times hallowed by tradition. It makes us realize that all prayer, insofar as it is personal at all, is not individual but collective and social.[116]

Finally, the life of prayer brings out the need for discernment[117] and ascesis in the apostolic life.[118] Obviously this does not mean that we want to turn the religious life into some form of asceticism. Unfortunately spirituality and spiritual human beings were equated all too often with asceticism and mortification. Because liberation spirituality is a paschal spirituality, it does incorporate the transforming experience and perspective of the cross. However, asceticism, suffering, fasting, and renunciation are not means or instruments of sanctification; instead they are the results, the consequences of mission. Only in those terms are they able to express the profound liberative intent that animates every apostle and motivates every religious.[119]

And of course there can be no real Christian life centered in Christ without a Marian dimension. On our continent the Virgin Mary is a key

---

the comments on the document of H. Uribe, "Oración y vida religiosa," in *Vinculum* 117 (1973): 52–73.

116. *CLAR*, no. 14, p. 48: "Hence all personal prayer is somehow communitarian just as all communitarian prayer is also personal." In talking about formation *CLAR*, no. 31, p. 21, n. 9, rightly reminds us that "an evangelical value is always communitarian, and broader than the individuals who incarnate it." The collective and communitarian structure of the evangelical values enables us to better appreciate the collective structure of Christian existence and holiness. Also see Boff, Spindel, Dreier, Harada, *A oração no mundo secular* (Petrópolis, 1972).

117. *CLAR*, no. 14, pp. 53–58.

118. Ibid., pp. 59–61.

119. Ibid., p. 61: "Perhaps the most effective way of living a life of asceticism today and shouldering the cross of Christ is to sincerely live out one's vows as demands imposed by obedience and to live in solidarity with the marginalized people of our continent—sharing their labors and both the personal and communitarian risks involved." In other sections, however, this view is not maintained—at least not in such clear-cut terms. See E. Hoornaert, "Origem da 'vida religiosa' no cristianismo," in *Perspectiva Teologica*, no. 5 (1971), Recife Institute of Theology, p. 232. J. Aldunate, "Una nueva ascesis para el mundo de hoy," in *Cuadernos Testimonio* (Santiago de Chile) 4 (1972): 15–23. Maria Angela, "Una ascesis para los años de formación," ibid., pp. 24–32, offers more practical suggestions. C. Hallet, "Para una renovación de la ascesis de la vida religiosa," ibid., pp. 3–12.

part of the religious experience of the masses. A liberation spirituality must reformulate and include this Marian tonic. While this feature is present in theological reflection on the religious life, it may well be true that it has not been explored and spelled out enough. Hopefully this situation will soon be remedied.[120]

Approaching the religious life as a life according to the Spirit is another way of understanding the religious life as sign, prophecy, and the concrete embodiment of the new human being. In this case, however, the new human being is present only insofar as a "new heaven and earth" is being fleshed out on our continent today. It must entail the historical transformation of Latin America. That is holiness. That is salvation.

CONCLUSION

Here I should like to offer a summary overview of the situation in Latin America insofar as consideration of the religious life is concerned.

First of all, we must realize the importance of the 1968 Medellín Conference for all subsequent reflection on the religious life. It was not simply a problem of a practical nature, of what adaptations to make and how to do it. The clearly pastoral concern of the Medellín Conference required that we examine our criteria in greater depth and provide more solid theological grounding.

The basic context for our reconsideration and renewal of the religious life is clear enough. It is the vivid awareness and the concrete experience that our continent is fraught with exploitation and injustice, that the mass of people live in an inhuman situation.

For this reason the meaningfulness and caliber of the religious life in Latin America is bound up with its effectiveness in helping to transform this real-life situation. We cannot theologize about the religious life while turning our back on the surrounding reality. We cannot revitalize the holiness of our religious communities while remaining aloof from the general situation. The religious life cannot be a sign of the kingdom if it does not participate in the effort to transform our scandalous history.

Thus an option for the poor is an essential component of the project of

---

120. See *CLAR*, no. 14, pp. 34–35: "María, figura y modelo de la vida según el Espíritu," *CLAR*, no. 13, pp. 28–29,34. *CLAR*, no. 3–II, on training dedicates three lines to her, pp. 21,36,42. *CLAR*, no. 4, p. 39. *CLAR*, no. 16, devotes some eighteen lines to her, pp. 130, 150, 151. *CLAR*, no. 20, does not include some of the most significant religious aspects of Latin American life to which the religious life should correspond. Mary, for example, is not even given honorable mention!

the religious life. To the concrete difficulties of living out such an option are added different levels of understanding its political side. That explains the hesitation and vacillation of many. Increasingly, however, this commitment is becoming the focal point for theological reflection on the central themes of the religious life: the following of Christ, flight from the world, consecration,[121] life in fraternal communion, small communities,[122] and so forth. It is from this standpoint that we are looking hopefully, though not without conflict, at the future of the religious life.[123] We religious must be linked intimately with the poor in the midst of their struggles to fight injustice and build a new continent.

It is there that many religious are now living. It is there that many involved communities feel themselves being reborn to the gospel message and returned to history. It is there that many of them are becoming increasingly politicized, finding that this enables them to explore more deeply the collective and universal perspectives of their commitment to the poor. On this more highly social and political level of commitment to the poor we find a new and more fruitful link between prophecy and utopia, two key elements in the Christian and the religious life on our continent.

It is not just that we have a new context in which to discern the primacy of mission.[124] We are also more deeply concerned to rethink the theology

---

121. E. Delaney, "Los religiosos y el pueblo argentino," in *Vida en Fraternidad* 17 (1974): passim.

122. See CLAR, no. 1, p. 13. CLAR, no. 3-I, pp. 35–36. CLAR, no. 14, p. 58. CLAR, no. 20, pp. 39–42. On small communties see CRB, "Encontro sobre pequenas comunidades empenhadas diretamente na pastoral," in *Convergência* 75 (1974): 1163–67. CLAR, no. 31, pp. 45–47.

123. See M. Perdia, "Los religiosos del futuro vistos desde Latina América," in *Razón y Fe* 904 (1973): 387–92. M. Edwards, "La religiosa del futuro," in Supplement 15 of the Boletin CIRM, 1973, pp. 10–11. J. Domínguez, "El futuro de la vida religiosa," in *Christus* (Mexico City) 465 (1974): 23–26.

124. As M. Agudelo points out, "the guiding norm is the quest for liberation." That is the challenge to be posed to both natives and foreigners. See Agudelo, "Integración del religioso no nativo en la Iglesia local," in *CONFER* 11, no. 40 (1972), fasc. 3; in *Vinculum* 115 (1973); and in *L'apporto dei religiosi italiani nella chiesa dell'America Latina*, documents and proceedings of a meeting held in Rome, 1972, pp. 131–48. See A. Cuzzolin, "Validità del contributo dei religiosi stranieri," in *L'apporto dei religiosi italiani*, an interesting paper which reflects all the sensitivity and sincerity that should be evident in those who choose to come to Latin America. See E. Vigano, "Contribuição dos religiosos e das religiosas estrageiros a América Latina," in *Convergência*, 48/49 (1972): 41–42. Idem, "El papel del religioso

of the religious life from that context. It is a relatively recent phenomenon in the history of the religious life and its theology in Latin America; it is also being lived out and shared "in the flesh" more than it is being written down.

The demands confronting religious in our countries have been well summed up by the theological committee of CLAR. It calls for a religious life that is more authentic, more Latin American, more integrated into pastoral activity, and more fraternal. [125] However, it is on a different level that we discover a whole series of questions which are being gradually clarified on the basis of various concrete experiences. It is the level of describing, analyzing, and interpreting Latin American reality insofar as it relates to us as religious. It is not simply a matter of possessing some vision of reality or of taking due account of the political dimension in the religious life. Much more important is the relationship between the religious life and a political line of action. What demands are imposed by communal life, obedience, and so forth when they are considered in terms of political pluralism, and when we have already made a basic option for the poor and oppressed and for a socialist society? The renewal of religious life in Latin America cannot dodge this context without giving up its mission to be a sign and prophecy of the kingdom. [126] The contribution of the religious life to the process of Latin American liberation does not have just socio-political dimensions that need to be evaluated. The

en la tarea de liberación," *Testimonio* 9 (1970): 7f; it contains reflections designed to introduce the work of the committees, but it does not broach the more political perspectives of liberation.

125. *CLAR*, no. 20, reflects on the way CLAR sees its role in Latin America and present-day religious life on the continent. Rather than an evaluation it sets forth the lines that mark its present and that should characterize its near future. The sequence and order of the features mentioned might have been a bit different. Once an option for liberation has been made, then all the features must be judged in terms of their authenticity, their pertinence for Latin America, and so forth.

126. See S. Galilea, "Algunas condiciones para la renovación de la vida religiosa," in *Servir*, 1972, pp. 45–52. C. Caliman, "A prudencia na renovação da vida religiosa," in *Convergência* 52 (1972): 20–30. C. Perani, "Missão: proclamação do reino ou promoção humano," ibid., 58 (1973): 265–73. Though he does not diagnose the crisis, Perani maintains that the religious life, as an eschatological charism, cannot take on the social, political, and economic realms simply as part of our commitment; they must have a central place in the religious life. He admits that the religious life places us in the bourgeois class. He also proposes to hold a class vision, taking mission as human promotion for the starting point in trying to reconsider the religious life.

effectiveness of the contribution by Christian religious to our continent is much more global, but no less concrete. Within the mediation of political and cultural factors it must point up the meaning of the liberation effort.[127]

The best current efforts at Latin American reflection on the religious life are trying to start off from this frame of reference in order to find a response to the issues raised. The reception is very uneven, and more than a few tensions are being generated. That is the case with CLAR, for example.[128]

Finally, I should like to point up three features that reflection on the religious life must keep in view and that take on new force in the light of liberation theology. In a sense it is a question of emphasizing and visualizing certain points better, points that were initially worked out in Latin American theology. Only then will we explicitly draw nearer to the theology of liberation as a theology of the religious life.

In the first place theological methodology inexorably confronts us with a life option. We must opt for the oppressed, for the popular classes and their liberation project. Without this historical praxis the other levels and the very sense of our methodolgy will not be comprehensible. The peculiar thrust of liberation theology is not to offer us a scientific analysis and a political interpretation of reality. It is to show us that this option for the poor requires an analysis of reality which starts off from the dominated classes and cultures.[129] The various sociological theories of analysis and

---

127. L. Boff in *Vida en Fraternidad*, no. 13, p. 28: "If we approach the nature of the religious life in terms of its purpose or usefulness, . . . we run the risk of not grasping anything about its foundation or essence. To put it another way, . . . the religious life is useless, yet its chief richness and its radical meaningfulness lies in that uselessness. It is useless for technical enterprises, for the conquest of economic problems, and as a point of departure for liberation from underdevelopment. But this note of uselessness is not exclusively confined to the religious life, because God, his grace, Jesus Christ, and his message are useless in the same sense. But in fact they possess deep meaningfulness."

128. See "CLAR, o que e CLAR? " in *Convergência* 53/54 (1973): 33–37. This article explains what CLAR is and presents some of the criticisms directed against it. It is accused of not being representative enough, of tending toward secularization and dangerous experiences, of losing its own proper charism, and of being based too much on liberation theology. There is a partial response to these objections in *CLAR*, no. 20.

129. Besides the works cited in note 32 of chap. 1 in this volume, see J. Van Nieuwenhove, "Le projet théologique de Gustavo Gutiérrez. Dialogue avec sa théologie de la libération" (Brussels, 1972), 23 pages, mimeographed. Reprinted

interpretation may well change, but that does not invalidate the methodological perspective or the question that triggers our theological effort. In the light of faith we must ask ourselves: What am I doing? What ought I be doing? What do I think? How do I regard this situation? How does it give impetus to faith itself and raise problems for it?[130]

Clearly this approach inaugurates a new way of doing theology and exegesis. The revolutionary practice of Latin American Christians opened up a style and, even more importantly, a content to which we were not accustomed in the interpretation of Scripture. It was not simply that exegesis now started off from life. The life in question was lived out amid violence, torture, oppression, and the struggle for rights. It involved training groups and mobilizing the masses. In the light of harsh but hopeful experiences numerous peasants, workers, and students lived out in their own lives the most concrete sort of exegesis and the most difficult sort of interpretation. They thus covered the fuller spiritual and theological sense of the Lord's word. Without spurning the scientific rigors of modern exegesis, liberation theology roots itself in the exegesis of the militant people. Without a "militant" exegesis Latin American theology loses its spiritual impetus and vitiates its historical contribution. One author has described it quite aptly:

In liberation theology, particularly that of Latin America, the contacts and linkages with biblical hermeneutics are quite original and autonomous. . . . Its point of departure for a new hermeneutics of the biblical message is not based on stimuli of a cultural sort as is the case in the "new hermeneutics" of Germany, France, or England. It is based on the situation in which the Christian communities on that continent find themselves. There the socio-political factor predominates. This leads to a frank and open orientation to "praxis," . . . which serves as the "hermeneutic criterion" not only in theology but also in the interpretation of the biblical message.[131]

---

as "La théologie de la libération de Gustavo Gutiérrez. Réflexion sur son projet théologique," in *Lumen Vitae*, 1974, pp. 200–234. The author maintains that Gutiérrez's method is not reductive but rather based on reciprocal implications.

130. See Gutiérrez in "Diálogo sobre la liberación" CELAM, 1973, pp. 68–85. S. Galilea, "Teología de la liberación y nuevas exigencias cristianas," in *Medellín*, 1, 1975: "Theology starts off from fact, not from a theory of dependence. That will enable it further on to avoid the dangers of an 'ideologized' theology and to maintain its prophetic level. There Christians with differing ideological commitments concerning liberation will be able to meet each other" (pp. 38–39).

131. R. Fabris, "L'ermenutica bibblica," in *Vita e Pensiero*, new series, no. 1, 1975, pp. 92–93. This author uses the term "liberation hermeneutics" for what

Militant exegesis has the following characteristics among others. First of all, it is a theological exegesis in Karl Barth's sense of the term.[132] That is to say, it is an effort to hear the word of God in the text, to comprehend it, and then to interpret it in favor of other human beings.[133] But it is not enough that the comprehension and communication of the message be done by the community.[134] It is the mediation of liberative praxis which provides this theological exegesis with its content and its concrete historical embodiment.

It was Bultmann, whose major concern was clearly pastoral, who advocated the shift to an "existential," "demythologizing" exegesis. His central question was: Does Jesus' preaching on the kingdom still have meaning for people today? Bultmann did not hesitate to say that it did, so long as the message was demythologized. Militant exegisis also starts off from a missionary concern: Are faith in Jesus Christ and the proclamation of his gospel experiences capable of transforming the history of our continent in political and cultural terms? Our answer is yes, provided that the message is "de-ideologized," stripped of its bourgeois weight and reading. The only ones who can effect this theological exegesis are the poor and the oppressed. It is they who will restore to the masses and all their human brothers and sisters a liberative gospel message that can give meaning to the liberation struggle as a whole. The militant comes to the message with a prior understanding of humanity and history. The starting point and locus of verification for the militant's hermeneutic circle is the fruitful but nonetheless painful relationship between our continent today and the utopia of their liberation project with its tactical and strategic approximations. Militant exegesis is not simply an existential exegesis in general. It is a hermeneutics that clearly stresses the political character and the liberation orientation of the message when viewed from the standpoint of the poor classes and the marginalized races. And it recognizes the language problems underlying this militant perspective.

In the second place militant exegesis, though it seems to approach only a relatively few texts,[135] is an exegesis that positions us within the

---

Gutiérrez calls "militant exegesis." See his lecture in the P.U.C. theology course of February 1975, mimeographed.

132. See K. Barth, *Credo* (Munich, 1935), p. 153.

133. R. MacKenzie, "La autocomprensión del exegeta," in *Concilium* 70 (1971):449; Eng. trans., "The Self-Understanding of the Exegete," *Concilium* 70:11–19.

134. See G. Hawenhüttl, "Dialogo entre el teólogo y el exegeta," ibid., p. 447.

135. See Gutiérrez, lecture in the P.U.C. theology course, Lima, 1975, where he

dynamism that runs through the whole text, overflows it, breaks down its forms and redactions, and thus makes possible "full access to the whole reality of Scripture." [136] When we say that any particular line of Scripture opens us to the message as a whole, we are simply reminding people that no aspect or line can be separated from the whole. It is illuminated by the rest of the text even as it sheds light on it in turn. Exaggerated as it may seem, this is basic to any militant exegesis; it is its way of understanding the *sensus plenior* of biblical exegesis. [137]

Thomas Aquinas states that the act of the believing person, the act of faith, does not terminate in what is enunciated or proclaimed but in the reality that is enunciated. [138] Vatican I made use of the principle known as the analogy of faith, which proposes that any given affirmation must be understood in terms of all other affirmations. [139] Vatican II directs our attention toward an organic and intrinsic conception of dogmatic reality.

Thus the expression *articulum fidei* ("article of faith") used by medieval theologians directs us to the "whole" of which an article is part. Every article is meaningful insofar as it is related to each and every other article taken singly and as a body; in this case the reference is to the Creed and its articles. [140]

With due reservations we can say that this is what the militants are doing when they compare their lives and struggles with the word of God in a particular passage. Every passage is simply a point of entry for contact with the Lord.

The perspective that derives from liberation praxis as an overall praxis is affected by the fact that liberation and its content is a totally unifying dimension. This means that militant hermeneutics stresses both its locus of verfication in the historical transformation of the people and its spiritual character, that is, its concern to live in the Spirit who pervades, animates, and overflows the text at every level.

---

discusses the use of Scripture in the documents of such Christian communities as those represented in the two anthologies *Signos de renovación (Between Honesty and Hope)* and *Signos de liberación*.

136. R. Ware, "La escritura en la teología actual," *Concilium* 70 (1971):562.

137. For a different approach to the import of the *sensus plenior*, see P. Benoit, *Exégèse et théologie* (Paris, 1961), 1:21. For him the *sensus plenior* should be restricted to advances in the texts within the body of revelation. It should not be applied to later theological reflection.

138. "Actus credentis non terminatur ad enuntiabile, sed ad rem."

139. DZ 3016.

140. See Thomas Aquinas, *Summa Theologica*, 2a II, q. 1 ad 6.

This approach to exegesis, which is the basis of liberation theology, enables us to reconsider the religious life as a living exegesis, as a militant hermeneutics of the gospel message to be applied to our people's life today.

In all its manifold forms the religious life in Latin America is a kind of *articulum fidei*. That is to say, it is a partial and formal enunciation of an organic unity: the gospel message, the Lord Jesus. As theological exegesis, the religious life is the original expression of the dynamism that finds fragmentary and often muted expression in any given text. Thus Latin American religious life presents itself as a militant interpretation by believers, as contemplative and combative interpretation of the message and meaning of salvation, as the added value or surplus value of which MacKenzie speaks.[141] Religious themselves will be a theological exegesis of God's word when this added value is divulged and shared in liberative praxis and the task of evangelizing the people. It is this praxis that will have enabled us to draw out this added value from the Scriptures. The religious life would then be a kind of *sensus plenior* exegesis of the gospel message. It is a way of understanding the dynamism of the Lord's message and, above all, of the Lord himself who is announced and communicated in the message.

This may enlighten us as to how to rethink the value of the specific charisms of a given community or the spirit of a given congregation. In giving privileged stress to some aspect of the gospel, they are simply looking for some tiny entry into the gospel and some little window through which they hope to offer the whole message of God's love to the common people and the world. Perhaps we can also get a better understanding of the way in which the religious life is a radical living of the gospel message. As we see it, to radicalize the letter of Scripture is to undertake a militant exegesis, to read its *sensus plenior* from the standpoint of our option for the marginalized classes and races.

However, we want to avoid any trace of illuminism when we refer to the religious life as a living exegesis of the gospel message. That tendency proposes to flesh out the gospel message while completely disregarding the history, Scripture, and tradition which explains it. When our scientific exegesis becomes theological exegesis, we also want it to be stamped with the people-oriented perspective of our militancy.[142] Bultmann's exegesis

---

141. R. MacKenzie, "La autocomprensión del exegeta," *Concilium* 70.

142. See, for example, S. Croatto, "El mesías liberador de los probres," *Revista Bíblica* 31, no. 137 (1970): 233–40. Bojorge, "Goel: dios libera a los suyos," ibid.,

is grounded on Heidegger's philosophy; ours is grounded on a politico-cultural perspective: the struggle of the oppressed for liberation.

The theological exegesis of militants also calls into question mythical representations of God's word and ideologized presentations of it. But this is a result of its radical critique of society, a society where religion and the Bible have been captured by the dominant classes in order to legitimate their position, their interests, and their living conditions. In that sense militant exegesis is a political and prophetic exegesis, one that subverts the long-standing practical hermeneutics that the dominant classes have provided for themselves and the people.

As a spiritual theology, liberation theology has its own methodology, ecclesiology, and Christology. It offers the lives of religious exciting possibilities for renewal, and it creates conditions permitting them to rethink their theological framework.[143]

The central challenge is highlighted and its exigencies are underlined. It is to bear witness to the love of the Father and the fecundity of the Spirit of the risen Christ in the very liberation efforts of the marginalized masses on our continent. Our lives centered in Christ will be recognized and made fruitful in the difficult synthesis of a generous commitment to the historic cause of our people and our effort to build up the church from that standpoint.

32, no. 139 (1971): 8–12. Idem, "Para una interpretación liberadora," ibid., 32, no. 139 (1971): 67–71. L. Rivera, "Sobre el socialismo en Santiago," ibid., 34, no. 143 (1973): 3–11. A. Moreno, "Jeremías, la política en la vida de un profeta," in *Teología y Vida*, 12, nos. 3–4 (1971): 187–208. R. Sartor, "La epístola de Santiago releída a la luz de la condición latinoamericana," in *Nueva Mundo*, no. 2 (1971): 275–90. Idem, "Culto y compromiso social según Santiago," in *Revista Bíblica* 34, no. 143 (1972): 21–30.

143. S. Galilea, "Teología de la liberación y nuevas exigencias cristianas," in *Medellín*, 1, 1975, reminds us that many of us got involved in liberation theology out of missionary concerns. As time went on, however, we realized that liberation theology "must have an impact on other areas of pastoral theology, particularly on ecclesiology and the theology of the sacraments. Liberation theology is increasingly an impetus to missionary reform within the Latin American church. That is one of the reasons, I believe, why so much conflict surrounds it at present" (pp. 35–36).

4

A Life Dedicated to the Poor of the Land

The outstanding constant in the quest of Latin American religious is their restless uncertainty and their effort to incarnate themselves in the world of the poor. This is the decisive step in renewal as far as I can see, fostering hopes and obstacles for many religious communities. Concrete understanding of this exigency and the actual living of it in the objective conditions of our continent are a source of scandal for many and of personal and collective tensions for more than a few. For a growing majority, however, it is their principal task. Without it they feel that they cannot be faithful to the Spirit.

The overwhelming fact about our continent is that the majority of its people are poor, exploited, and marginalized. This forces us to recognize the chief sign of the times in all its force and meaning. That sign is Christ the poor person. We cannot dissociate the condition of the poor and oppressed from the mystery of Christ. Christ presents himself to us as the chief liberator, and we can recognize him as such. His condition of poverty is not an accident. It is a necessity of all salvation history, an option of God's unfathomable love. The liberating love of God is ever linked historically to the poor.

In Christ we find an indissoluble link between unconditional surrender to the Father and real, unlimited self-giving to the poor.[1] This link is the

---

1. R. Muñoz, *Nueva conciencia de la Iglesia en América Latina* (Santiago, 1973; Salamanca: Sígueme, 1974): "Love for God and effective love for the poor are inseparable. It is not just that God has established this as the norm, requiring some proof that is not intrinsically related to love for his own person. They are inseparable because God himself took on our humanity in Christ and chose to identify himself personally with the needy, the suffering, and the oppressed. This identification is total, as we know from Jesus' parable of the last judgment.

concrete historical embodiment of his universal, liberative love. The sign of his filiation goes by way of his condition of poverty. It unfolds and develops for all human beings through the poor. In his consecration to the poor, Christ's consecration to the mission entrusted to him by his Father possesses the sign that verifies it historically. In that the presence of the kingdom can be recognized. It is in this framework that the title of this chapter should be interpreted.

Ignatius of Antioch displayed profound evangelical sensitivity when he wrote these words to the poor of Ephesus: "We need to be anointed by you."[2] We have a credible sign of consecration by God when the poor and the lowly and the despised recognize us and themselves as trustees of the good news. We share it with them and they return it to us so we may become even more radically converted.

They are the humble of the earth of whom Zephaniah speaks: "Seek the Lord, all you humble of the earth" (Zeph. 2:3). Isaiah also alludes to them: "The Lord has established Zion, and in her the afflicted of the people find refuge" (Isa. 14:32). The same note can be found in Jeremiah 40:7 and 2 Kings 25:12,22–26,30. After the sack of Jerusalem and the second deportation, "some of the country's poor, Nebuzaradan, captain of the guard, left behind as vinedressers and farmers" (2 Kings 25:12).

To be consecrated to the poor of the land means to have opted for those who not only are the favorites of Yahweh (the just, the blest, the upright) but also will inherit the land. The promise and the fulfillment of liberation is linked with them. It is they who are involved in the transformation of history, the creation of a new heaven and earth.[3] In Christ the poor are identified with the breaking-in of definitive salvation and the inauguration of a world which is undergoing a transformation to justice and liberation.

A theology of the religious life in Latin America should begin where the presence of religious on this continent began historically: at the side of the native masses, the poor of the land. Despite its limitations and blind spots, this was the most original and faithful evangelical awareness of the

---

. . . Thus when we serve the poor, we are serving Christ himself even though we may not realize it. This is the only criterion by which our entire life will be judged" (p. 260).

2. Ignatius of Antioch, Letter to the Ephesians, in the volume of his letters in *Sources Chrétiennes*, Greek text trans. and ed. T. Camelot: "It is I who must be anointed by you with faith, exhortation, patience, and longanimity" (III,1).

3. See J. Dupont, *Les Béatitudes* (Paris: Gabalda, 1973), 3:430–48. He studies the relationship between the "people of the land" and the "poor in spirit."

early missionaries. We today, of course, cannot imitate some of the conditioning impulses and loyalties that weighed down on many religious of old.

The historical practice of liberation on our continent has left a wealth of valuable experiences. To this can be added advances in the social sciences and the maturing presence, reflection, and activity of Christian communities. That should enable us to follow in the footsteps of Bartolomé de Las Casas and others like him, to improve the motives, scope, and socio-political implications of our option for the Indians of Latin America, for its marginalized races and exploited classes.

This is the framework within which we ought to redefine our self-understanding, our activity, and our life as religious. It will put us in continuity with the best missionary tradition and in line with the novel realities of our continent today.

The theological and evangelical content of our commitment to the Indian and the native population has been deepened and enriched by an increasingly more numerous and more lucid presence in their life and by our efforts to reinterpret the gospel message from their point of view. We have thus come to see the gospel challenging the life and structures of the church. But this evangelical content has become more vital and problematical because we have come to see more clearly the complex political consequences of being on the side of the poor and defending their cause. In the liberation movement we have been visualizing and trying concrete ways of expressing our solidarity with the weak.

Thus the option for the poor of the land is shedding new light on our lives as Christians. It presents itself as an authentic evangelical conversion and as an unavoidable political stance. This is the initial step in the following of Christ. Being on the side of the exploited people is the sign of the kingdom's presence and proof that the Spirit of the risen Christ is at work in the history of our continent. This option becomes the fundamental act of our existence as Christians; it is both theological and political, cultural, and spiritual.

Though it does not work mechanically, solidarity with the poor is the necessary precondition for the renovation of the church and a profound change in our lives. After that, and again not automatically, it is the locale where it becomes possible for us to re-create the religious life and the theology that expresses it. Rethinking the religious life from the perspectives of our liberation theology means that we accept the fact that theological methodology first requires us to make an identification and adopt a social and historical stance. The theology of liberation can be done only in this involvement and this praxis which, on our continent, has a very specific political and cultural sign and color: i.e., the popular classes, marginalized sectors, dominated races, and oppressed people. Without such an option there can be no theology, i.e., force, life, light, and faith that transforms history. Without such an option there can be no liberation, i.e., a total alternative project. However, I do not mean to suggest that the two are separate when I present them in this way.

In this chapter I should like to consider what our consecration to the poor brings out very clearly. It is the conviction that the poor are the ones who change the sense of history into a more humane and universal one, and that the kingdom grows and finds expression in the struggles to humanize the world which the poor and the lowly initiate with their lives.[4] From this practical profession of faith, hope, and love for the poor I shall attempt to consider some of the central themes of the religious life on our continent.

THE POLITICAL OPTION

Medellín unhesitatingly indicated the will of the church to shoulder the cause of those without a voice on our continent. The deep Christian roots of this option, far from concealing its conflict-ridden character, bring it out more clearly and force us to make it explicit. To link one's fate with a conflict-laden history such as ours is to make a choice that involves conflict and perhaps crucifixion. The social character and political content of our solidarity with the oppressed is embedded in the very heart of its evangelical inspiration.

Aware of this, the bishops at Medellín declared that they were ready to side with those priests and religious who were being criticized or persecuted for living their lives with the poor.[5] Thus the Medellín context creates new reasons for Christians to enroll in the struggles of the poor on our continent.

The *very dynamism of faith itself* has prompted many religious to side with the oppressed. The life of certain Christian communities and a certain pastoral sensitivity has also affected them. This fact does not invalidate or undermine the legitimacy of our further evolution toward politics. What has happened to us is that the picture has grown more

---

4. R. Muñoz, *Nueva conciencia,* pp. 326–27, where he cites a text of *CLAR,* no. 4, p. 56, n. 103.

5. Medellín document on the "Poverty of the Church," n. 11: "We express our desires to be very close always to those who work in the self-denying apostolate with the poor in order that they will always feel our encouragement and know that we will not listen to parties interested in distorting their work."

complicated for us. The obviously political nature of our presence and activity among the popular classes has amplified both the motives for solidarity and our concrete historical embodiments of that solidarity.

Paradoxical as it may seem, lengthy battles had to be fought even in religious orders founded to serve the poor before we were truly able to integrate ourselves into the lives of the poor. Many communities that sought to inculcate the charism of serving the poor would repeatedly remind their members that this commitment was not a political one and that their apostolate to the poor should avoid every taint of politics.[6] Every political motive or criterion was viewed as undermining the specifically religious intuition of our mission and our identity.

Today, however, we must point up another touchy aspect that is no less important in the eyes of many religious confronting their communities. It is not simply a matter of recognizing and accepting the inevitably political dimension of our presence and our work among the common people. The touchy issue is the partisan embodiment of our option for the exploited classes and the range of lines and programs being opened to us. This issue is having a profound impact on our experience of faith and our community life. It is challenging our vocation to life in common and altering our conception of fraternity. It explains many of our tensions, our silences, and our feelings of aloneness; but it also reveals our hopefulness, our mysticism, our dynamism, and our impatient stubbornness in the face of mediocrity and defeatism.

It is not enough to say that we are following the liberation line, which is already a common platform. We must try to spell out how this perspective is implemented concretely and organically. The horizon is further complicated by the fact that we continue to be unhesitatingly interested in our religious community, each of its members, our fraternal life together, and our proclamation and celebration of God's word. We have not lost that concern in our quest to serve the poor. Herein lies the paschal experience of many Latin American religious. It may seem cruder but it almost certainly is also more meaningful and fruitful for them, for the people to whom they have dedicated their lives, and perhaps some day also for their religious communities. In the near future that will be the experience of many more religious. The future of the religious life on our continent will be decided in these terms because it is in these terms that the present and future of the common classes of people are being defined.

Our option for the oppressed has had its impact on us religious. In

---

6. *CLAR*, no. 8, p. 70.

general we do not come from the proletariat. Moreover, our training for the religious life has been very successful in inculcating the ideology of the petty bourgeoisie in us. That is the price we have had to pay because the religious life, as an institution, occupies a place of prestige in our societies. Our option for the poor, then, entails a process for us all, including those from the common people who do not possess a clear class consciousness.

We have often been deeply influenced by the view of reality held by our chief benefactors. We have paid court to them so that their voluntary contributions might support our apostolate to the poor. Or else we have come to judge situations under the influence of others, e.g., former students now in high positions, their parents, or local authorities with whom we are on friendly terms. We have been far less influenced by the perhaps crude way in which the poor themselves analyze and interpret their situation. We have not paid much attention to those who questioned our stance or saw it as a defense of the interests of the dominant classes. Though this picture has begun to change, the fact remains that the view of reality held by many of our religious communities is not only naive but politically reactionary.

To immerse one's life in the common classes is to creatively assume their vision of reality. *This amounts to adopting a qualitatively different understanding of the history of our continent,* both its past and its present history. We opt for the oppressed classes to comprehend history insofar as it has a message, offers hope, and is salvation history. To paraphrase the classic dictum *credo ut intelligam,* [7] we are opting for the poor in order to understand reality and our faith in Christ.

Here I want to focus a bit on the process of politicization, the process of understanding Latin American reality and transforming it. I want to discuss some of the elements of this process that have enriched our solidarity with the poor.

From Integration in the World of the Poor to Historical Liberation Project

No renewal of the religious life would have taken place without the insistent summons to incarnate ourselves in the life of the poor and the subsequent implementation of it. This summons was never intended to canonize the condition of poverty, exploitation, and wretchedness; nor

---

7. G. Gutiérrez, "Praxis de liberación, teología y anuncio," in *Concilium* 96, pp. 363–64.

was it meant to serve demagogic purposes or simply win people's good will. Integrating ourselves into the world of the poor was a positive way of expressing our conviction that only from the standpoint of the poor can we ourselves be reborn, only from there can we revitalize the hope that it is possible to change society, and only from there comes liberation. Liberation does not come from money, prestige, or the great of this world. If we had not immersed our lives in the living conditions of the poor, we would certainly never have heard the clamor of their voices. CLAR rightly points out that a basic precondition for immersing the religious life in the world of the poor is that first there must be a clear-cut personal option for the poor. We must be in solidarity with them, with their problems and struggles and commitments.[8]

A significant number of religious have been turning to the impoverished sectors of society in recent years.[9] Sometimes the old limitations have cropped up in somewhat different terms in the process. People have rightly pointed out that superficial adaptation and assimilation is not enough. Besides learning the local language and customs, we must immerse ourselves in the inner dynamism of the people.[10] One criticism of missionary work is that evangelization has tended to westernize native communities too much. True as that may be, it does not go far enough. A more comprehensive political view is needed. We must incarnate ourselves in such communities without destroying the aboriginal culture,

---

8. *CLAR*, no. 1, p. 34. J. Leclercq offers a different outlook, stressing not a dominating concern for the poor but involvement with the poor as a precondition for inspiring and animating the world today. See Leclercq, "La influencia de los religiosos en la animación espiritual de nuestro tiempo," in *Presencia de los religiosos en una nueva sociedad* (Madrid, 1975).

9. C. Palmes, "Una vida religiosa más auténtica," in *Vida en Fraternidad*, no. 18 (1974): 43f. L. Boff, *A vida religiosa e a Igreja no processo de libertacão*, CRB (Petrópolis: Ed. Vozes, 1975), pp. 38, 85–88, 97–99.

10. E. Pironio, *Invio di personale apostolico in America Latina*, 1972, p. 28. However, he does not elaborate a more political view of what it means to "incorporate oneself into the creative process of God's people." His view of the political dimension comes down to a relatively quick and ingenuous politicization of foreign clergy, religious, and lay people. M. Agudelo sees liberation as the guiding norm, discusses joint pastoral effort, and stresses the urgent need to close ranks in the fight to achieve justice on our continent ("Integración del religioso no nativo en la Iglesia local," in *CONFER* 11, no. 40, 1972). For a more political perspective see G. Mugica, "Figura y labor del misionero en el marco de una teología del la liberación," in *Misiones Extranjeras* 16–17 (1973): 135–50.

and we must try to rescue the priceless values of the native population. Insofar as the reality of such aboriginal communities is concerned, perhaps we should devote more effort to the categories used by the social sciences for diagnosis and liberation strategy.

The situation poses real difficulties for many of our religious who are trying to integrate themselves into the life of the native Amazonian tribes. There are many barriers—cultural, religious, and economic. And the tension deepens as these religious become more and more aware of the political exigencies bound up with their work in such regions.

A certain effort at acculturation is not enough.[11] Nor is it enough to accept and refine the ideological and political presuppositions of the people. Solidarity with the common classes requires that we immerse ourselves in their cultural universe, their overall context of life. The religious and psycho-social milieu of the Latin American people forces us to reconsider the effectiveness of certain orthodox notions in the social sciences and the tactical and strategic demands entailed. How are we to rethink the historical project of liberation from the specific viewpoint of our native Indians, mestizos, and aborigines?

Making a choice is not enough. We must also make an effort to incarnate and live it with the people. The cultural experience of the poor and the marginalized classes does not just give "objectivity" to our commitment. It also forces us to reformulate our analysis and interpretation of the situation, as well as our political views, in truly operative and effective terms.

The fact is that many religious are already there with the poor. What, then, do they think? Having shared something of the sufferings of the poor, they have felt an urgent need to move ahead, to frame their motives and experiences and contributions in a broader perspective. Such a perspective would offer glimpses of more solidly grounded alternatives.

---

11. In the days of Toribio de Mogrovejo the provincial Council of Lima stipulated that religious were to provide the catechism, confession, and sermons in the language of the Indians. This stipulation, set forth by the 1583 council, was reiterated in 1591. The first diocesan synod (Chapter XX), prohibited holding blacks for gain or profit. See *Lima Limata Conciliis* (Rome, 1673). The outlook of Las Casas broke new ground in the effort to adapt to the Indians. See E. Hoornaert, "A tradição lascasiana no Brasil," in *Revista Eclesiástica Brasileira* 35 (1975). A conception of mission as a transcultural activity was held by many missionaries to Latin America up until the 1960s. For a new perspective see G. Gutiérrez, "De la teología de la misión a la teología del encuentro," in *Estudios Indígenas* 1, no. 1 (September 1971): 9–16.

They are moving from integration into the system to an active effort to "disintegrate" the system. It is the existing system itself which is responsible for the present living conditions of the majority of people, which thereby ensures progress and well-being for a small minority.

This point becomes all the more obvious as people come to realize that we cannot look to the gospel message for a political project. It becomes clearer that the historical liberation project of the oppressed is the pathway and the process ensuring cohesion to our efforts on behalf of justice and development.[12] So we move from involvement in the world of the poor to a decision to embrace their political project on behalf of liberation. This significant transition is complicating and enriching our lives, immersing us squarely in the historical thrust of a people fighting for their just interests.[13]

Thus our option for the poor and oppressed is not one task among many others.[14] It is the key act, and it represents a qualitative leap. It becomes such, however, only when we make their historical project of liberation our own, and that entails more than merely physical involve-

---

12. See L. Gera, "La misión de la Iglesia y del presbítero a la luz de la teología de la liberación," reprint from *Seminarios*; also in *Pasos* (Santiago de Chile), no. 14, pp. 12–13: "The history of this people is at a point where they are led to face up to the struggle for their own liberation. . . . Their collective life is sealed with the sign of liberation, of a freedom they seek to win. The church must flesh out its gospel message in the reality of the people. Hence the pastoral option of the moment is to assume the historical project of the people."

13. For the major outlines and features of the liberation project see G. Gutiérrez, *A Theology of Liberation* (Maryknoll, N.Y.: Orbis Books, 1973), chaps. II, VI, XI, XII, and XIII. Idem, "Praxis de liberación, teología y anuncio," in *Concilium* 96, pp. 356–60, 372–73. J. L. Segundo, "Capitalismo—Socialismo: Crux teológica," ibid., pp. 403–22. For another perspective see H. Assmann, *Proyecto histórico*, ed. MIEC-JECI.

14. That is how some present it. M. Agudelo ("Integración del religioso no nativo en la Iglesia local") mentions seven major lines of actions for our continent. Involvement with the poor is the last mentioned, alongside such proposals as travelling teams and the use of married deacons. Aside from this, however, the article offers many worthwhile practical suggestions.

I also disagree with the view that an option for the poor is to be derived from the vow of poverty. This is maintained by J. M. Guerrero, "El religioso y la política," *CONFER*, Arequipa (October 1974), mimeographed, p. 8. On the contrary, it is within an option for the oppressed that the vow of poverty comes to express in history what it signifies evangelically: i.e., solidarity with the poor, the following of Christ, and a fight against exploitation.

ment with the people. This option for the oppressed is the starting point for theological discourse[15] and for the historical project of liberation.

From an Option for the People to a Class Option

When we talk about the necessity of incarnating ourselves in the world of the poor, certain questions arise spontaneously. Who are the poor and the oppressed? Whom do we mean when we talk about "the people"? To what extent are we to live as the people do when they themselves despise and reject their present situation?

The answers given to these questions by many religious individuals and communities bear witness to the different standpoints and criteria adopted in trying to flesh out our basic option for the people. It is precisely here that the contributions of the social and political sciences combine most fruitfully with evangelical sensitivity to ensure that the struggle for liberation will be effective and that all segments of the popular masses will make their contribution to it.

The people in question here are those on our continent who are suffering the cumulative effects of poverty, oppression, discrimination, and exploitation in all their forms. In Latin America more than anywhere else the term "people" is taking on growing importance and expressivity.[16] As a general term, it takes in a broad gamut of traits. For us here it means the poor, the neglected, the masses of peasants and laborers, the marginalized, and the oppressed. It also means the unknown actor and agent in freedom fights that have marked our history: the unknown soldier, if

---

15. See. G. Gutiérrez, "Praxis de liberación," *Concilium* 96, p. 360.

16. "From the start the Mexican revolution pointed up the fundamental concept of Latin American revolution: the concept of the people. We should work on an historical, social, and cultural analysis of this concept, which has no equivalent on other continents" (J. Comblin, "Movimientos y ideologías en América Latina," in the El Escorial anthology entitled *Fe cristiana y cambio social en América Latina*, Salamanca: Sígueme, 1973, p. 103).

More recently J. B. Metz has offered very interesting observations that might erroneously be labelled "populist." But he does not offer a political vision of the destiny of "the people" in history. He duly notes their character as a "suffering people," but he does not allude to their class-character or their historical project of liberation. See Metz, "Iglesia y pueblo o el precio de la ortodoxia," in the anthology *Dios y la Ciudad, nuevos planteamientos en teología política* (Ed. Cristiandad, 1975), pp. 117–43.

you will.[17] Even more importantly, perhaps, it means the human beings who should be the agents of revolution in Latin America today.[18]

The creole expression *"ésa es gente del pueblo"* leaves us with no doubts about the socio-cultural connotations of the term "people." It means the simple people of humble birth, those in "shameful need" according to Catholic documents of the late nineteenth century.[19] It means the inhabitants of the interior and the highland provinces. In short, the term "people" takes in living conditions, race, and even geographical location. It not only includes the note of "proletarian" but also the collective structure of the poor and their character as protagonists in the struggle for liberation.[20]

Three factors are at work in their distinctive ways to highlight the potential ambiguity of the term "the people" in each of our countries. One factor is the leadership role attributed to the middle classes in the political project of certain social movements or currents in Latin America. Associated with this is another factor: the exaggerated populism of various governments and political programs. The third factor is the various nationalist movements.[21] All these factors suggest that our communities

---

17. See E. Dussel: "The 'national emancipation' was neocolonial and oligarchic; it was not a people's revolution. . . . The common people of Latin America . . . did not participate in the process. They were now dominated by new lords. . . . They are the 'poor' of the gospel message in whom we must believe ("Historia de la fe cristiana y cambio social in América latina," *Fe cristiana y cambio social,* pp. 89–90).

18. This is the outlook of the Medellín Conference and many other documents put out by Latin American bishops and Christian communities.

19. Among other things the First Catholic Congress of Peru, held in Lima in 1896, set up the *Olla de los Pobres* ("pot for the poor") for their benefit. One of its purposes was "to provide food for people in dire need, a task of the utmost urgency. This duty falls first and foremost on the charitable heart of Christian women" (p. 322, Section Four).

20. When talking about the participation of the common people in the process of liberation, the Peruvian bishops remind us that it must be real, direct participation in revolutionary activity against oppressing structures and attitudes. See *Justicia en el mundo,* no. 9.

21. A nationalist ideology was ably implemented by the dominant classes throughout the period of emancipation in our nations. It has left a deep imprint on our people and it makes it more difficult for them to develop a class-oriented perspective. Incorporating the values of "national identity," a class-oriented perspective frames them within a project that embodies the interests and aspirations of the common people as classes.

must be careful and conscientious in using political terms to express our solidarity with "the people."

However, social analysis does enable us to give rich and specific content to our use of the term "the people."[22] Our own pastoral documents take advantage of this analysis, though they may add their own emphases and connotations. The Medellín document on religious urges us "to serve, educate, evangelize, and assist the socially marginal classes."[23] We are coming to see ever more clearly that we cannot deal with the poor as poor people ourselves through merely private actions when in fact the poor constitute a collective reality, when we see their situation in terms of an objective, structural view of society.[24]

Change cannot come from a vision centered on the individual. It can come only from a view centered on social class. Our perspective must be a collective one, taking in the interests of the poor as a whole.[25] This class-oriented view enables us to grasp the exploited, marginalized, and alienated character of the people. It also highlights the interests of the dominant class which are at work, and which also leave their imprint on the political cast of the liberation project.

This class outlook goes hand in hand with one of the most significant and conflict-ridden phases in the politicization of Christian communities and many religious. Our analysis of the situation and our view of the possible alternatives takes a decisive turn. Moreover, we are suddenly

---

22. R. Ames: "Liberation implies the full realization of all the dimensions of human beings. The active subject of liberation is the oppressed human being whom social analysis reveals to be an exploited class. Action taken by and with the exploited classes is the central practice in the liberation process" ("Factores económicos y fuerzas políticas en el proceso de liberación," in Fe cristiana y cambio social, pp. 53–54).

23. Medellín document on religious, no. 13.

24. CLAR, no. 4, p. 48.

25. C. Perani, "Missão: proclamação do reino ou promoção humana," in Convergência 58 (1973): 271: "The required conversion must take in all that. It cannot be reduced to an attitude of greater generosity." R. Ames ("Factores económicos y fuerzas políticas en el proceso de liberación," in Fe cristiana y cambio social, pp. 53–54) says that once the objective contradiction is recognized, a class option becomes imperative. He feels that socialism is an orientation that seeks to render the liberation praxis of the people effective on the economic and political levels. From a theological perspective see G. Gutiérrez, "Evangelio y praxis de liberación," in Fe cristiana y cambio social, pp. 234–35; idem, "Praxis de liberación," in Concilium 96, p. 356.

made aware of the underlying and dramatic import of social confrontation on our continent as well as our place in it.

The historical project of liberation entails a struggle against the historical project of oppression upheld by the dominant classes.[26] It is in that sense that solidarity with the poor is a class option.

We have no intention of suggesting that the term "the poor" is to be restricted to the proletariat, the lower working class in the strict sense.[27] But it certainly does include them, along with the subproletariat, the unemployed, the impoverished peasants, and neglected peoples and races. The class content of our historical involvement with the poor and the oppressed embodies our rejection of the existing system and the political purposes which sustain it.[28] It also embodies our desire to offer a truly human and universal alternative. We face the challenge of fashioning a new project, a new way of being humans, Christians, and members of a people.[29] For that very reason our identification with the common people as a class is a denunciation and condemnation of the selfish interests of the dominant classes. Yet paradoxically enough, this class option for the poor is the only one which situates us in the framework of a project, an experience, and a message of liberation that is universal, collective, and evangelical. For the Lord's salvation is a universal and collective gift.

Our involvement with the poor in terms of a class option is the most solid proclamation of our evangelical conviction that a society divided into classes is inhuman and that a classless society is not only possible but feasible. Any hesitancy here reveals our lack of belief in the power of the Spirit that is revealing itself in the liberation struggle of the exploited classes on our continent.

This class-oriented vision, then, helps us to keep check on a certain tendency toward "populism" in our option for the poor.[30] It also helps us

---

26. G. Girardi, "La nuova scelta fondamentale dei cristiani," trans. and abridged in *Selecciones de teología* 54 (1975): 179–93.

27. See B. Sorge, "Evangelio y pobreza hoy," in *Criterio,* April–May 1973. However, his approach distorts the political and classist perspective of the option for the poor. This perspective is also neglected by T. R. Hamey, "Politicizing the Reform of Religious," in *Review for Religious* 3 (May 1970):124f.

28. Peruvian bishops, Document *Evangelización,* no. 1.6.

29. As G. Gutiérrez ("Praxis de liberación," *Concilium* 96, p. 335) rightly says, "This option constitutes the axis of a new way of being human beings and Christians in Latin America."

30. The lack of a structural and political vision in our presence among the

to avoid a certain "interclassism" in the ideological suppositions we use to justify the type of work and the functions performed by our communities.[31]

In any case our class solidarity must focus our attention on the poor. They must increasingly become the object of our conscious awareness. Indeed they must become the standard by which we evaluate our lives as individuals and communities. Otherwise our contribution to the liberation of Latin America and the transformation of the church will not really be credible.

The Political Dimension and Political Organizations

Many factors have been at work over a long period of time to keep us religious from devoting serious attention to the socio-economic and political reality of our countries. There was the traditional conception of convent, cloister, and withdrawal from the world. There was the insistence that our vocation was to be men and women of peace. Our lives were supposed to orbit around God, and so we were not to be concerned about the squabbles taking place in the world. Even when there was real concern for the social situation, we did not always manage to perceive the real facts of history. We did not see the real relationship between the complex and conflict-ridden reality of our people and our own interior life and religious vocation. The world of politics remained alien to us. We could not get a real handle on it.

That situation is changing rapidly. The social and political process going on here has shaken even the most solid of our communities. The dominant note today is an urgent desire to know what is going on, to be informed, to form some judgment about reality at the local or continental level. What had happened was that for centuries theology—and hence

---

people, combined with generous zeal in serving the poor, accounts for a populist strain in our apostolic efforts and our mode of working.

31. See the reservations and conciliatory tone of the reflections in Cecilio de Lora, "Alcuni puni base per inquadrare la situazione pastorale della America Latina," in the proceedings of the 1972 convention in Rome, p. 74. After pointing out that there is no reason why we must abandon the upper and middle classes, C. Palmes ("Una vida religiosa más auténtica," in *Vida en Fraternidad*, no. 18, 1974, p. 43) goes on to say that the whole religious problem as well as the socio-political situation can be summed up in the need to make clear-cut options in favor of the poor and to live out this option in whatever line of work we are doing. See P. Bigo, "Vida religiosa y liberación," *Mensaje* 226 (1974):25.

spirituality and pastoral activity—had been elaborated without paying any attention to social and political analyses of reality.[32]

The bishops of Peru have focused on this lack of clearsightedness and serious analysis of reality as one of the principal reasons why we today cannot offer an answer to grave problems confronting Latin America.[33]

Now most of our communities are realizing that the historical dimension of our evangelizing mission is a necessary correlate of the message we preach.[34] We now know that the gospel message inevitably possesses a political dimension, as do faith, the presence and activity of the church, the works and services undertaken by our congregations, and so forth.[35] It is not just that pastoral activity possesses salvific content and a political dimension.[36] The fact is that the political realm also possesses evangelical density.[37] In its deepest sense political action is a praxis designed to transform reality in terms of the interests and the liberative message of the oppressed; hence it expresses the conviction and the will to create a

---

32. See R. Bosc: "Even up to the major theologians of the sixteenth century it could be said that theologians studied political reality. After the sixteenth century we find a great void in history. . . . From the sixteenth century to the time of Pius XII we find theologians merely repeating the same formulas of the past and showing no knowledge or study of social reality. So we find a real void in Catholic thinking for three centuries insofar as politics, society, and economics is concerned. Christians got nothing from the church's magisterium on these topics, and so we find them following all the errors of their age: nationalism, imperialism, and the re-establishment of slavery."

33. See the document of the Peruvian bishops: *Evangelización*, no. 2.4.1.

34. Ibid., nos. 3.4.2 and 3.4.3.

35. The Peruvian bishops, *Justicia en el mundo*, no. 28; *Evangelización*, no. 3.4.2: "Hence the task of salvation cannot be indifferent to the existing social order." See J. P. Martin: "There is not one single prophetic judgment that does not deal with concrete political realities. The transcendent aspect of the prophet's political judgment does not lie in its alienation from the world and its pure eschatology. It lies in deepening the political picture by giving it an eschatological sense" (In *Liberación, salvación y escatología*, Buenos Aires, 1973, p. 126). Also see S. Amsler, "Les prophètes et la politique," in *Revue de Théologie et de Philosophie* 1 (1973): 14–31.

36. See S. Galilea, "A los pobres se les anuncia el Evangelio," IPLA, 1972, p. 47f. Also see the anthology entitled *La vertiente política de la pastoral* (IPLA, 1970).

37. See the priestly movement ONIS, Document no. 1, "Opción por los oprimidos" (Lima, 1973), mimeographed; Document no. 2, "Evangelización liberadora" (Lima, 1973); for the relationship between salvation and liberation see G. Gutiérrez, *A Theology of Liberation*, chap. IX.

fraternal society, to unite human beings. For us, human brotherhood is a sacrament of the irrevocable love of Jesus' Father. Our discovery of the political realm as a historical project and as an immersion in the world of the poor[38] brings us face to face with something difficult and fraught with conflict, with a scene that becomes increasingly complex and demanding, and with a viewpoint that takes in everything.

In this connection it would be interesting to deepen our reflection on political action as prophecy and the political movements of the poor as authentic prophetic movements.

To open one's eyes to Latin America is to find oneself in a more problematic situation. Life suddenly becomes more complicated. We cannot lightly dismiss what is happening, nor can we disregard the causes of the present situation or possible alternatives. Even the theological commission of CELAM clearly sees that there are two general constants in present political awareness on our continent. First, there is an increasingly clear awareness of the antinomy between oppression and liberation. Second, there is the deep conviction of the exploited themselves that they are victims of injustice and that it is possible for them to liberate themselves from this situation.[39] As religious increasingly concretize their option for the exploited classes, these two constants continue to raise new questions and create different conditions for life in community, for activities and tasks, and even for our understanding of political reality.[40]

---

38. The same point is brought out by the theology committee of CELAM in "Iglesia y política," Document no. 13 (Bogotá, 1973): "Two closely related levels can be distinguished in the area of political activity. One is what we call here the scientific level, the level of the positive sciences with their modern advances and technological resources. The other is the level of the historical project itself, with the qualitative changes it entails in social life" (pp. 34–35).

39. Ibid., p. 19: "There is a new aspect here that goes beyond the positions considered at the Medellín Conference. It can give rise to a relatively new diagnosis. While there admittedly are different points of view and emphases, the basic tendency is a dynamic, creative, revolutionary approach to the various forms of political activity and political events."

40. In their document on the ministerial priesthood, prepared for the 1971 Synod, the bishops of Peru saw politics first and foremost as the realm in which human beings become masters of their own historical destiny and share in the work of giving direction to the society in which they live. In our case we seek to make society freer, more fraternal, and more just. This, then, would be an obligatory dimension of all human activity. On a secondary level politics would involve partisan options, concrete models of social organization, and specific ideologies and agendas (see no. 4.3.6).

It is also becoming clearer to us religious that we cannot validly judge reality from the safety of an apolitical trench, from the parapets of some alleged neutrality, or from some disengaged religious or evangelical position.[41] Judgment of socio-political reality must come through the mediation of the political realm, and we must be aware of the ideological and political presuppositions underlying our analysis and our proposed alternatives. The best efforts of political theology have brought out the fact that the critical reservation of the church within society is a function of a political nature. Precisely because its criticism is framed against the horizon of eschatology, it is exercised in history here and now. What I should like to bring out here is the fact that this critical reservation operates under the politico-cultural sign of the oppressed classes on our continent.[42] Thus our critical reservation can be exercised simultaneously in terms of the historical project of liberation and in terms of its own eschatological vocation. For the critical function certainly cannot act to negate the historical, causal, and efficacious character of liberation in building up the kingdom.[43]

This means that we cannot allow ourselves to be restricted to the realm of the spiritual. To shun the political demands of the real-life situation under the pretext of preserving the prophetic freedom of our mission would be to bear witness to a freedom that does not free and a prophecy that does not transform anything.[44] As CLAR puts it: "Historical, temporal commitment in the realm of 'the flesh' and the politico-prophetic function of religious are the real-life sign of their commitment to the kingdom and its eschatological function."[45]

---

41. See J. Batista, "Vida religiosa y testimonio público," *CLAR*, no. 19, Bogotá, 1974, p. 103.

42. See *Testimonio*, no. 150, p. 17: "Any critical attitude toward change based on ethical or technical reasons should be respected and upheld. But we cannot understand those religious who criticize change because of family or emotional solidarity with the ruling class" (meeting in Padre Hurtado, January 1972).

43. See J. L. Segundo, "Capitalismo—Socialismo," in *Concilium* 96, pp. 409–11.

44. See J. Batista, "Vida religiosa y testimonio público," p. 13. Also see the working draft of CLAR, "Vida religiosa y situación socio-política en América Latina," pp. 18–19, no. 76. There is some ambiguity in the remarks of J. M. Guerrero, "El religioso y la política," in *CONFER*, Arequipa, October 1974, p. 10. On the one hand he says that in certain circumstances it is up to religious to foster struggle and even violence. On the other hand he seems to denigrate the prophetic freedom to engage in criticism in favor of non-activism in politics.

45. "Vida religiosa y situación socio-política en América Latina," *CLAR*, no. 77 p. 19: "Historical, temporal commitment in the realm of 'the flesh' and the

Many Christians in our countries have gone beyond the mere realization of the political dimension of their faith and of their involvement with the poor. Practice itself has helped them to discover the importance of a more organic effort and a more formal militancy. On the basis of their professional work or their membership in such Christian communities, they have felt the need to direct support for the poor into more organic channels and programs that are better defined socially and politically.

The problem is not a new one in Latin America. Our history bears ample witness to the fact that individual religious and whole religious communities have envisioned collaboration with political movements and emancipation struggles in a variety of ways.[46]

This participation is not just occasional, though it has had its high points and highly motivated times. The facts and events of past history are not normative in any strict sense for today's religious. However, they do represent a heritage of experience and practice that raises doubts about any attempt to condemn the direct participation of religious in politics on the basis of casuistic reasoning or allegedly theological principles: "Strictly speaking, we can say that there are no absolute or radical incompatibilities between the priestly ministry and active participation in politics."[47] This concession is not based on any principle of

---

politico-prophetic function of religious are the real-life sign of their commitment to the kingdom of God and its eschatological function."

46. Ibid., no. 69, p. 17: "These examples should make it clear that historical situations are complicated. They have their own exigencies. Involved in the problems we face today are the same principles of old, even though circumstances may have changed.

47. Document no. 13 of the theology committee of CELAM, "Iglesia y política," p. 49. Even taking due account of the Chilean situation at the time, I do not find admissible the overall stance presented by G. Cifuentes, "La religiosa y la política," in *Testimonio,* no. 17, 1972. He offers a variety of reasons why religious women should not participate actively in politics. By lending their moral weight to a given party, he says, they would be exercising a spiritual form of dictatorship. They would cut themselves off from other people and give people the impression that they are acting outside their realm of competence. They would be suggesting that laypeople are children in need of guidance. They would be putting the banner of their message at the service of one group, when in fact it should not be expropriated by any one group. Being women, they could easily be manipulated by politicans; and they would be breaking the unity that should exist between human beings. As representatives of the church, they would be involving it in an area where it does not directly belong—just as the Armed Forces do not belong directly in politics. Such is Cifuentes's position.

secularization.[48] The political dimension of our mission is rooted in the very core of our commitment to love the poor and effect the transformation of history as a result.[49] For many religious, the seeds of direct militancy as a charism lie buried at the heart of the motives and the concrete embodiments surrounding our option for the oppressed.[50]

The exercise of judgment and discernment regarding the timeliness and effectiveness of religious participation in some organized political activity is based on circumstances of time and place. It should take in such factors as the charisms of individuals for this type of work and our relations with the Christian community as well as our own religious community. There is no doubt that our status as religious is not an obstacle to radical historical involvement in the struggles of the oppressed. There is no doubt that it does not justify our being mediocre or conservative with respect to this commitment. But it certainly can affect and modify the channels or platforms through which our political action is exercised.[51]

---

48. F. Boasso, "Sacerdocio, y política," in *CIAS* 220 (1973): 18: "The legitimacy of a political option by priests is not to be found in the secularist notion that they, as citizens, possess certain rights. . . . It lies in the connection between such an option and the mission of the church. . . ." See García, Borrat, Palacios, and Pelegri, "Ministerio sacerdotal, justicia y política," in *Misiones Extranjeras* 11–11 (1972): 113–30.

49. See G. Gutiérrez, "Praxis de liberación," *Concilium* 96, p. 369: "The political dimension lies in the very dynamism of a divine message that seeks to incarnate itself in history."

50. See A. Rotzetter, "La fraternidad franciscana de hoy en el contexto eclesial," in *Cuadernos Franciscanos de Renovación,* September 1973, p. 165: "The first rule does not talk about politics. However, our concern for peace and nonviolence does give a political dimension to Franciscan life. Later Franciscan theologians, such as Adam Marsh, Roger Bacon, and Ramon Lull, analyzed this dimension and even worked out a huge political plan. They even ventured a radical critique of the notion of the crusade." See also the text requested by the Franciscan Provincials, "La vocación de la orden hoy," in *Cuadernos Franciscanos de Renovación,* no. 20 (December 1972): 227: "With regard to political commitments in the strict sense (i.e., to a specific political party), we recognize the right of every Franciscan to have such commitments so long as they are not contrary to the gospel message and Franciscans . . . subordinate them to our essential options and our life of brotherhood. It seems to us that, except for rare exceptions, our fraternities as such cannot adopt a political option binding all their members."

51. Document no. 13 of CELAM's theology committee ("Iglesia y política") refers to relative incompatibilities on page 41. We obviously get little help with

We must recognize that the political option of religious does not absolutely have to take the form of party affiliation. That is not the only channel open, nor the one required to prove real radicalism.[52] Moreover, the political stance taken by each individual or each community cannot be normative. It is not even normative for us as individuals in the same way in the various stages of the militancy process.[53]

The most important thing is that we not lose sight of the guiding perspective: i.e., the poor, the humiliated. We are confronted with an ongoing demand to see the relationship between the people and political organizations.[54] We must be tireless and creative in comparing political activities with the needs, interests, and aspirations of the poor and their cultural world. The evangelical depth and richness of our conversion to

---

this problem from the theology that assigns the earthly city to the laity and the heavenly city to priests and religious. Also inadequate is the distinction between the church as an institution and the church as a people composed of the faithful. See Y. Congar, "Evangelización y humanización—Salvación y liberación," in *Evangelización y humanización,* Twelfth meeting of USIG, Rome 1973, mimeographed, p. 3ff. J. Fernández, "Criterios para ayudar a definir la actitud del religioso frente a la política," in *CONFER*, Arequipa, 1974, no. 24, pp. 16–21; he makes the charism and the pastoral function a restrictive element.

52. S. Galilea, "La fe como principio crítico de promoción de la religiosidad popular," in *Fe cristiana y cambio social en América Latina,* pp. 151–52: "Political action in Latin America today requires awareness, organization, and activity of those who are suffering from oppression. This is what we call political mobilization or 'politicization.' It may not necessarily be channeled through political parties, though that has been the usual thing. It may also find expression in labor organizations and neighborhood groups, for example. In short it may be channeled through groups seeking to influence the power structure through varied forms of political action."

53. J. M. Guerrero ("El religioso y la política," *CONFER*, Arequipa, October 1974, p. 6) makes a proposal that deserves further elaboration. He talks about two major types of communities: the kind already familiar to us on the one hand and service-oriented communities that would assume some sort of politics on the other. It is only to be expected that relations between the two would not always be harmonious. We simply cannot standardize the political commitments of religious or their communities.

54. See CLAR, "Vida religiosa y situación socio-política," p. 19, no. 80: "In exercising their political and prophetic function, religious take a stand outside the established order of injustice and turn toward the poor." Document 13 of CELAM's theology committee stresses that in the political realm religious must strive for solidarity with the poor and the marginalized (p. 54).

the Lord in the poor opens up unforeseen possibilities for sensitivity and solidarity with the people, for a deeper understanding of life and the underlying meaning of history. This should foster and activate the project of the new person and the various struggles for the vindication of people's rights. Of course the associated programs will not be solely economic ones.

The content and authenticity of our evangelical and political radicalism will come from our ability to be faithful to the poor and to the great liberation movement stirring in the dispossessed masses on our continent.

Conscious awareness of the political dimension of our mission and, even more, our organic participation impose an urgent demand on our communities. They must have a clear understanding of what pluralism means here. It does not mean that our congregations can play any political role whatsoever; not all such roles are compatible with the gospel message or with the basic charisms of a religious congregation.[55] The process of apprenticeship is a costly one. The universal and collective perspective of the basic project advocated by political organizations does not always succeed in dispelling sectarianism, factional deviations, and the fanatic tendencies that are often evident in the heat of the liberation struggle.[56]

In Latin America we find that the concrete political embodiment of our pastoral options poses important and delicate challenges to obedience, dialogue, and fraternal life together. The disenchantment of an increasing number of religious toward renewal is rooted here. Even changes in the existing structures of training and administration and the creation of new forms of community life do not get to the core of the question. In the eyes of those who belong to powerful international congregations, the guidelines set forth by chapter meetings and international congresses

---

55. See A. Durand, "Ambiguité du pluralisme et exigences politiques des communautés chrétiennes," in *Lumière et Vie* 20, no. 105 (1971):116–30.

56. See J. Batista, "Vida religiosa y testimonio público," pp. 103–4. J. A. Saez, "Reflecciones ante nuestro pluralismo y la formación permanente," in *Confragua*, 1974, Guatemala, p. 36: Saez maintains that pluralism in the religious life derives from the decision to offer witness centered around the most radical values of the gospel message. I would only add that the radical attitude toward history and the kingdom is a part of that message insofar as it is posed and lived from the standpoint of the poor. See J. Míguez Bonino, "Visión del cambio social y sus tareas desde las iglesias cristianas no-católicas," in *Fe cristiana y cambio social en América Latina*, p. 202.

increasingly seem to be compromise conclusions in the light of varied real-life situations. Yet those conclusions purport to offer common criteria that will preserve the original spirit and charism of the given congregation.

It would be naive, however, to think that the disagreements and discrepancies divide along neat geographical lines. The problem is more or less the same everywhere. One gets the impression that people are willing to do anything in the way of modernizing forms but not to accept the social, political, and cultural consequences of real class solidarity with the exploited on the international level. Perhaps this explains the mediocre cast of our evangelical conversion to the Lord and the scarcely captivating aura of the "models" of holiness that we display in our showcases. Many of the concessions granted to the grassroots level possess the same sort of ambiguity. On the one hand they give the image of a certain amount of freedom. But they also make it a bit more difficult to keep demanding change. They seem designed to keep us from seeing where our process of renewal will take us in the end, where the qualitative leap lies. It must entail an authentically evangelical option for the oppressed races and classes of the world, and that option must be fleshed out politically in the historical struggle for their liberation.[57]

There must be pluralism in our forms of work, community, dress, and sharing responsibility. But the pluralism that concerns us most today is that which is entailed in our common option for the liberation of the oppressed classes on our continent. Here is the source of our most upsetting tensions and our most evangelical uneasiness. What comes to our aid here is the openness that derives from the eschatological content of our message and the universality of the new human being and the new society envisioned by political action. These two factors are constantly at work to overcome the retrogressions and the absolutizations that would negate the pluralism needed for the cause of the oppressed and the renewal of our religious life.

---

57. The feelings of many Latin American Christians are summed up well by R. Muñoz (*Nueva conciencia de la Iglesia en América Latina*, p. 299): "We must find a democratic socialism oriented toward the people. It must be an original brand of socialism that suits our qualities and that avoids the oppressive excesses which have accompanied its concrete application in other countries. It must avoid the totalitarian and bureaucratic rigidity that precludes real participation on the part of the common people. It must avoid dogmatism that imposes the views of one group while claiming to uphold science and the interests of the people, or which insists that the Christian faith can only be a product of bourgeois ideology."

Perspectives for the Religious Life

Obviously there are other ways to broach the topic we are considering here: i.e., the politicization of religious and the correct way to live the relationship that exists between faith and politics, between commitment to the poor and a political line of action.

What I have done above is to focus on three factors: the historical liberation project, the class character of our solidarity with the people, and experience of concrete political involvement. Now I should like to consider some of the perspectives that open up to various aspects of the religious life when one attempts to live that life on the basis of a historical and cultural option for the oppressed.

a. Religious life on our continent does not become Latin American primarily because it adopts the uses, customs, and languages of the people. Mimicry and the adoption of folklore do not make us more Latin American. We become more Latin American by grasping, deepening, and making our own *the historical vocation of the peoples of Latin America* in the international struggle for a human, just, and fraternal world. Only thus do we affirm both the particularity of being Latin American and the universal scope of the horizon within which we act both as Latin Americans and as members of the human race. It is the historical project of liberation undertaken by our masses that defines the Latin American nature of our religious life.[58] It is in that context that it becomes meaningful to incarnate the cultural forms of the people. There we can express the tasks of liberation in the language and color and flavor of our peoples.

b. It has been rightly pointed out that two phenomena characterize our continent today: *poverty and youthfulness.*[59] We confront popular classes

---

58. See *CLAR*, no. 20, p. 30. There we are reminded that Latin American religious life cannot be laid down in advance. It can only be discovered gradually insofar as "we are attentive to the Spirit and incarnate ourselves in the lives of our people in order to reinterpret the gospel message from there."

59. Ibid., p. 28: "Suffering from the consequences of this dependence, the church is being prodded by young people and the poor to reflect on this new phenonemon that is having such an impact on the Christian people. This prompts the church to re-examine the gospel message in the light of the new and unforseen context, for which theology has little real help to offer." See *CLAR*, no. 8, pp. 82–83: "The Salesian community in Latin America is confronted with two typical phenomena throughout the continent: a numerical preponderance of young people and the urgent need for the betterment of the common classes of people."

that are poor and a population that contains a very high percentage of young people. These two phenomena pose a direct challenge to the history of our religious congregations in Latin America. Even more importantly, they impose demands on us for the present and the near future. The two phenomena are not separable. They combine to give shape to the most dramatic situation existing in our countries and to form the basis for our hopes for the future.

Our congregational identity and our basic charisms will be operative and fruitful only if we are willing to reformulate them in terms of the common classes of the people. Congregations created to serve young people must reconsider their particular charisms in terms of the poor and the oppressed insofar as they are working in Latin America. There is no other option for them. In affluent areas of the globe these same congregations may work with wealthy young people who are "poor in spirit" and "oppressed" by the corruption of a society based on consumption. That is their business. We must leave them to bury their dead. Here the reality of the common people, of the despoiled and impoverished, is the category of life and the criterion for reformulating our specific congregational attributes. This is the concrete starting point for facing up to the distortions that we may have allowed to creep into our basic charisms or to undermine the full potentialities. The maladjustments will not be corrected overnight, but we must be clear about the proper starting point.

c. In its document *Perfectae caritatis,* Vatican II offered us three criteria for satisfactory renewal: the gospel message, the charism of the congregation's founder, and the signs of the times today. I think they are valid. When adopted in terms of our concrete situation, they take on force and greater exactitude. Our option for the common people paves the way for a very precise reading of the signs of history today; from there we must go on to explore the spirit of our congregation's founder and the demands imposed by the gospel message. But when we try to give this solidarity with the poor its full political weight, and when it finds expression in well defined political activities, we sense that these criteria fade away into vagueness and neutrality. They seem to become too ingenuous and ineffective for any real renewal.

The problem comes from the third criterion. We must make it clear that it is a matter of reading and interpreting history from the standpoint of the exploited classes and their historical project. Otherwise our spiritual, theological reflection on charisms, the gospel message, and "terrestrial realities" will turn aside from, or perhaps even against, the liberation movement where the kingdom's presence and construction is taking place.

d. Here we have the crucial point of all religious training. It is not a matter of adding a dash of political information and training or instructive tidbits about national and continental realities to the intellectual, human, and spiritual training of religious. The political content of our option for the oppressed must become the cornerstone of our training. From there we must rethink the other aspects of training and the charism of our congregation, even though the founder of our congregation may never have thought in such terms.

The point is not to prepare religious for the realm of politics as they were once prepared to face temptation and disordered affections. The challenge posed to us is one of creativity, which does not mean that we simply give up on living perspectives and ways of being faithful to the Lord that were used by older generations to respond to the needs of their day. In the radical needs of the poor on our continent we must rediscover the Lord's summons to live out his mystery of self-surrender to the Father, contemplation, and fidelity to the mission. In the highpoints of the struggle for liberation and the steps forward being taken by the people we must bring out the richness and fruitfulness of Christian love and the full historical and political implications of the following of Jesus.

e. As Vatican II reminds us, the active religious life gains renewed vitality from its mission. This principle takes on historical form every time we recognize that the liberation praxis of the oppressed is the locale where our mission is verified, where the promises are proclaimed and fulfilled, where the message becomes credible and universal. It is "the apostolate," understood in those terms, that is destined to revitalize our religious life.

f. To follow Christ in the poor is to plunge into the thickets of life where the common people suffer their passion and death; but it is also to make their hope in ultimate victory our own. There is clear and unmistakable stress on the paschal experience, the meaning of kenosis, and the summons to generosity, fidelity, and gratuitousness.

The historical project of the lowly and the abandoned is not an alternative project alongside that of following Christ. What is ultimately at stake in the political project of the oppressed is wholly in tune with what is involved in the following of Christ. To follow him is to do what he did: i.e., transform human history into a history of brotherhood. Solidarity with the poor is the historical—hence complex and conflict-ridden —expression of our following of Christ.

g. Consecration to God finds its concrete sign in our consecration to the poor. As religious we are "reserved" for them. The older themes of consecration and flight from the world sometimes connoted a somewhat negative understanding of the world and life on earth.[60] But the kind of perspective opened up to us by the yearnings of the poor for liberation enables us to rediscover the deeper and more positive sense that those two themes have had in the history of the religious life.

Flight from the world is in fact a protest, a refusal on the part of Christians to settle down comfortably in society. It was a religious protest containing an element of political criticism. Insofar as many Christians stopped supporting society and the status quo, their flight from the world was not simply an evasion. Because it stood for countervailing values and a different project, it was a contribution to the transformation of existing society.

So it is with the *fuga mundi* of Latin American religious today. Their solidarity with the oppressed, their commitment to the liberation project, means that their flight from the world takes on the nature of a *break* with society and embodies a *historical alternative* as its content. The political perspective bound up with our new solidarity has contributed important correctives to the wrongheaded and ingenuous outlook in the older notion of flight from the world. The rational scheme of the social sciences places us in a different vision of history, free of subjectivist, Manichean, Stoic, and Neoplatonic tendencies. It is a political vision of history with the transformation of the world in mind. It also envisions a historical alternative, the project of liberation, which gives social dimensions to the gospel values that had been overly spiritualized by the older notion of flight from the world. It is in this sense that the new notion of flight from the world, connoting a break with existing society and a historical alternative as its aim, finds embodiment in the transformation of the world.

The oppressed of our continent are becoming increasingly aware of their vocation to be transforming agents of history. The vocation of religious, as followers of Christ and people consecrated to God, should be lived out within the common vocation of all to transform Latin America.

Instead of "spiritualizing" our flight from the world, then, we must work every day to make it more historical, social, and political. In short, it must increasingly subvert the existing situation.

h. Solidarity with the poor puts us outside the system and the law. It sets us against many people, even our fellow religious. It breaks our identity and our identification with the system itself and with specific

---

60. See the summary of V. L. Gutiérrez, "El proyecto de vida evangélica y las opciones profesionales y apostólicas del religioso," in *Presencia de los religiosos en una nueva sociedad* (Madrid, 1975), pp. 317–74, especially pp. 337–38.

groups within that system. Our option for the poor inaugurates a new identity in each of us as individuals and in our religious communities. Our identity becomes more and more bound up with our capacity to identify with the poor and the oppressed, to accept their standard of living, their justifiable aspirations, and their efforts to attain them as our own. Ours is an identity on the move, a "nomadic" identity, an "unstable stability."

Our crisis of identity is a crisis of choosing. To decide in favor of the poor is not so much to find an identity. It is to set out on the task of fashioning a liberation project that will identify us with all our fellows and the Lord. It is in and through this course of action that we will find our lost identity as priests and religious.

i. With its historical ideal of liberation, solidarity with the poor forces us to explore and deepen the experience of *koinonia* ("fellowship" and "communion") with the rest of humanity. Closer to home, it forces us to explore and deepen that experience with our fellow religious in the same community.

The political demands of this identification raise a whole series of questions about the real possibilities of our communities to continue to summon us to *koinonia*. Friendship, for example, is an expression, a sacrament, of *koinonia*. But while on the one hand it finds a chance to grow and intensify in political radicalism, it also calls for maturity and openness if it is not to grow cold and disappear.

Many religious men and women are living the harshest kind of loneliness with their fellows because the latter's political posture is incompatible with the most elemental demands of the poor. But the real depths of the experience of these men and women lie in their unquenchable fidelity in spite of such silence and scandal. The most militant members of the exploited also know what it is to experience the indifference, lack of understanding, and empty response of their companions and those closest to them, including their families.

Involvement with the oppressed broadens *koinonia* and gives it universal horizons. It opens us up to new friendships, isolating us on one front and uniting us in solidarity on the other. The love we find in communion with the poor should give us the strength, the joy, and the courage we need to shoulder the loneliness we face in our religious communities. Our loneliness can then become a sign of hope, availability, and gratuitousness that will make it possible for others to believe in the things we believe.

It is a paradoxical situation. On the one hand the political project of liberating the oppressed produces tensions and even breaks in our communities. On the other hand it also raises the necessity and the possibility of living as brothers, of giving historical and collective expression to *koinonia*.

j. Our option for the poor and their historical project of liberation also opens us up to the theme of the new person, which is a central one in the religious life. The perfection to which we are summoned by our rules and constitutions is nothing else but the commitment to fashion the new human being in justice and holiness.

The political aspect of our option for the poor helps us to discover some very concrete features of this new human being. Certain evangelical features now prove to have profound political import and efficacy: e.g., a sense of community, the value of gratuitousness, a sensitivity for justice, the capacity for wonder, concern for the lowly and the weak, the power of love, the liberative content of an activist death, friendship as a substitute for master versus servant relationships, etc.

We are obliged to move forward toward the perfection of the new human being in Christ through the building up of the new human being that is already under way among the poor.

THE EVANGELICAL OPTION

Our solidarity with the poor and the oppressed, with sinners and the suffering, with the persecuted and humiliated, has real historical import because it is a truly evangelical option and the fulfillment of the Good News.[61] Its subversive force derives from the fact that it is caught up in the prophetic dynamism of the promises and the transforming power of the kingdom.

Here I shall confine myself to a summary overview of some of this evangelical content and its relevance for reflection on the religious life.

A Qualitatively Different Understanding of God's Word

The experience of immersing ourselves historically in the exploited classes constitutes a new way of understanding reality and situating ourselves in the ongoing process of history. When we opt for the poor, we choose to comprehend the deeper meaning of their hopes and struggles; but we also choose to comprehend the dynamic activity of the Father's

---

61. See J. Dupont, *Les Béatitudes*, 1969, 2: 216, 276–77. The author shows that the people in question are not people who are better disposed spiritually but those who are suffering and who make up the lower end of society.

grace and love throughout the course of salvation history. As I see it, in the absence of solidarity with the oppressed there can be no liberative understanding of the gospel, no comprehension of the Christ of history and his message.

a. The Christ-event—the historical, earthly Christ who came as a poor man—is an irrevocable and decisive happening in salvation history. It leaves its abiding mark on any interpretations or tendencies relating to the Scriptures. Most important, it lays down the criterion, the norm, for faith: for its way of life, its fidelity, and its liberative practice.

Christ's advent as a poor man is fully in line with the logic of the promises. Only in this way can the authenticity of his message be recognized and verified (Isa. 61:1f; Luke 4:16). His choosing to be poor is the first gesture of fidelity to his Father and his people. For the poor represented those who were sensitive and open to Yahweh's love, who were convinced that the fulfillment of his promises would change their lives and transform history.

Christ enters humanity historically through the mediation of the poor. He is a poor person, not just a member of humanity in some vague, undefined sense. He is a member of a poor nation and a poor people. The historical humanity which he takes on himself is the humanity of the poor—the human, or rather, inhuman conditions in which the marginalized classes and the oppressed common people live their lives. This fact itself is a real-life, theological exegesis of the whole prior tradition. It is the hermeneutic criterion governing any attempt to comprehend the mystery embodied in his message.

b. Christ's incarnation and life as a poor person assures us that the hope of the poor in the Messiah is authentic, that it is indeed the bearer of liberation. Christ is the Messiah of the poor.[62] That is the current of thought which Christ guarantees and fulfills in his person. This Messiah will have two features, according to Deutero-Isaiah (Isa. 40–55). He will be a servant, and he will undergo suffering. Now these two features themselves have characterized the living situation of the poor in all ages. They are servants by definition, and the fact of being poor entails concrete experience of suffering, privation, and exploitation. Thus the Messiah would be the Poor One *par excellence,*[63] and every poor person in history

---

62. See C. Duquoc, *Christologie, Le Messie* (Paris: Ed. du Cerf, 1974), p. 245. S. Croatto, "El Mesías liberador de los pobres," in *Revista Bíblica* 31, no. 137 (1970): 233–401.

63. See A. Gelin, *Los pobres de Yahvé,* Spanish edition published by Nova Terra,

is, as it were, a sacrament of that Messiah. Salvation would come through the Messiah of the poor, who is poor himself. Liberation, then, coincides with the messianic era in which the poor would hold the central place.[64]

Christ's life and death as a poor person confirms these experiences of the people who truly belong to Yahweh. God is faithful and does not abandon his people. The poor are the trustees of his promise and its fulfillment. Human beings are faithful to God if they respect the poor, the lowly, the helpless, and the simple. God's faithful love is revealed and realized in the toils and struggles of the poor for justice and their own liberation. They are the centerpiece in salvation history, the necessary mediating link in the relationship between God and human beings, between human beings themselves, and between human beings and nature. The universe can no longer be the stage for relations of injustice, inequality, and discrimination. It must become the new earth, the setting for relations of authentic kinship.[65]

The reality of Christ the poor person shatters any hope confided in the power of the great, the force of a king, and the sharp wits of the wise. Neither the great ones of this world nor the poor themselves believed that the fulfillment of the promise, the transformation of the world, would come from the weak and the lowly. Thus belief in the Messiah as the Messiah of the poor represents a gift and a conversion. The same applies today: belief in today's poor and conversion to them is a grace of the Spirit, a gift to be welcomed and nurtured.

c. The way in which Christ becomes the "collective property" of humanity is paradoxical. He does so by making himself poor even unto death (Phil. 2:6f) and turning the poor into agents of redemption, the sacrament of liberation, and the locus of salvation.[66] The universality of Christ and his message is played out in a complete and perduring option for the poor. Faith without the poor is dead faith. It is faith devoid of hope, universal perspective, or fulfillment.

1965, p. 138; Eng. trans., *The Poor of Yahweh* (Collegeville, Minn.: Liturgical Press, 1964). H. Bojorge, "Goel: Dios libera a los suyos," *Revista Bíblica* 32, no. 139 (1971): 8–12. R. Lepointe, "Pauvreté et messianisme," in *Kerygma* 5 (1971): 37–50.

64. A. Gelin, *Los pobres de Yahvé*, p. 101.

65. P. J. Proudhon described the God of the gospel message as "the God of the poor and the worker, ever the God of sinners and the oppressed, . . . of all who suffer, . . . of those who are denied self-expression, robbed, imprisoned, and calumniated." See J. Duquesne, *La gauche de Christ* (Paris: Ed. Grasset, 1972), p. 159.

66. Matt. 25. See A. Gelin, *Los pobres de Yahvé*, p. 138.

Christ revitalizes the universal vocation of the chosen people, helping them to break with every narrow interpretation of Scripture and every sectarian attitude. He reads the Scriptures as a poor man in the tradition of the prophets.[67] His exegesis brings out the universal and collective character of its message and of salvation. It makes clear the conflict-laden character of liberation, which is the work of the poor and the suffering. In Christ the poor one we find the place where God's eternal love is concretized and made universal.

d. In the case of Christ the condition of poor human being and servant holds true for his life even beyond his death and resurrection. His exaltation[68] does not invalidate it; instead it confirms the fact that the fulfillment of the promise is to be found therein.

The raison d'être and underlying meaning of Christ's historical life was the fight for justice.[69] That is why Jesus came into the world and died. His quest for justice became a real fight as soon as he presented himself as the poor Messiah, unmasked the alleged "justice" of their opponents, and denounced the use of religion to justify unjust attacks on the poor and heavy legal burdens on the lowly. In Christ we see the profoundly biblical roots of an option for the poor and its subversive overtones in the society of his own day.[70] The proclamation of the kingdom necessarily involved these two dimensions. What is more, historical changes effecting liberation for the poor are the place where the word of God and his promise become historical, credible, efficacious, and a challenge to the whole world.

e. If we all have died and risen in Christ, then we all have been saved in the cross and resurrection of a poor man. Our liberation comes through the condition of Christ as a poor person, which finds its fulfillment in pain-filled humiliation and lordly exaltation. The promise is realized insofar as the mighty are cast down and the lowly exalted. The lordship of Christ is the lordship of the poor, a very different kind of lordship. It does not subdue and oppress people as the lordship of the mighty does. It confers strength and lordship on those who accept it, making them free, responsible agents rather than slaves. The lordship of the poor Christ is

---

67. See. C. Duquoc, Christologie, p. 244.
68. Ibid., Chapter II, pp. 71–169 and 228.
69. Ibid., pp. 227 and 239ff.
70. See A. George, "Le problème politique dans le milieu de Jésus," in Lumière et Vie 20 (1971): 6–17. From the same standpoint see P. Bigo, "Jesús y la política de su tiempo," in Medellín 1 (1975): 51f. From the standpoint of liberation theology see G. Gutiérrez, "Jesus and the Political World," in Worldview 9 (1972): 43–46.

different because it is born of an experience of real poverty and is connected with a different kind of project. It seeks to inaugurate a new type of human being, living in fellowship with other human beings and recognizing all as children of the same Father. Such is what the experience of the poor in spirit is meant to be.

Implications for the Religious Life

a. Paradoxically enough, this option for the poor is not "optional." It does not depend on personal inclination, good will, a personal charism, or socially concerned people. The reality of Christ the poor one and his message means that such an option is an essential element in our option for him through faith. He has made it clear that the kingdom comes by way of the poor, that only through them can we open our hearts to the biblical message, and that our fidelity to him must be defined in terms of the poor. We have fought long battles in many of our religious congregations to get their chapter meetings to make such a definition. The only real concession so far has been that they have allowed our involvement with the poor so long as the utmost prudence is exercised.

b. It is in solidarity with the poor and the oppressed that we are saved.[71] It is there that we realize our encounter with the Lord (Matt. 25). Thus only in the light of that experience can we understand God's message and share it. That experience is the nourishing wellspring of our spiritual life and the revitalizing basis of theology. Only there does the experience of the religious life have any possibility of renewal.

The evangelical aspect of this encounter is further enriched when we consider all that is involved in a historical option for the poor. It also includes the paschal experience because it assumes the socio-historical implications of liberation and the politico-cultural implications of proclaiming the kingdom.[72] Liberation praxis is the hermeneutic tool for

---

71. A good point was made by the participants at the first Latin American seminar on training for the religious life: "The option for the liberation of the oppressed can be understood only by those who live and bear witness out of hope. To do this is to proclaim that brotherhood is possible, to receive the salvation that comes from the poor" (*Vida en Fraternidad*, 20, 1974, p. 22).

72. See H. Borrat, "Las bienaventuranzas y el cambio social," in *Fe cristiana y cambio social*, p. 216f: "The beatitudes are completely and radically Christocentric. They impel his disciples to the following of Christ, and his disciples, like him, must take the pathway of self-humiliation, poverty, persecution, and a state of want. . . . They will be deprived of everything, perhaps even of their freedom,

discerning, understanding, and living by the voice of God in and through the voice of the people. We accept and share the word of God as a word that is for the poor and their deepest aspirations.

c. An option for the oppressed is also a precondition if we wish to give real meaning to what is called the vow of poverty.[73] Solidarity with the poor does not derive from the vow of poverty. There is a curious thing going on here. On the one hand an option for the poor and the oppressed is being carefully examined and weighed in some of our communities. On the other hand the vow of poverty is increasingly equated with "poverty of spirit." Thus the vow of poverty is stripped of its historical and political content because it is not rooted in a commitment to the exploited classes; and it also ceases to be an effective means of holiness and the spiritual life. Historically speaking, we can say that spiritual poverty has arisen and grown out of the concrete experience of real poverty.[74]

We have not been without saints and people who have contributed to the transformation of our continent. The real challenge facing those who regard an option for the oppressed as the qualitative leap in their lives is to accept the consequences of that decision. For it entails the demands of an austere, impoverished life stripped of all pretension and motivated only by love for the people. Just as Paul warns that it is not enough to hand one's body over to be burned (1 Cor 13:3), so we might say that it is not enough to become proletarians; we must also accept the subversive implications of austerity and poverty in an unjust society.

their physical integrity, and their lives. This progressive emptying is the inevitable course of those who adopt the beatitudes because they are following in the footsteps of Jesus. He was born poor and grew poorer throughout his life . . . until his death on the cross." See G. Fourez, "La vie évangélique comme signe de contradiction," in Supplement to La Vie Spirituelle 110 (1974): 304–13.

73. See Cecilio de Lora, "Alcuni punti base per inquadrare la situazione pastorale della America Latina," in the proceedings of the 1972 convention in Rome, pp. 74–75: "How can poverty be expressed in community terms in Latin America? It can be considered from many points of view, . . . but the first and most important consideration is that the Gospels do not talk about poverty but about the poor."

74. See A. Gelin, Los pobres de Yahvé, p. 138. H. Borrat ("Las bienaventuranzas y el cambio social") points up three different readings of the beatitudes. One centers around the private individual, one centers around the church, and one centers around classes. My approach is a combination of the second and third readings, stressing that we must build up the church on the basis of the poor and inject political content into our mission on this continent. From a historical standpoint see N. H. Pipo, "Los pobres en la Iglesia," in Teología (1964), 2: 1–5, 3–31, 107–49.

d. The evangelical richness of solidarity with the poor requires that we not equate it with a political rationale.[75] The salvific dimension of the political realm does not strip it of its own specific character. All too often we tend to stress the religious and pastoral side of our presence among the poor while deliberately contrasting it with its real political and ideological implications.[76] We can barely tolerate these implications. For a growing number of religious, however, we must do more than simply tolerate these implications. We cannot keep our evangelical motives completely separate from our political ones. The militancy of religious is part and parcel of the political vocation that they take upon themselves.

However, when our commitment to the oppressed does not involve a partisan option or even a program, we find it more difficult to find criteria for choosing our commitments and our signs of solidarity. Of course we have generosity and a certain amount of freedom in choosing to side with the poor. But it frequently happens that what we have to contribute as individuals and communities is also the source of our perplexity, vacillation, and error in the face of more specific situations.

We must endure a trying apprenticeship. Those in our communities who do offer more direct witness will challenge our communities' capacity for acceptance and dialogue. Warnings against naiveté and anarchy should not rob us of fidelity to the Spirit. It is the Spirit who summons us to segments of the populace which may not be of primary political importance in the takeover of power, but which will indeed contribute to the project of liberation and the creation of a new human being.

e. To be for all, religious must be for the poor. To be a member of

---

75. See D. Hervieu-Leger, "¿Signos de un resurgimiento religioso contemporáneo?" in *Concilium* 89 (1973): 325; Eng. trans., "Signs of a Contemporary Religious Revival," *Concilium* 89: 11–25: "Frequently religious reactivation seems to be accompanied by a contraction of militant activity in the specifically political realm. It is not surprising to find this happen in the case of those whose revolutionary commitment never became anything more than a projection of their own religious fantasies. It never developed into class solidarity. This is not surprising when we consider the social strata in which this movement developed."

76. See J. M. Guerrero, "El religioso y la política," who maintains that denunciation must be forthright, true, effective, and based on the gospel message rather than on ideology. See J. L. Segundo, *The Liberation of Theology,* Eng. trans. (Maryknoll, N.Y.: Orbis Books, 1977), chap. 4, the section subtitled "Faith Without Ideologies: Dead Faith." Also see J. C. Scannone, "Teología y política," in *Fe cristiana y cambio social en América Latina,* p. 259.

humanity, religious must be of and for the weak and the humiliated. To be brothers and sisters to the whole world, religious must be part of those who possess a message and who are fashioning world kinship. In the history of nations it has been the poor. In salvation history it was to them that the promises were made, and it was in them that those promises were fulfilled.

Gutiérrez has rightly pointed up the need for a collective, social appropriation of the gospel message in terms of the common people.[77] In like manner we religious must belong to the lowly of our continent. Both as an institution and as an overall phenomenon, the religious life is not one of the things that the people feel to be theirs. As is the case with the church, they come to religious as clients. The social appropriation of the gospel must also find expression in the people's appropriation of those institutions whose underlying inspiration comes from the gospel message. The religious life is one such institution. This is especially true since we often say that we religious are examples of the gospel lived in all its radicalism.

This outlook might seem to be very unrealistic. But some of us feel that if we approach the renewal of the religious life from this perspective, many other features of that life will be seen in a new light: e.g., religious consecration, obedience, and flight from the world as transformation of the world. I do not suggest that anything will happen automatically. I am simply saying that the social appropriation of the gospel goes hand in hand with support for the people's liberation project. Latin American religious must allow the common people to fashion their own ways of living the gospel, to which our own experience has many valuable elements to contribute. By the same token their ways of living the gospel are a summons from the Lord to us, urging us to renew the structures of the religious life, our spiritual life, and our evangelical identity. The close participation of Buddhist monks in the lives and struggles of their people in Southeast Asia offers us much food for thought in this connection.

Finally, I should like to offer a brief summary of this chapter. Our consecration to the poor has evangelical roots. We comprehend the Scriptures insofar as we read them in terms of Christ the poor human being. Such a reading sheds new light on what it means to follow Christ and to live in poverty, chastity, and fraternity. The same thing holds true when we start off from the poor of our continent as the historical mediation of our encounter with the Lord. We discover and opt for an interpre-

---

77. See G. Gutiérrez, "Praxis de liberación," in *Concilium* 96, p. 373.

tation of Latin American reality that has new emphases and consequences for many. The concrete practice of many religious has led them to rethink and rework their evangelical option for the poor in terms of its social content and its political rationale. They have come to focus on such things as a class-oriented outlook, a projected socialist society, and closer collaboration with others. This has complicated the picture, but at the same time it has also given concrete historical embodiment, and hence credibility, to the gospel message and their witness.

Steeped in this basic outlook, we face the Lord's summons to renew our lives, to grow in the Spirit, and to mature in the struggle for justice and the kingdom. We are not without questions or tensions, of course. But our consecration to the poor bolsters our hope that we religious in Latin America may be able to be revitalized with a holiness that will transform our continent. [78]

----

78. A. Tortolo objects to the idea of consecration to the people in commenting on an article by Delaney, "Los religiosos y el pueblo argentino," in *Vida en Fraternidad* 19 (1974). Tortolo feels that such a focus is completely anti-theological. He reiterates the dictum of Thomas Aquinas that one makes one's vows to God alone: *votum soli Deo fit.* The dictum is true enough. But what concerns us here is the historical mediation that will make our consecration to God meaningful, efficacious, and sacramental. In the following of Christ this mediation, which is thoroughly theological, is self-surrender to the poor. In their flesh Christ became the brother of all and expressed his filiation with the Father.

5

The Liberation Project and the Project of the Religious Life

In this chapter I propose to offer some considerations on the religious life as a way of life based on the exigencies of the kingdom. I do not intend to offer a presentation of the religious vows as such but to point up the general outlook that derives from a liberation perspective.

When we talk about liberation at its various levels of historical expression,[1] we are referring to the historical project of the popular classes both as a general design and as the reference point of the liberation process. It is social praxis that maintains the dynamism and ongoing creativity of that process.

The perspective adopted by liberation theology concentrates on liberation praxis in history and begins its reflection from that praxis. The point is worth emphasizing because the idiom of liberation theology has been taken over by some theologians who clearly dissociate it from the historical practice of the common people. In any case the focus of authentic liberation theology on praxis opens up a new perspective on the religious life. Religious life can be viewed as a project that incorporates the challenges and achievements embodied in the struggle for political liberation on our continent.

The People's Project as a Sign of the Kingdom

A ceaseless quest for justice and peace lies at the heart of the aspirations and struggles of the oppressed. The historical project of liberation has a popular cast since it is the work of the common people and expresses their

---

1. See G. Gutiérrez, *A Theology of Liberation*, Eng. trans. (Maryknoll, N.Y.: Orbis Books, 1973), chap. 2.

real soul. When we contemplate this project from the standpoint of faith, we see in it the presence and power of the Spirit. What is implied in this experience is an acceptance of the kingdom that finds historical expression in this project.

The Kingdom and Liberation

One of the most original biblical and theological contributions of Gutiérrez is his stress on the theme of the kingdom and political liberation. His work contains pages that are deeply rooted in the Scriptures, and his reading of the Scriptures is profoundly marked by the impact that political liberation had on the chosen people and their understanding of God's promises.[2] The key axis is the kingdom and political liberation. It is this axis that gives meaning to any theological focus on salvation, to Christology as a consideration of Christ as the liberator, and to the eschatological promises as the historical fulfillment of the divine promise and the spiritual life. It is also the key to overcoming the old theory of the distinction of planes.[3]

I believe that this focus opens up new pathways for reflecting on the experience of the religious life, and I shall try to show how in the pages that follow.

The kingdom of God is the promise of salvation that has already been fulfilled in history through the death and resurrection of Christ and that will be completely fulfilled by Christ when he returns. In his preaching Jesus describes the kingdom as the time of salvation, the consummation of the world, and the restoration of communion.[4] We cannot spiritualize that reality to the point where it ends up confined within the heart of the human individual. When Jesus tells us that we cannot hasten the coming of the kingdom or circumscribe it in some geographic location, he is definitely not implying that it is to be found in the heart of human beings.[5] As Jeremias points out, "the kingdom is not a spatial or a static concept

---

2. Ibid., Chap. 9, especially pp. 155–78.

3. Congar seems a bit perplexed when he attempts to evaluate Gutiérrez's theological contribution to this issue. See Y. Congar, "Libération et Salut" (Bulletin de Théologie) in *Revue des Sciences Philosophiques et Theologiques* 58, no. 4 (1975): 657–71.

4. See J. Jeremias, *Teología del Nuevo Testamento*, Spanish trans. (Salamanca: Sígueme, 1974), 1:125; Eng. trans., *New Testament Theology* (New York: Scribner's, 1971).

5. Ibid., p. 125. See Gutiérrez, *A Theology of Liberation*, pp. 160–68.

but a dynamic one."[6] This means that we will recognize it wherever we find the dynamism of love, goodness, and fraternal communion operative in history.

At the same time, however, the kingdom is not to be confused or equated with any specific one of its concrete embodiments in history. The kingdom can be recognized in political liberation in history. Partial though they may be, liberation happenings in history do give real, effective human reality to the kingdom and God's promise. In the dynamism of these partial historical embodiments we remain open to further attainments of liberation and to the underlying sense of the kingdom that finds fruitful expression here and now. In short, there is a relationship between liberation and the growth of the kingdom.[7]

The kingdom of God is proclaimed as a new creation precisely because it is the fulfillment of the promised liberation.[8] Historical realizations of the kingdom indicate that something new is being fulfilled, and that something new points up the deeper meaning of the partial historical realizations that are part of the overall process. Far from exhausting history, the achievements of the liberation process open it up to the fuller meaning that gives direction to those achievements and lends credibility to such openness. At the same time, however, there is a tension between what we experience in the present and what we hope for in the future.[9] Thus we can say that the kingdom is not to be reduced to any given historical stage,[10] while still rejecting excessively spiritual reductionism and historical embodiments that are either apolitical or innocuous with regard to the existing social order.

It is not just that the kingdom has some vague connection with concrete historical achievements. The growth of the kingdom takes place in those historical happenings that produce growth in humaneness, justice, fraternal solidarity, and love. The efficacy of the kingdom is bound up with those historical happenings even though it is not wholly exhausted by them. We can go so far as to say that there is a causal relationship between total political liberation and the growth of the kingdom.[11]

---

6. J. Jeremias, *Teología del Nuevo Testamento*, 1:121–22.

7. G. Gutiérrez, *A Theology of Liberation*, pp. 168–78.

8. C. Duquoc, *Christologie, Le Messie* (Paris: Ed. du Cerf, 1974), 2:227; G. Gutiérrez, *A Theology of Liberation*, pp. 175–78.

9. G. Gutiérrez, *A Theology of Liberation*, chap. 9.

10. Ibid., Chap. 11, pp. 232–39.

11. J. L. Segundo, "Capitalismo—Socialismo: Crux Theologica," in *Concilium* 96, pp. 410–11, 421.

The Kingdom and the Historical Project of Liberation

The reign of God consists of the liberation that Jesus brings to the oppressed. We know that Jesus' whole life was oriented around the kingdom and its meaning, that is to say, around the struggle to re-establish communion between human beings themselves and between them and God. To be this fraternal communion, the kingdom in history must coincide with the establishment of justice. To establish justice means to shoulder the consequences of all liberative action against evil: i.e., persecution, trial before the authorities, betrayal, and death.[12]

But there is something else that represents the novel aspect of the good news and that is an essential feature of the kingdom. The kingdom itself is a gift and a promise that is given and fulfilled in the poor and the oppressed. The kingdom—as salvation, communion, and the transformation of the world—is offered to the poor, and that is an intolerable scandal. Worse still, the kingdom is uniquely theirs.[13]

The radicalism of the kingdom lies in the fact that it is at the root of liberation. In the good news fulfilled in the poor and oppressed we find the roots of our hope and of the world's salvation. The crowning point of the demand for conversion was the requirement that we accept the fact that the kingdom of God will come from the poor and oppressed. There is no access to the kingdom apart from this option for them. That is why the option is not "optional." That is why evangelical radicalism in every age must start off from the poor people's struggle for justice; otherwise it may turn into a ladder of purely spiritualist asceticism and a concrete negation of the kingdom.

The kingdom is not merely an interior reality; it is a social fact. Christ's preaching is not the proclamation of an ideology designed to camouflage injustice. Jesus proclaims and establishes a new way of living.[14] He was persecuted, not only for his vocabulary but also for its concrete content. For Jesus related his words to the lowly and the poor, making them the only inheritors of the kingdom. To take sides with the poor is to unmask social injustices, to spotlight the crimes and abuses committed under the guise of religious observance and scrupulous fulfillment of the law, to

---

12. See J. Mateos, "Algunos conceptos del Nuevo Testamento," in the New Testament of the *Nueva Biblia Española*, published by Ed. Cristiandad, 1974, p. 768.
13. J. Jeremias, *Teología del Nuevo Testamento*, 1: 122 and 133.
14. Matt. 7:21,24,26; 13:20–21.

show how all that may represent irredeemable infidelity to God.

The kingdom of God is revealed and concretized in history in the struggle of the poor and the exploited for justice, freedom, and love. This is the historical liberation project of those who seem to be the refuse of the world. [15]

With all its human limitations and contradictions, the common people's historical project of liberation represents an alternative. Its universal character, its utopian perspective, and its collective structure enable us to recognize signs of the kingdom's presence and fruitfulness. For it points toward a fraternal, classless society and a new kind of human being. The fundamental thing is the kingdom. But the mediation of the historical liberation project, of the social praxis of the oppressed, is historically decisive.

The Historical Project as a Sign of the Kingdom

The three characteristics of the people's liberation project just mentioned—universal, utopian, and collective—mean that it is the chief sign of the fulfillment of God's promises, of the kingdom's growth. Insofar as this historical project retains its universal perspective, its communitarian content, and its prophetic message, it becomes the locus of fidelity to the kingdom and its demands for us here in Latin America today. It is the place where the transformation of history and fidelity to the Lord meet, the locus of spiritual experience, childlikeness, and poverty of Spirit.

In the historical practice of the exploited the liberation project of the lowly finds a partial but transforming conversion of its message. For there it seeks to turn human love into a historical, universal, and communitarian reality. That is why the utopia of the poor is a sacrament of the kingdom.

We know that the kingdom and the divine promises are a universal gift with a collective structure. We cannot enter the universality of the kingdom without entering into communion and accepting the call to be a community, a people. We accept the kingdom as a gift insofar as we see and accept ourselves as a single people called to be one heart, one body, and one spirit in communion with our one God and Father.

We are called to be new human beings: just, living in fellowship, and motivated by the force of love. This summons means that the historical

---

15. 1 Cor. 1:27–28.

project of the people and its embodiments[16] are the privileged place for the fulfillment of the promises, the locus of renewal for the charisms, and the concrete expression of the power and prophetic inspiration of the poor in spirit.

The liberation project of the exploited gives historical expression to the hope and conviction of the people. They believe that transformation of the existing situation can come from the poor. They know that every effort at liberation must incorporate the deeper aspirations of the dispossessed masses on our continent; otherwise it will have no meaning, no subversive force, and no power for real conversion. In historical terms acceptance of the kingdom implies this basic attitude. We must believe and hope, against all hope, that salvation has come and that the liberation of the poor is its unmistakable sign.

Implications for the Religious Life

There is no doubt that the kingdom cannot be reduced to its historical expression as social, human, and religious liberation. But there is also no doubt that we see its concrete embodiment and growth in such historical expressions. Every way of life that purports to be grounded on the kingdom and its demands must operate in and through the concrete embodiments and demands of historical liberation. Liberation is the guiding historical thread, bearing witness to the dynamism of the kingdom, grace, and the power of the Spirit.[17]

Since the religious life is a sign of the kingdom, it must also look to the liberation project of the oppressed. There it will find the place where its purported meaning and its message are fleshed out concretely. In the religious life we are called upon to recognize and make explicit the meaning of the kingdom that already finds expression in the advancing struggle of the poor to obtain freedom, solidarity, and love.

In their liberation project we find the historical locale of our fidelity to the kingdom and our own history. It is a fidelity lived out in the tensions, contradictions, and hopes of a people who have suffered long centuries of submission, deception, and false illusions. To immerse ourselves in the real-life project of the people is to immerse ourselves in all these circumstances, many of which are signs of sinfulness.

---

16. G. Gutiérrez, *A Theology of Liberation*, Chap. 11.

17. See A. Durand, "En busca del sentido de la vida religiosa," *Selecciones de Teología* 40 (1971): 356. Durand tries to show that the religious life acquires its eschatological import insofar as it posits positive, social human mediations.

Much has been said about the religious life as a way of life that takes evangelical radicalism as its guiding norm. My impression is that this approach in itself does not point up what is truly radical about the good news: i.e., an option for the poor as the verification of the kingdom. As I see it, there is no evangelical radicalism if one strips away this central feature. It must entail an option for the oppressed and for their project: the creation of a new human being and a fraternal, classless society based on justice. Otherwise the doctrine of evangelical radicalism is simply a reworked version of an older theology of the religious life, one that viewed religious life in terms of asceticism.

Asceticism and the cross are requirements of the gospel message only insofar as people choose to live by its radical focus on the experience of the poor and their need for total liberation. The gospel loses its prophetic radicalism when it is not lived from the standpoint of the poor. It then ceases to be the good news for all, and it can readily be turned into an ascetic code for a politico-religious ideology. We religious in Latin America are called upon now to rediscover the radicalism of the gospel through our option for the oppressed masses here. Radicalism is not to be measured by our exaggeration of the letter of the gospel message. It hinges on our discovery of the Spirit, on a change in outlook. We must come to see that the promise and fulfillment of the kingdom is bound up with the poor.

The religious life does indeed represent a distinctive expression of the prophetic charism enjoyed by the people of God. But it does so only insofar as it recalls and recognizes the divine promise, opening us up to the hope that it will continue to be fulfilled today and tomorrow as it was yesterday. We cannot dissociate the charism of prophecy from the fulfill-ment of the promise, that is, from the historical events of liberation and the struggle for justice.[18] It is in this struggle that the prophetic charism fulfills its role of shedding light and spelling out the underlying import of events. It is there that the prophetic charism tells us that historical events express the meaning of the kingdom and embody its persistent summons to live in accordance with the demands of the divine promise.

But how are we to turn the liberation of our continent into a prophetic

---

18. See C. Duquoc, *Christologie*, 2:238–48. He makes it clear in what sense the prophetic life of Jesus was a fight for justice, prophecy, and liberation. Compare the opposing view of R. Schnackenburg in *God's Rule and Kingdom*, Eng. trans, (New York: Herder and Herder, 1963). Schnackenburg thinks that Jesus com-pletely eliminated the earthly, national, and politico-religious element from the idea of the kingdom, rendering it a purely religious reality.

sign of the kingdom's presence and growth? If our message is to be credible, we must spell it out by immersing our own lives in the life of the people who are trying to build a future based on freedom and love. As a life-project grounded on God's promise, our religious life will take on historical consistency and make a real contribution only if we live it out in the historical liberation project of those who are oppressed.

It seems to me that no renewal of the religious life can be meaningful to the people of Latin America unless it takes place within their own struggles for liberation. Hence the theology of the religious life can be revitalized only insofar as it is a theology of liberation.

THE PEOPLE'S PROJECT AND THE FOLLOWING OF CHRIST

Christ's life as the suffering Messiah and the gospel message corrected certain distortions in the religious life and thinking of his people.[19] In so doing it turned the kingdom of God into the full and complete response to people's deepest and most authentically human aspirations.[20] The kingdom of God finds historical articulation in the liberation project of the poor insofar as this project expresses and realizes the utopian element in the hearts of all human beings.

It is important to remember that the term "kingdom of God" is equivalent to "the following of Christ" or discipleship. The demands are the same in both instances.[21] Not only have we spiritualized the kingdom, turning it into a purely interior experience. We have also turned the

---

19. See C. Duquoc, *Christologie*, 2:263–80.

20. See L. Boff, "Salvación en Jesucristo y proceso de liberación," in *Concilium* 96, p. 378f; Eng. trans., "Salvation in Jesus Christ and the Process of Liberation," *Concilium* 96, pp. 78–91. Boff rightly reminds us that the expression "kingdom of God" alludes to the utopian side of the human heart. Thus Jesus articulated a radical datum of human life: its principle of hope and its utopian dimension. But Boff also stresses that the kingdom is not an intrinsic extension of the present world. It breaks in as a revolutionary overturning of the world's existing structures.

21. Luke 18:22–24; 14:33; Matt. 18:4,20. I cannot get a clear picture of the view which maintains that the following of Christ is a qualified expression of one's acceptance of the eschatological character of the kingdom and also the fruit of a special vocation. In this vein see J. L. Aurrecoextea, "La vida religiosa como seguimiento de Cristo," in *CONFER* (Madrid) 12, no. 45 (1973):53. He does spell out clearly the development of the whole theme of discipleship in the postpaschal period. While discipleship was universalized, it also lost its roots in history when it was reduced to an inner, spiritualist attitude.

following of Christ into a formal imitation of Jesus' life, suggesting that we must shape our own inner life in conformity with his virtues. But if the kingdom is fleshed out within the process of liberation,[22] then the following and imitation of Christ cannot be realized outside the historical liberation project of the poor. It is there that we accept the following of Jesus, which is a gift even before it is a task. It is there, too, that the following of Jesus unfolds.[23]

One fact is historically irreversible: the following of Christ as a physical discipleship and companionship ended when the Lord returned to his Father. After that the Christian community extended the obligation to all Christians, as we read in Luke's Gospel and the Acts of the Apostles.[24] Now we must shape our whole life in terms of the same outlook that Jesus had when he came into the world. Sharing that outlook, we must now shoulder the historical tasks that flow from it. Two features are inextricably bound up with that outlook. One is the proclamation of the kingdom as a promise that is on its way to fulfillment. The other is the poor as the historical locus of verification for the prophetic character and the liberative content of the kingdom. The historical task that flows from that outlook is the transformation of history, the creation here and now of a new society and a new human being.[25]

The proclamation and fulfillment of liberation in Christ also leads us to

---

22. L. Boff, "Salvación en Jesucristo y proceso de liberación," *Concilium* 96, p. 387. E. Rasco, "Jesús y el Espíritu, iglesia y historia, elementos para una lectura de Lucas," in *Gregorianum* 56, no. 2 (1975):360f: "The kingdom of God is not a dimension external to history. Luke does not introduce it into history by some process of moralistic or spiritualistic interiorization. Instead he makes it something that really enters into history and is close to human beings within it."

23. Following Jesus can mean three things, according to T. Aerts, "Suivre Jésus," *Ephemerides Theologicae Lovanienses* 42 (1966): 472–512. In the case of the prepaschal Christ, it means abandoning everything and accompanying him wherever he goes. In the case of the postpaschal Christ it means following his demands to deny oneself and take up the cross. In the case of the postpentecostal Christ, it means following the Christ of faith and history morally, spiritually, and physically. In the last instance, however, I do not think it brings out a clear-cut reference to historical reality, human aspirations, and the transformation of the world as signs of the kingdom, as social and collective embodiments of the kingdom's presence and growth.

24. See, for example, J. Galot, "El Evangelio: norma suprema de la vida religiosa," in *Cuadernos Monásticos* 27 (1973):559–70.

25. See E. Samain, "Manifesto de libertação: o discurso programa de Nazaré," in *REB* 34 (1974): 134.

situate Jesus' struggle for justice in the framework of his resurrection. It is there that the good news once and for all takes on its historical, cosmic, material character and its universal dimension.[26] Hence we cannot turn the following of Christ into an inner, spiritualist mimesis in the post-pentecostal economy. To do so would be to refuse to follow Christ, to deny the force and novelty of the resurrection, to take the life out of our faith in Jesus and the kingdom, and to nullify our proclamation of liberation to the people of today.[27] Christ's exaltation and ascent into heaven do not justify any such interiorization or spiritualization of Christ. The Lord's resurrection establishes an inseparable and comprehensible relationship between justice and liberation. The two together provide a synthesis of his message and a concrete experience of the kingdom.

To follow Christ is to become converted to his love by trying to take the dynamism of his death and resurrection and make its impact real and effective in Latin American history today. His death and resurrection offer us the certainty that the lives of all human beings find meaning and fruitfulness in the struggles of the poor for justice and a more fraternal world. This is the principle that moves history. It is the wellspring of human hope and the historical embodiment of human love as something stronger than death, something stronger because of the death that is found in the experience of our people as victims of brutal repression.

The warm, human love that inspires and crowns the irrepressible liberation process of the oppressed clearly constitutes a collective experience of the resurrection already at work in the history of the poor. They suffer the pangs of childbirth as they strive to make sure that today love will be stronger than death, than injustice, than exploitation, than racial discrimination. In his resurrection Christ won out over all that once and for all. In the struggle of the poor for liberation, his resurrection takes on its collective, historical embodiment.

Thus the following of the dead and resurrected Jesus inaugurates a new kind of presence in the world and in history. It commits us to the task of giving historical reality to the kingdom in the eyes of the people on our continent. It commits us to transforming an unjust reality and creating a new human being.

---

26. In his *Christologie* (2:248–62) C. Duquoc responds to Marxsen's objections to the way in which the resurrection is presented. On the basis of Christology Duquoc solidly establishes the relationship between justice and the resurrection. He also casts doubt on any attempt to empty the formulas that present the resurrection of their cosmic and historical content.

27. Ibid., p. 256. Proclamation of the message does not annul or erase injustice and exploitation. It reminds us that we cannot pretend that the promise has been

The historical setting for our following of Christ is provided by the historical liberation project of the common people. But in the light of Christ's message this project acquires a horizon and an import that is packed with human richness.

Some theologians who stress evangelical radicalism and make this the distinctive feature of the following of Christ for religious do so in the broader context of the universal vocation of all human beings to follow Christ. They may also stress the christological perspective of the resurrection. However, while this perspective may indeed bring out the original thrust of the biblical message as opposed to Platonic thought and others, it does not put enough emphasis on the historical and cosmic structure of discipleship and on the transformative character of flight from the world. Moreover, it usually does not consider the liberation project of the poor as a historical expression of that perspective today. It does not see the transformation of the world and of human relationships as a concrete way of fleshing out the radical option of the gospel message for the poor.[28] Yet it is precisely there that the following of Jesus acquires for religious all the force and radicalism that is needed today if we are to shoulder the challenges posed by our continent.[29] It is there that we come to realize anew that following Christ in the poor is a gift, that our option for their liberation project must be lived as a gift-experience and their victories celebrated as the content of our thanksgiving to the Father.

Viewed in that perspective, the following of Christ will mean some-

-----

fulfilled so long as our struggle against injustice and exploitation has not succeeded in eliminating them.

28. That is why I find Tillard's exhortation to be "for the world" as an excessively poetic view of the religious life and its project. Perhaps the most serious flaw in his fine study and his view of evangelical radicalism is his failure to pinpoint the radical, original, and scandalous aspect of the good news in the poor. His approach, in my opinion, lacks the evangelical aggressiveness that derives from the poor and the historical perspective which derives from their historical project of liberation. See J.M.R. Tillard, *Devant Dieu et pour le monde* (Paris: Ed. du Cerf, 1974), p. 400f. Also see B. Rigaux, "Le radicalisme du règne: la pauvreté évangélique," in *Lire la Bible* 27 (1971):135–73.

29. See L. Boff, "La vita religiosa nel processo di liberazione," *Noticeial* (CEIAL), April 1973, p. 4: "Following Jesus means following his options. He opted for the poor, the lost sheep, the prodigal son, and all those who were on the margin of social and religious society. If religious propose to live as his disciples, then they must try to identify with the lowliest and the weakest because that is what the Son of Man did. Following Christ means accepting as normal the possibility of persecution, calumny, prison, and even death for the sake of human beings. . . . In Latin America today sacrifice and martyrdom can assume a variety of forms." Also see *CLAR*, no. 6, p. 19.

thing very different as a primordial value of the religious life. It will mean making every effort to turn our communion with our fellow human beings into the locus of our communion with God.[30]

My feeling is that the historical project of the people and its demands provides us with a standpoint for re-examining and interpreting the various elements that have traditionally been associated with the following of Christ in the religious life. While these elements deserve systematic treatment, I simply want to offer a few preliminary reflections here.

The Following of Christ as Total Self-Surrender

As a universal summons to live as he did, the following of Christ expresses our total consecration to the Lord. In the religious life we have all too often neglected baptismal consecration, both in its basic nature as consecration and its total character. Vatican II restored these two dimensions to baptismal consecration and its work of configuring us to Christ.

The presentation of the religious life as consecration, usually in terms of one or more evangelical values, has led us to view the following of Christ in fragmented terms. We are now involved in a long process of clarifying the nature of the evangelical counsels, their number, their scriptural foundation, and their theological import.[31]

---

30. See G. Turbessi, 'Prefigurazioni bibliche e fondamenti evangelici della vita religiosa," in the anthology *Per una presenza dei religiosi nella Chiesa e nel mondo* (Turin, 1970), p. 223. V. Ayel, "La exigencia evangelizadora de la vida religiosa 'en acto,' " in *Evangelio y Vida Religiosa* (Rome: USIG, 1974), pp. 4–34: "Thus the religious life will be the following of Christ only if it is inserted in the full reality of the world and its needs, there manifesting the coming of the kingdom" (p. 19). See *CLAR*, no. 1, p. 9.

31. See I. Mennessier, "Donation à Dieu et voeux de religion," in Supplement to *La Vie Spirituelle* 49 (1936):277–301; idem, "Conseils évangéliques," in DS (Paris, 1953), 2:1592–1609. E. Ranwez, "¿Tres Consejos evangélicos?" in *Concilium* 9 (1965):74–81; he examines the outlook of Vatican II and concludes that the evangelical counsels are not exclusively those professed by religious congregations. F. Sebastian Aguilar, "Valoración teológica de los consejos evangélicos," in *CONFER* 7 (1965):353–75. J. M. Ranquet, *Conseils évangéliques et maturité humaine* (Tournai: Desclée de Brouwer, 1968). K. Rahner, "Sobre los consejos evangélicos," in *Escritos de Teología* (Madrid) 7 (1969):45; Eng. trans., *Theological Investigations*. E. Quarello, "Il significato dei consigli Evangelici," in the anthology *Per una presenza*, pp. 391–413. A. Turrado, "Teología, antropología y consejo evangélico," in *Revista Agustiniana de Espiritualidad*, 1972, pp. 9–32. J. Isaac, *Réevaluer les voeus* (Paris, 1973). M.C. Cymbalista, "Consejos del evangelio y

Throughout the course of history the vows have served as an expression of our surrender to the Lord. Far from minimizing the force and total nature of this consecration, they have simply brought out various ways of comprehending and fleshing out the overflowing richness of Jesus Christ, the one we seek to follow. While it is true that the three vows of poverty, chastity, and obedience do express vital levels of human existence, they have never exhausted the manifold forms of the evangelical life.

As I pointed out earlier, any line of the gospel message that is lived in depth will enable us to recapture the whole message and its exigencies. This is true even though we find different theologies in the final redactions of the New Testament as we have it. Any point of entry brings together the overall dynamism of the Christ-event and the Christ-mystery. It has happened historically to all sorts of people. Some have read the Gospels with a special sensitivity for the poor. Some have been particularly impressed with Jesus' openness to the will of his Father. Some have been struck by his concern for the sick, the lowly, and the abandoned. Still others have been impressed with his total dedication to his mission. No matter what the different emphases may be, it is always one and the same Lord we are called upon to serve.

The religious life is a way of understanding, proclaiming, and living the whole of the gospel message and its total impact on human life. It is one way of acting out the totality of the Christian life. The problem is not to see what it selects out of the Christian life but how it recaptures the *totality* of the gospel through concrete forms and points of entry that must necessarily be partial and varied. Theologically speaking, we can say that being religious means being Christians who accept their overall baptismal vocation by choosing a particular approach as the way that leads to the total Christ. From the standpoint of church history, poverty and chastity and obedience and life in common have been concrete ways of approaching the totality of the gospel message. They are features of the religious life that have gained official recognition from the church.

These partial and particular entry-points into the overall dynamism of the gospel give shape and stress to differing perspectives in the project of the religious life. It is through these entry-points that we propose to read and bear witness to the Lord's message for our own sake and for others.

---

consejos evangélicos," in *Cuadernos Monásticos* 27 (1973): 625–37. J.M.R. Tillard, *Devant Dieu*, pp. 142–52, 387–97. L. Boff, "La estructura antropológica de los votos: un voto en tres," in *CLAR*, no. 22 (1975):9–19.

The novel feature does not lie solely in being faithful to the overall dynamism of the gospel, but also in being faithful to the entry-points that the Spirit has brought to life: i.e., the vows of poverty, chasity, and obedience. Being faithful to these entry-points means being able to re-create the power of the gospel and to reveal its unsuspected contributions to human life.

My belief is that the option for the oppressed and their liberation project can serve as the starting point for a reinterpretation of the "classic entry-points." These points can then be reinterpreted and revitalized as the synthesis of a life-project based on the totality of the gospel message and its radical concretion in the history of our people. The religious life and each one of us religious must be the living and militant exegesis of the all-fulfilling dynamism of the gospel. Every line of that message can give character to our project of following Christ, which is to say, our project of building the kingdom and radically transforming the lives of our people. Thus it is valid to stress certain particular aspects, so long as we remember that each aspect finds its full meaning in the underlying dynamism that calls it into being, i.e., in the totality of the gospel message and the radicalism of the kingdom.

Koinonia as the Historical Project of Liberation

The fulfillment of the promise lies in the fact that communion with God perdures as a vocation, i.e., as a gift and a process. In the proclamation and fulfillment of liberation in Christ, communion between human beings perdures as the locale of communion with God. The life and mission of the church is to see to it that human brotherhood makes it possible for others to believe in the experience of filiation. This is the deeper sense of *koinonia*. Here is how the bishops of Peru describe it in their document on evangelization (3.3.5):

As the saving work of Christ, liberation is the process through which human beings draw closer to full communion with God and each other. By means of Christ's truth and the ministry of the church they overcome all the obstacles to becoming full human beings—from the personal sin inside themselves to the social repercussions of sin.

Koinonia means turning human *agape* into an experience of divine *agape*. This is the content and the task involved in the following of Christ. The lives of human beings become the conscious following of Christ when we recognize and celebrate the liberation of the poor as the sign of our acceptance of the kingdom and the locus for the proclamation of the promise. It is the living context where we shoulder and live out the consequences of our option for Christ as an option for the oppressed. That is the human brotherhood we mean when we talk about *koinonia*.

The liberation project proposes to change the social relations existing between human beings. It seeks to eliminate the selling of some human beings to others, the submission of oneself to another for the sake of mere subsistence. The utopian aim of the oppressed is to eliminate a society divided into classes and to establish a world where we human beings act in terms of gratuitousness, creativity, real friendship, and brotherhood. Many of those who are sharing the yearnings and struggles of the downtrodden at close hand know that this utopian ideal is gradually becoming a reality. Dedication to the cause of the downtrodden is a concrete experience of gratuitousness. More than the embodiment of an ideological conviction, it expresses deep sensitivity and unswerving confidence in the downtrodden; and thus it makes their historical project believable.

Human brotherhood is the core of the poor's project. The political praxis and the broad-scale liberation movement of the poor are a sign of the living presence of the kingdom. Their project compels us to join our lives to theirs, to join in their struggle for a society marked by brotherhood, solidarity, and human love. Evangelical *koinonia* is not credible apart from the dynamic thrust of the liberation struggle that occupies the history of the common people on our continent. Their liberation project gives concrete historical embodiment to God's *agape* in the form of human brotherhood. And communion with God opens up fraternal love to its deepest liberative sense and its most subversive dimension: i.e., its capacity to be stronger than death itself.

The religious life has correctly been presented as an experience of *koinonia*. At one time it may well have been difficult to assimilate *koinonia* to life in communion, to life in community.[32] But the fact remains that life in community can have real meaning only if it is an experience of *koinonia*, of fraternal love. In the concrete, life in community must be dedicated to fashioning human brotherhood in the real-life history of our peoples. Life in community can serve as a sign to the extent that it is the concrete—

---

32. For a better understanding of what life in common means, see A. Restrepo, *De la "vida religiosa" a la "vida consagrada," una evolución teológica,* pp. 53–54. He borrows some of the views of A. Larraona regarding the *lex peculiaris* of secular institutes. Larraona introduces the notion of an ordinary life in common that is not contemplated as such by the Code of Canon Law (can. 487, 673 ff). It would be based on the constitution of a given institute or other forms of particular law.

though incomplete—embodiment of brotherhood immersed in the struggle of the common people. Religious community is an experience of *koinonia* insofar as our commitment to the oppressed and their quest for a fraternal society is recognized and celebrated as God's *agape*, as a sacrament of the kingdom.

When the religious life is characterized by communion with human beings and their struggle for justice, it will cease to be a purely inner way of life or a purely intramural reality. There can be no credible religious life without total dedication to the struggle for a more fraternal society. The source of the tensions we are experiencing now is to be found in the historical, collective, and conflict-ridden aspect of the liberation task. If we wish to re-examine the communal religious life and its fitness for its mission, we must do so within the context of the historical project that seeks to build a society of truly fraternal human beings.[33]

Pages filled with learning have been written about communal religious life as *koinonia*, and many valuable observations have been made. My impression, however, is that consideration of the fraternal dimension does not get beyond personalist remarks about "being with others" or being "a subject related to others." In talking about Christian brotherhood, people do not seem to bring out the fact that the poor are the bearers of the message of human solidarity, that their concrete achievements are signs of *koinonia*. While writers indicate that the religious community is theocentric and a locale for reconciliation, they do not seem to realize that such reconciliation signifies a subversion of the existing social and historical order on our continent; for the existing order is clearly a denial of human fraternity. Though they frequently point out that community entails a single, common ideal and a shared project, they do not see the historical and political roots of the project aimed at human *koinonia*. They propose an irenic vision of historical reality and fall back into the framework of intra-community personalism, even when they go so far as to remind us of the historical side of the grace we received at baptism. Theirs is a spiritualist conception of *koinonia* even though they may talk about apostolic commitment. That is the impresssion I get of Tillard, for example. His description of the religious life and its project as being "for the world" seems too vague, and hence his talk about religious life "before God" seems too ahistorical.[34]

---

33. Though his context is different than ours, see E. Bianchi, "Una comunidad interconfesional en Italia: Bose," in *Concilium* 89 (1973): 416–17; Eng. trans., "Bose: An Interconfessional Community in Italy," *Concilium* 89:111–19.
34. See J.M.R. Tillard, *Devant Dieu*, pp. 223–33, 234–54, 263–64, 278f. In the

For others and myself the process of liberation is a historical experience of communion and fraternity. Our option for the common classes establishes a camaraderie between ourselves and many other human beings. How can we turn this revolutionary comradeship into the living expression of a fraternity that will concretize the presence of the kingdom in history?

The judgment scene in Chapter 25 of Matthew's Gospel is the recognition of the salvific content of camaraderie. It confirms the sign-function of evangelical *koinonia*. What is at stake in the solidarity and camaraderie of liberation praxis is human brotherhood envisioned as a project, an ideal, and a way of life. It is there that we recognize the gift of *koinonia* and its terrible demands. For we may have to go as far as to offer up our lives.

From this standpoint, then, the liberation project of the poor is the locale of fraternal communion. Insofar as the religious life is lived out there, it too will serve as a locale for the following of Christ and will assume its subversive character as a discipleship lived in and with the oppressed.[35]

Many religious men and women are now living as members of Christian communities made up of the common people. There they are simply militants alongside other militants. Far from draining our religious communities of meaning these experiences are enabling us to view our religious communities calmly and hopefully, though not without serious questions. Many would like our religious communities to possess the simplicity and the apostolic vitality we find in the people's communities. The lifestyle of militant peasants and workers shows us that there are simpler ways of being religious in the very midst of the people. We cannot help wonder if the canonically recognized form of religious life has not met its match in the vitalized community life and the fraternal experience of the common people and their church.

---

same vein see J. M. Guerrero, "Vida religiosa en el mundo secularizado," *CLAR*, no. 9, pp. 51–59. V. Gambino, "La dimensione comunitaria o di koinonia della vita religiosa," in the anthology *Per una presenza*, pp. 555–58. Like the above, Gambino does not see *koinonia* including communion with the poor as a mediating sign of communion with God. The religious community can evade all the conflict-laden elements of reality. A political perspective is totally lacking in his work. By contrast G. Gutiérrez reminds us that *koinonia*, as an encounter with the Lord, is lived out in human brotherhood and celebrated in the Eucharist.

35. See R. Garaudy, "La base en el marxismo y en el cristianismo," in *Concilium* 104 (1975):62–75; and E. Dussel, "La base en la teología de la liberación," ibid., pp. 76–89.

The people's communities do not claim to monopolize certain charisms that have dropped straight out of heaven. They do not dwell on ways of winning over the "influential" people in society and the church so that these people will protect their organizations. Their annals do not narrate the shrewd ability of their founders to win ecclesiastical or papal approval of their constitutions and rules. The Christian lifestyle of these grassroots communities raises serious questions about the solemnity and complexity of our monumental institutions. The church of the people is already arising as a sign of liberation out of these militant communities. It is not arising out of our high-sounding institutions, which are often more preoccupied with completing picture-galleries of saints from other centuries. Is it possible that once again the Lord is throwing the wise and the powerful into confusion?

The answer, I think, is to be found at the very point where the question arises. Many religious orders and institutions were born in the same sort of simplicity and fraternal dedication. Their own success, and perhaps other historical factors of a more general nature, led them further and further away from their original ideals. The poor on our continent, who have now gathered in communities grounded on faith and active struggle, challenge us to be faithful to the evangelical ideals that gave rise to our religious institutes. Will we accept that challenge?

Many religious men and women feel the challenge posed to their communal religious life when they opt for the exploited people and live in their communities. There they discover the rich treasure of their order's basic charisms and the real meaning of a life dedicated wholly to the Lord. How are we to reformulate communion for our own religious congregations in this new context? How can we religious feel united when there is no force in any of the signs that served historically as expressions of our congregation's charism? We seem to be in the same plight as the chosen people: How can we go on believing when there is no temple, no cult, no prophets, and no priests? How can we go on believing when we are exiled in a strange land?[36]

---

36. The type of apostolate and the needs to be met are not the main things driving religious out the door and away from their cloisters. The main factor is the ideological and political aspect entailed in their option for the exploited. They get permissions and temporary dispensations until they finally leave or submit and return. Perhaps we should adopt the idiorhythmic lifestyle of certain Eastern monks. They govern themselves, relating to the community as they see fit. It is another kind of lifestyle alongside the eremitic and the cenobitic. See P. G. Cabra, "Reflexión sobre el estado actual de la vida religiosa en cuanto a su fuerza

This is the challenge facing many religious in Latin America who are trying to be faithful to the people while still remaining loyal to their own option for the religious life. *Koinonia* lived out in terms of the poor and their project does not just take on concrete historical shape. It is also a source of strength on the one hand and a summons to fidelity on the other.

Liberation Praxis and Human Love

We know that ultimately the lives and struggles of the exploited in history represent an awesome, conflict-ridden act of human love. Love is the wellspring and the aim of their right.

An option for the oppressed and their liberation project entails an option for human love. It means that we firmly believe that this is indeed the vocation of every human being. Solidarity with the poor implies a commitment to turn human love into a collective experience from which there is no turning back. Human love is the basic, perduring reality that ensures that social and political praxis will be truly liberative, that it will transform existing social relations and create a new way of being human.

This is the prophetic message engraved on the flesh of the oppressed. Herein lies their universal vocation, the reason why they are the sacrament of a new humanity. To believe in this is to begin the complete subversion of history as human beings have known it.

Thus human love is not simply an inner reality of the individual. It implies the establishment of just and fraternal social relations on every level—economic, social, political, and cultural. It is within this framework that sexual maturity becomes indispensable as an embodiment of the total vitality of men and women. It is here that love takes on its full human warmth, its genial and inexhaustible embodiment in history. It is here that new vitality is injected into both its private and its universal dimensions.

Here again sexuality turns out not to be a purely individual problem or a purely inner reality. Its structure is collective. Because we have turned sex into a motel-problem, we have failed to see its underlying relationship with the social and political awareness of the masses. We have failed to see the link between the liberation project of the common people and the

---

evangelizadora," in *Evangelio y Vida Religiosa* (Rome: USIG, 1974), p. 35f. See A. Büntig, "Las comunidades de base en la acción política," in *Concilium* 104 (1975):111–21.

creative features that men and women are capable of injecting into such values as solidarity, generosity, and fidelity.

The liberation project summons us to rectify this failure. It is a task for all, for both the married and the celibate. Our option for the oppressed is not an abstract, intellectual option. It is not concerned solely with changing ideas or clarifying our mind. It is much more profound and all-embracing. No part of our life can be left outside, neither our emotions, nor our sexuality, nor our sensitivity, nor our aesthetic sense. The historical project of the oppressed summons us constantly to re-examine our own understanding and experience of human love and human emotional life, particularly since it is something which we must live out today in concrete practice.

Let us begin with the assumption that opting for the oppressed means belonging to them. How are the common people to feel that our affective life belongs irrevocably to them? How are they to know the convergence of our life-giving forces as men and women is really a contribution to their struggle? How are we to live this obligation if we are celibates? How are we to live it if we are married?

Sad to say, we have tried to answer these questions in terms of available time, proper working conditions, and personal availability. To do that, however, is to evade the whole import of our presence among the people and the impact of their liberation project on our lives as married people or celibates. The problem is not one of available time. It is one of meaning and purpose. Its political effectiveness, its historical impact, and its human content are rooted in that.

Insofar as Christians are concerned, both marriage and consecrated celibacy are options made out of love for the kingdom or they are not options of faith at all.[37] Love for the kingdom does not mean love for the next life, however. It means love for history, for the lowliest and simplest human beings, and the transformation of the existing world into a world of brotherhood, justice, and liberation.

That is the way in which two young Catholic activists understood their marriage commitment. They chose each other in a total commitment as a

---

37. See J. M. Pohier, "Le célibat consacré comme discours sur Dieu et sur la sexualité," in Supplement to *La Vie Spirituelle* 110 (1974):275f. Also see F. Monnover, "Reflexiones sobre el celibato involuntario," in *Matrimonio y Celibato*, 1967, pp. 269–75. On tradition with regard to matrimony and celibacy see E. Lopez Azpitarte, *Sexualidad y matrimonio hoy* (Santander, 1975), pp. 349–52. For a view of recent exegesis on celibacy in the New Testament see the writings of T. Matura in *Nouvelle Revue Théologique*, 1975, pp. 481–500 and 593–604.

way of giving new life to their class option. Marrying a woman of the common people meant accepting her as a member of a certain class. Marrying a common working man meant uniting with all the common people in their struggle for justice and brotherhood. For this couple marriage meant a way of being present within their own class. Their marriage project was a sign and a concrete embodiment of the liberation project of the oppressed. The radical seriousness and particularity of the love of one man and one woman for each other reinforced the class perspective, the collective horizon, and the universal content of their love. Their matrimonial experience was a privileged way of revitalizing their option for the common people and their struggles. On the one hand it would reinforce their ideological position and their political praxis. On the other hand it would fructify their emotional life, their human tenderness, their sexual experience, and their understanding of fatherhood and motherhood. Understood in this sense, love in the flesh and the lot of man and woman in marriage led them to extend class camaraderie and solidarity into friendship and real brotherhood. We are reminded that this is the kind of love involved in the revolutionary option.

Proletarian marriage is a sign of the kingdom insofar as it is a concrete experience of love that transforms history in the light of God's promise and impresses its dynamism on human life as a whole. For couples who do not come from the common people, the perspective is the same even though their starting point is different. In the last analysis the project of conjugal love seeks to express the same values of the new human being that the liberation praxis of the oppressed seeks to inaugurate. The point is that human love is a collective experience, and that it is the meaning of the life of every human being.

Am I talking about vain illusions? No. However vague my words may be, I am trying to express the rich and fruitful experience of many young militant couples.

It is certainly true that neither continence nor celibacy is inherent in consecration or self-surrender to the Lord, though they are required in the canonically recognized forms of religious life.[38] Though this may change, the fact is that there will always be men and women who choose to make virginity their way of life. And it will always be difficult for people

---

38. See G. Lafont, "La institución del celibato religioso," in *Concilium* 97 (1974): 72f. B. Gardey, "Conditions nouvelles d'un célibat permanent," in *Supplément* 78 (September 1966):453–58. S. Villatte, "Redonner sens au célibat religieux?" in *Vie Consacrée* 3 (1971):129–57.

to understand the underlying meaning of this option and its historical significance.

While the celibate aspect of our religious life is not its basic foundation, it is the most striking aspect on the social and cultural level. Therefore, if the liberation project confers historical meaning on the religious life, religious celibacy must be meaningful in that context or it will say nothing at all to people.

The project or ideal embodied in the celibate life is something that is also present in the liberation project of the common people. Both seek to make clear that human love is the meaning and goal of human lives, and that this experience of love is not bound to relations of blood, family, kinship, race, class, or nation. Human fraternity, solidarity, and love are grounded on gratuitousness. The problem is how to make this contribution historically real and effective on the basis of a commitment to the common people.

The underlying reason for choosing the celibate life has nothing to do with greater availability of time or even the desire to live as Christ did. The underlying reason has to do with why Christ himself led a celibate life. Of course his dedication to his mission called for complete availability. More important in my opinion, however, is the fact that the aim of the divine promise and the kingdom is to establish relations based on total gratuitousness between human beings themselves and between them and the Father. Brotherhood and divine filiation are nothing else but the outcome of opening oneself up wholly to gratuitousness. Thus the celibate life challenges any and every attempt to restrict the fulfillment of the promise and the covenant to the adherents of one race or tribe or people or creed.

Christ's option for celibacy, then, has profound religious, social, and political import. It is framed within the kind of messianism that he himself opted for; and though it is not normative, it is profoundly meaningful. Its historical import lies in the fact that it fleshes out in history one of the major aspirations of the poor of the land. It signifies that we human beings are to relate to each other as brothers and sisters, and thus it breaks down the sectarianism of clan, tribe, race, and nation. In short, it opens us up to the gratuitious character of human love. That is why Christ could ask married people to conduct themselves as eunuchs out of love for the kingdom. He wanted to show that human love, fidelity, and solidarity do not grow solely in the symbols and gestures of married life or within the ties of kinship and race.

Viewed in these terms, our lives as celibates can do much to subvert the ideological structure of society. In the midst of political efforts and commitments on behalf of the common people we tend to believe that we can contribute only what is immediately demanded of us: e.g., available time, expertise, and other human qualities. Moreover, there is no reason why a commitment to the people should mean going without marriage or a partner. Indeed the more primitive the group with which we work, the more difficult it is for them to understand how anyone can deprive himself of the fruitful benefits of the flesh.

How can we communicate the value and import of our option for celibacy to individuals and the people as a whole? Our option for the exploited classes summons us to camaraderie. But perhaps it is not the best atmosphere for sharing life-experiences that can best be understood and communicated when they are coupled with ties of trust, friendship, and affection. Class solidarity, too, must take on a human face.

Perhaps that is why we have not been able to spell out what human warmth and tenderness mean to us in response to the affection of others. Perhaps we do not know how to do it. Perhaps the political struggle has hardened us. Perhaps we have succumbed to the propaganda that says that the takeover of power is the first priority, that there is no time for sentiment and romantic twaddle. Perhaps we have not found the right cultural expressions of the common people to get across our own emotional and sexual experience, which is so deeply imprinted with our petty bourgeois origins. Perhaps the need for security measures in the liberation struggle allows us to share our deeper self with only a few. But the difficulty of the task does not excuse us from attempting it.[39]

Neither marriage nor celibacy exhausts the full dimensions of our life.[40] Both, however, do point up something that animates our whole life, i.e., human love as an experience of liberation. What is at stake in one lifestyle can be lived in the other also, though the signs and points of emphasis may differ. The universal perspective of human love takes on different tones and connotations in the married life and the celibate life.[41] Human

---

39. If we do not attach due importance to affection, kindness, and the tender warmth of human love, how can we in practice proclaim love of God as an experience of freedom and of profound meaning for our lives as human beings?

40. See A. Durand, "En busca del sentido de la vida religiosa," p. 355.

41. I think it is important to stress universal openness as a central feature of the religious life. But in historical terms the universal operates by way of the particular, and specifically by way of the common people. See, for example, A. Durand, "Recherches sur le sens de la vie religieuse," in Lumière et Vie 96 (1970):59f. Examining the outlook and import of the celibate life and the married state, he realizes that we cannot simply talk about universal openness in general terms. The common people will never believe that our love is universal unless they feel that we are totally with each one of them. Thus I disagree with R. Schultz's

love takes on particular strains of tenderness and affection in a man and a woman. There it points up and energizes aspects that can be fulfilled only by choosing some life project, be it marriage or celibacy. Neither the particular nor the universal dimension can be automatically realized by either celibates or married people. Both the celibate life and the married life represent one particular option taken out of love for the kingdom. Human love embodied in concrete gestures is the verification of charity, and charity ceases to be communion with God when it does not operate through the experience of human love.

The point is that human love must be made meaningful to the poor, so that it can transform history. Only then will they be able to believe the message of filiation and brotherhood which we, as followers of Christ, proclaim in our words and our way of living.

Fidelity and Liberation Praxis

The life of *koinonia* as an experience of human love expresses and calls for an attitude of unconditional fidelity. The history of God's love for human beings is the history of a faithful love. God's fidelity to his promises and his people is the wellspring of our own fidelity. In Jesus Christ God's loving fidelity blossomed in all its saving force. It is the Father's fidelity that gives full meaning to the Son's obedience.

The fact is that we live in an economy of fidelity, of gratuitousness. To say fidelity is to evoke a context of trust and a relationship of friendship. The relationship of master and servant is gone. Fidelity reminds us that we must not only persist but move forward. We must keep moving in the dynamic track of that for which we have laid down our lives. Fidelity means more than response and execution. We must preserve and deepen our underlying motivation, our conviction of mind and heart, and the mystique that is at work in the task we seek to fulfill. If obedience is not real fidelity, then it turns into mere observance, infantile subjection, legalism, and passivity. We observe the law but we run the risk of not being faithful to God's plan, of never entering into the experience of his liberative love.

To talk about obedience in the religious life is to talk about fidelity. Only in that context can obedience be creative and transforming. Christ's obedience expressed the fact that he had made the Father's plan his own.

---

description of the universal aspect of celibate love: "It is opening one's arms to all without extending them to anyone" (ibid., p. 144).

Obeying meant being faithful to that plan and its implications. Fulfilling the Father's will did not mean palming responsibility off on the other person. Instead it meant pointing up the source that gave meaning to the project for which he was laying down his life. It meant highlighting the tender, faithful love of God for human beings.

Christ's obedience was not passive resignation. It was the synthesis of his fidelity to human beings and his fidelity to God. Obedience was a transforming action that created communion. Christ was obedient so that the promise might move on to fulfillment. We cannot dissociate Christ's obedience from the Father's project, the kingdom. There it becomes fidelity: an act of love, trust, and openness.

Precisely because obedience is fidelity, Christ was often extremely disobedient. He was disobedient in order to remain faithful.[42] Even when his obedience seemed to be nothing else but allowing things to take their course (e.g., his passion and death), it was for him a gesture of freedom and fidelity: "No one takes my life from me. I give it freely."

Christ's obedience is linked with his lordship, as Paul reminds us.[43] It is comprehensible only as fidelity to his mission, to the fight for justice. Some exegetes see obedience as the synthesis and explanation of Christ's life. That is why they present it as the key element in their explanation of the religious life as well.[44]

Be that as it may, obedience is a thorny topic today in our Latin American religious communities. The ongoing thrust of our commitment to the common people and our work among them is raising a direct challenge to overly legalistic and formal conceptions of obedience in religious community life. The issue at stake has to do with discerning the will of God in the historical mediations created by our solidarity with the exploited. Stress is shifting to fidelity to the people's liberation process as the prime thing. Fidelity to the demands of religious community follows from there.[45]

---

42. See K. Rahner, "Jesucristo, modelo de obediencia," in *Cuadernos monásticos* 25 (1973):271–72.

43. Phil. 2:6–11.

44. See J. Cambier, "Théologie de la vie religieuse aujourd'hui," in *Etudes religieuses* (Brussels, CEP), pp. 39–41.

45. Though he is writing from a different standpoint, L. Boff offers interesting observations in his article entitled "Vida religiosa y secularización," in *CLAR*, no. 18, p. 5; idem, "Tensão entre a busca de realização pessoal e a obediencia religiosa," in *REB* 34 (1974):329–42, Spanish trans. in *CLAR*, no. 22. Also see B. Deleplanque, "La rénovation de la vie religieuse dans l'Eglise et le monde moderne," in Supplement to *La Vie Spirituelle* 78 (1966): 361–62.

The primacy of mission, as the synthesis of our consecrated life, is now the standpoint from which religious obedience must be defined anew. For many this mission is made concrete in their solidarity with the exploited classes, and liberation praxis becomes the place where the gospel is proclaimed and verified. We can see why the older notion of obedience, interpreted as observance of the rule and maintenance of order within the life of their religious congregation, would have little meaning for these committed religious.

The will of our heavenly Father is a will to transform human beings and history. We are now discovering that will where we find the historical signs of the growing presence of freedom, solidarity, and fraternity among those who are poorest. The course traced by our congregational rules should be no different; the chief concern of our religious communities should be the same. Faithful obedience in the following of Christ must take the form of fidelity to the historical process of building brotherhood and love between human beings. Unfortunately many of our communities are weighed down by traditions and prescriptions that dissociate religious obedience from the fidelity just mentioned. Even in some of the newer forms of consecrated life we find that obedience still remains deprived of its subversive impact on the existing social order. It is not viewed as fidelity to the liberation struggle of the poor. [46]

In the western world our concept of obedience and our cult of the rule has stripped the religious life of its ability to respond creatively to the most demanding challenges posed by our mission. We are unable to express solidarity with the oppressed. In eastern monasticism no rule plays such a shackling role. We say: "Show me religious who observe their rule perfectly and I will canonize them." Such a statement would sound meaningless or scandalous to eastern monks. [47]

---

46. There are many suggestive remarks made by G. Martelet in his article entitled "Pour une meilleure intelligence des instituts séculiers: la question de l'obéissance séculière," in *Vie Consacrée* 6 (1970):372f. However, he presents obedience as submission to existing society. He has no political vision based on the standpoint of the poor. Such a vision would call society into question and enable us to see obedience as a decision to be faithful to the task of transforming history.

47. The rule is of an indicative nature in monasticism. See A. Veilleux, "The Interpretation of a Monastic Rule," in *Cistercian Studies* 3 (1969). J. Leclercq, "Qu'est-ce que vivre 'selon une regle'?" in *Collectanea Cistercensia* 32, no. 2 (1970): 155f. A. Plamadeala, "La obediencia en la tradición ortodoxa ayer y hoy," in *Cuadernos Monásticos* 25 (1973): 288f. P. Deseille, "Los monjes de occidente,

In our case obedience cannot continue to be synonymous with observance of intramural rules and regulations. Such observance is meaningless for the people at large, and it does not create authentic *koinonia* in our religious institutions.[48]

Those who are asked to serve for a time as religious superiors must also recognize the new perspective proposed here. They must see the people's liberation project as the locale where we can be faithful to the gospel message and to the charism of our religious congregation. Up to now we have seen our religious superior and our brothers in the community as the place where we come to recognize the will of God. That is well and good up to a certain point. Unfortunately we have not always confronted our superiors and our fellow religious with the demands of the kingdom that find expression in the needs and demands of the people at large.

We cannot dissociate the rule, the criterion of discernment for the superior and the community, from the life and struggle of the poor on whose side we are supposed to be. To do that is to distort the criteria for our activity and to disfigure the evangelical perspective that makes obedience meaningful.

The proper perspective does not eliminate tensions, but it does put them in their proper place. It does not eliminate mistakes, but it helps us to correct them by showing us that our task is to transform history into a panorama of universal brotherhood. Obedience is the way to communion with God only when it is communion with the poor. The real-life problems of obedience—fidelity, interrelationship, and responsibility—are reduced to something else when they are tackled outside this framework. They become problems of group dynamics, social psychology, self-mastery, and socialization techniques.[49] All these cannot be neglected, but the point is that something more important and profound is at stake. What is at stake is the proper conception of the religious life itself. And our point here is that the religious life is a life-project in which we follow Christ by heeding the rhythms and emphases of the people's liberation project in history.

---

discípulos del monaquismo oriental," ibid., pp. 309–30. Deseille clearly points up the positive emphases of the eastern tradition.

48. See S. Galilea, "A los pobres se les anuncia el Evangelio," *IPLA*, no. 11, pp. 22–23.

49. Some fine observations are made by Thomas Merton in his article entitled "El lugar de la obediencia en la renovación monástica," *Cuadernos Monásticos* 25 (1973): 299–307. He says that all that will be useless if we do not acquire new theological perspectives.

Discipline is certainly necessary.[50] But to discipline means to create an awareness, to instill a mystique. Without some mystique, without some utopia, obedience transforms nothing and creates nothing; it is not an expression of freedom. At best it can only offer us security and camouflage our own immaturity.

On the one hand working with the people requires us to have stability. Thus the proper redistribution of personnel becomes complicated when we base it on the works to be undertaken or on the interminable search for personal identity and self-fulfillment. On the other hand working with the people also calls for a certain degree of mobility. The rhythms of daily life and of scheduling must remain a bit unstable at all times. Those who work with groups and organizations of the people know what this takes in terms of being available and rescheduling one's time. Thus there must be an ongoing effort to coordinate the life of the religious community and the work of its individual members. If our obedience as a community and as individuals is going to be filtered through our work with the people, we will not only have to make our structures more flexible but also find ourselves summoned to an ongoing process of conversion.

If we choose to reconsider religious obedience in terms of the demands made by our solidarity with the exploited classes, we will often find ourselves in extreme situations vis-à-vis our religious communities. But those situations can be extremely fruitful if we know how to be faithful to our original option—in short, if we remain bold and strong. Love for the kingdom may mean that we will have to be disobedient, for the sake of real obedience. But we will be disobedient without recriminations or rancor, fully confident that the irrepressible strength of the lowly and the dispossessed is imprinting the signs of the kingdom on history and tracing out the pathway of liberation for all of us—even our religious congregations.

Loneliness is not just the mark of the married people who choose to be eunuchs out of love for the kingdom (Matt. 19). It is also the mark of those religious who choose to go beyond the ties and structures and friendships of their consecrated life in order to express their fidelity in hopeful self-surrender to the people as well. When the cross is the consequence of

---

50. See P. Jacquemont, "Autorité et obéissance selon l'Ecriture," in the Supplement to La Vie Spirituelle 86 (1968): 340–51. A. Di Marino, "Autorità ed obedienza," in the anthology Per una presenza, pp. 483–513. J.M.R. Tillard, "Repenser le gouvernement des instituts," in Vie Consacrée 4 (1970): this article is a very practical one, practically a recipe book.

fidelity to our mission—the proclamation of the good news to the poor—it is always a path to liberty and life.

A Life in Solidarity with the Poor

Our previous reflections provide us with the basic perspective that can give meaning to the religious life as a life of poverty. On our continent today the social poverty of religious must serve as the sign that will make our evangelical poverty credible.[51] When poverty characterizes the human condition on the cultural, economic, social, and political level, it betokens some evil and it cannot be an end in itself.[52] If we take on poverty, we do not do so to idealize something evil and pretend that it is good. We are simply following Christ, who took on the bodily weight of sin in order to overcome evil, to liberate us from sinfulness, and to fight the underlying causes.

Our poverty will be meaningful only when it expresses both solidarity and rejection,[53] when it turns the struggle against injustice and exploitation into the historical mediation of its spiritual, evangelical content.[54] Otherwise it will simply be an ascetic exercise incapable of transforming the life of the poor. That may well have been our problem in the religious life so far. We turned poverty into an instrument of ascetic perfection and

---

51. This point is put well by I. Ellacuria, *Freedom Made Flesh: The Mission of Christ and His Church*, Eng. trans. (Maryknoll, N.Y.: Orbis Books, 1976): "So the poverty of Jesus' life represents a fundamental theological value. It is not a matter of some merely psychological or affective response whereby the Christian desires to be poor with Christ in order to be more like him. The whole matter goes much deeper. Jesus' poverty has a socio-theological import of major importance. On the one hand it is both a precondition for, and a result of, his absolute freedom vis-à-vis the powers of this world; on the other hand it is the condition for access to the only kind of life in which God reveals himself" (p. 34).

52. See P. R. Regamey, *La Pauvreté* (Paris: Aubier, 1941), p. 102. Some Franciscans propounded an exaggerated mystique of poverty as an end in itself, a view upheld by their General Chapter. However, John XXII declared it heretical.

53. Chap. 13 of Gutiérrez's *A Theology of Liberation* offers the best biblical and theological summary for any consideration of the religious vow of poverty.

54. See F. Boado, "Renovación doctrinal y práctica de la pobreza religiosa," in *CONFER* 10, no. 35 (1971): 344. L. Boff, "La pobreza en el misterio del hombre y de Cristo," *CLAR*, no. 22, pp. 39–62. Boff offers worthwhile considerations in this article, but he seems to put too much stress on the spiritual and interior aspect. That is not the case in his book, *A vida religiosa e a Igreja no processo de liberatação*, CRB (Petrópolis: Ed. Vozes, 1975), p. 94.

spiritual purification, accepting severe austerity on the personal level; but our poverty failed to have any impact on the life of the poor masses.[55]

Here I should like to add two observations. As religious we have been able to make vows of poverty and to live as poor people. But because we have failed to raise questions about a real-life situation that produces poor people, we have been poor people acting against the interests of the common classes. Today we are taking cognizance of that situation. Many religious in Latin America are now trying to live their vow of poverty in a different way. They are seeing its personal and communitarian implications when it is practiced in solidarity with the exploited classes.

Today the vow of poverty is a far cry from the old tack of asking for permissions. Much of what has been acquired by our communities has come to us through exemptions and permissions. Land, buildings, and stock shares have been acquired with the permission of the central government. When that could not be obtained, other ways have been found.[56]

The second point I should like to bring up here has to do with work as a form of poverty. One of the major points brought up by Vatican II with regard to the renewal of the religious life was that we religious must live by our own labor. This decision is embodied in the documents produced by many general chapter meetings and, even more importantly, in the practice of an increasingly large number of religious men and women.[57]

---

55. See E. Hoornaert, "Origem da 'vida religiosa' no cristianismo," in *Perspectiva Teologica*, no. 5, 1971 (Recife Theology Institute), pp. 231–32: "In an overall context of affluence and domination, the virtue of poverty was turned into a purely ascetic one. . . . Poor human beings were in the service of an affluent structure. Unable to reform the structure, people would turn poverty into a virtue 'for private use.' The poverty practiced by many monks and clerics no longer had any relationship to the real poverty of people outside the convent or the ecclesiastical structure. Poverty ceased to be a sign for the world and became an internal example designed to edify one's fellows in the monastery or religious institute. Evangelical poverty does not mean that certain people live as poor ascetics within an affluent system. It means that the gospel is lived among poor people, that 'the poor have the gospel preached to them,' and that the church takes sides with the poor and the oppressed. In Christianity poverty is the sign that God is walking with the poor as they journey toward their definitive liberation. In paganism poverty is simply a form of asceticism."

56. See V. Gomez Mier, "La pobreza en los institutos religiosos: estructuras tradicionales y nuevas perspectivas," in *CONFER* 11, no. 41 (1972):551–64, especially p. 558.

57. See *CLAR*, no. 1, p. 37; *CLAR*, no. 8, p. 16; *CLAR*, no. 13, p. 7.

There is a historical reason for this new emphasis on work. It has been hard for society at large to view the life of friars and nuns in their convents as work. This always compromised the credibility of their message and the content of the witness they claimed to offer. Many convents and monasteries sought to survive by a whole host of ingenious little projects: manual labor, farm work, handicrafts, and so forth. None of these efforts managed to break people's traditional image of religious as people who had managed to escape the law of work.[58] Today, by contrast, we are urged to work in the productive structures that will bring growth and development to our country. We are to be men and women of our time and place, immersed in the world of work.

Various theologies of work have come along to give doctrinal legitimacy to this way of interpreting religious poverty. They have exalted work as the place where people attain their human dignity and as a means of socialization. The bad thing is that in general they have not raised questions about the social, economic, political, and ideological structure in which work is carried out in capitalist society. The theology of work has tended to legitimate the exploitation inherent in the capitalist division of labor. Today the theology of secularization is urging us religious to immerse ourselves in society by engaging in work alongside our fellow citizens. Once again it seems that no questions are raised about the underlying structural reality.

If we need such appeals to engage in work without questioning the international division of labor, then we will be trying to be poor people in a way that goes against the best interests of the exploited. Once again we can glimpse the political outlook which is implicit in such theologies.

It is not enough to say that religious poverty means living by one's own work.[59] We must be aware of the nature of society and combat one that

---

58. See the pertinent observations of B. Deleplanque, "La rénovation de la vie religieuse dans l'Eglise et le monde moderne," in Supplement to La Vie Spirituelle 78 (1966): 357–58.

59. See A. Turrado, "Teología, antropología y consejos evangélicos," in Revista Agustiniana de Espiritualidad 12 (1971): 7–65; 13 (1972): 9–32; 14 (1973): 9–40; 46–47; 15 (1974): 32. He maintains that such realities of consumer society as work, wages, and social security should not be novelties for those living the life of the evangelical counsels. Referring to real-life situations such as those we find in Latin America, he says the work and witness of religious should take other forms: e.g., work done for free or for minimal compensation, active struggle against poverty and injustice, sharing the poverty of the needy, and so forth. This is a provincial and unscientific view of exploitation. In the same vein see V. Gomez Mier, "La pobreza en los institutos religiosos," CONFER 11:561–62.

allows exploitation and the alienation of human labor. Tillard shrewdly underlines the difficulties that can arise when we do not have clear-cut criteria governing what it means to live by one's own labor.[60]

What, then, are we to do? It is certainly not a matter of refusing to live by one's own labor. Instead we must be alert to the distortions that can arise or persist. Even more importantly, we must constantly remind ourselves that the social division of labor in the capitalist system is the root of class divisions and the exploitation of the majority, and that such a situation can and should be eliminated by the struggle of the exploited.

It is not enough to have work and to be efficient at it. We must also have a basic commitment to the historical project of liberation and seek to change existing social relations and production relations. Concretely speaking, such an outlook means solidarity with the exploited classes. It will provide us with criteria for evaluating our life of poverty as individuals and as religious communities. It will enable us constantly to redefine our role as, e.g., technical experts, professionals, and intellectuals.

The brain drain does not lie in the fact that our intellectuals are going off to other countries. It lies in the fact that the best trained people in our communities are not working close to the people. Fleeing up the ladder of success can be worse than fleeing abroad. To refuse to work with the poor and exploited is to rob the common people, for the money to train and pay us comes from them.

Another distortion might be brought up here. Thanks to their professional expertise, the members of our religious communities may often earn ten times what a manual laborer gets as a minimum wage. When those wages are placed in the community pot, we find that our religious communities and we as individuals are living a very comfortable middle-class life. It is not enough to practice religious "detachment" from temporal goods. In solidarity with the common people we must commit ourselves to the liberation praxis that is turning their historical project into a reality.

It is then that the following of Christ the poor one in the poor of our own continent will acquire the full historical dynamism that our vow of poverty seeks to express. A life of poverty and austerity is not just an evangelical practice. In our nations today it is a necessary precondition for breaking with the capitalist system and moving toward a truly just and fraternal society. Will we religious, through the witness of our poverty and our austerity, contribute to the development of the new human being who is rising out of the liberation efforts of our people?

---

60. J.M.R. Tillard, *Devant Dieu*, p. 48.

To be wholly poor is to be open to the lowly and the abandoned, to allow them to question our fidelity to the gospel message and demand solidarity from us.

I want to conclude this chapter by reiterating once again that the religious life, as one form of the evangelical life, finds its locus of verification in the historical project of the poor. But I also believe that the evangelical values fleshed out in various forms in the religious life throughout the centuries can flesh out and contribute to the underlying import of the liberation struggle. To say that the religious life is the following of Christ, that it finds its richness and novelty there, is to recall something that sounds rather traditional. But when we shoulder it through the mediation of the poor and exploited, it becomes quite original. It can then unfold its full transforming power and become a real experience of fraternal communion and union with God.

6

Liberation Praxis and the Pathway to Holiness

I have tried to show that the project of the evangelical life finds its place of permanent verification in the historical project of liberation. This means that holiness—as life in the Spirit, absolute fidelity to the Father's will, and the radical following of Christ—has an intimate relationship with history. Put more concretely, it has an intimate relationship with the life of the poor and the suffering. Remember that the Lord blest them because the kingdom was theirs, because the good news had been proclaimed to them, and because the Father's will had been revealed to them and hidden from the great and the wise.

There is nothing new about establishing a relationship between the spiritual life, our experience of God, and historical reality. That, in fact, is the only real Christian spirituality. It is rooted in the Old Testament and finds its confirmation in Christ. We cannot dissociate acceptance of the kingdom and its growth from the historical transformations that reveal its presence.[1] Here the fulfillment of the promises establishes an irrevocable link between fidelity to God and fidelity to human beings—to the lowly and weak in particular. Holiness and justice are not just themes of the promise; they are also the vocation of the collective group. The kingdom is a realm of holiness and justice, of complete and unreserved fulfillment

---

1. See the article of A. M. Besnard, "Tendencias dominantes en la espiritualidad contemporánea," in *Concilium* 9 (1965): 26–47; Eng. trans., "Tendencies of Contemporary Spirituality," *Concilium* 9, pp. 25–44. When he talks about a spirituality of life that is active in the world, he tells us that he is not talking about interjecting religious intentions or passing references to God into our spare moments at work.

of the Father's will.[2] Holiness and justice are the signs of the new human being, the human being of the kingdom.

The great contribution in Chapter 5 of *Lumen gentium* is its official insistence that there is a universal vocation to holiness. In an earlier day that vocation seems to have been restricted to those who formally vowed to seek perfection as a way of life.

The fact is that Christ did not come to call individuals to perfection. He came to re-create humanity as a whole in holiness and justice.[3] Needless to say, the theme of justice cannot be discussed with hasty exegetical accommodations based on a priori theological and pastoral suppositions. But it is equally clear that the dynamic thrust of salvation history, which finds its central happening in the dead and risen Christ, rules out any systematic attempt to treat justice as nothing more than an inner attitude toward God without historical roots. Justice must be mediated through a change in social relations with others, and it must be verified in deeds that eliminate exploitation, discrimination, and maltreatment of the poor, the widow, and the weak.[4]

The process of liberation, of justice, which is furthered by the struggles of the poor on our continent, is the historical expression of the message of salvation. We simply must fight for justice if we are to be just in the sight of the Lord. I maintain that the historical praxis that establishes justice between human beings is the path to holiness, the road that leads to knowledge and love of God.[5]

LIBERATION AND CONCRETE EXPERIENCE OF THE SPIRIT

The relationship between holiness and justice, as it is worked out in the mission, message, and life of Christ, shatters a certain pharisaical concep-

---

2. For a study of the relationship between "doing justice" and "doing the will of my Father in heaven," see Dupont, *Les Béatitudes* (Paris, 1973), 3:253f.

3. See S. Legasse, *L'appel du riche* (Paris, 1966); one chapter, pp. 113–46, examines the view of perfection in Matthew's Gospel. Also see Dupont, *Les Béatitudes*, 3:249f.

4. See C. Duquoc, *Christologie, Le Messie* (Paris: Ed. du Cerf, 1974), 2:238–63 ("Justice and Resurrection"). He notes that while Jesus is free and upright, justice as such does not interest him. What interests him is the poor, the despised, and the dispossessed. Jesus did not make justice a virtue of the Greek sort (pp. 258–59). Also see Dupont, *Les Béatitudes*, 3, chapter IV on Christian justice in Matthew's Gospel (pp. 211–305). Idem, "L'ambassade de Jean Baptiste," in *Nouvelle Revue Théologique* 8 (1961): 805–21, 943–59.

5. Bishops of Peru, *Justicia en el mundo*, no. 7.

tion of virtue and holiness.[6] Holiness does not consist in knowing the law, or even in observing it. It consists in accepting the kingdom. The life of the Spirit, not the law, is the path to holiness. Accepting the good news and opening oneself to the kingdom is a gift of the Spirit. Proclaiming and sharing it is also the fruit of the Spirit.

Accepting the kingdom means something more than being faithful to the law. It means immersing oneself in the transforming power of the Spirit and taking the first steps to becoming a new creation. As Paul puts it: "If anyone is in Christ, he is a new creation" (2 Cor. 5:17). It is Jesus who shatters the older Jewish conception of holiness as something bound up with knowledge of the Scriptures. For he focuses on those who do not know or understand the law as the inheritors of the kingdom and the recipients of the good news.[7]

In Luke's Christology the relationship between Jesus and the Spirit is central. But he also stresses the mediating role of Jesus' mission. His task is to proclaim the nearness of the kingdom, and this task entails certain consequences.[8]

Christ's experience of the Spirit is not only an act that takes place with his baptismal anointing but also a whole economy of the Spirit. It is bound up with his mission and sealed by his resurrection. Here I want to consider one text in Luke's Gospel (4:16f) which, in my opinion, sums up all the central themes of a life project centered around Jesus Christ. It also serves as the starting point and justification for any theology of liberation.[9]

The Lucan text is a bit ticklish because Luke himself had a hand in putting it together. Nevertheless many exegetes feel that this text does present very old elements in the gospel tradition.[10] It is clear that the

---

6. See F. Hauck, article "*osios,*" *Theologisches Wörterbuch zum Neuen Testament* (*TWNT*), 5:488–92, on the various meanings and uses of the words "holy" and "holiness"; Eng trans.: *Theological Dictionary of the New Testament (TDNT)*, 5:489–93.

7. See Dupont, *Les Béatitudes*, 2:137, 216.

8. See E. Rasco, "Jesús y el Espíritu, Iglesia e Historia, elementos para una lectura de Lucas," in *Gregorianum* 56, no. 2 (1975):374f. Dupont, *Les Béatitudes*, 2:134f. I. de la Potterie, "L'onction du Christ. Etude de théologie biblique," in *Nouvelle Revue Théologique* 3 (1958): 227–29 and 252.

9. See E. Samain, "Manifesto de libertação: o discurso-programa de Nazaré (Lk 4:16–21)," in *REB* 34 (1974): 261–87, especially p. 287.

10. See the bibliography of Samain, ibid., pp. 261–66; also Dupont, *Les Béatitudes*, 2:130–31.

presence of an Isaian text (Isa. 61:1f), words put in Jesus' mouth at his decisive moment when his mission was just starting, gives particular force and meaning to the passage as a whole.[11] The beatitudes, as presented by Luke, take on their full meaning when viewed in terms of the demands voiced by the Isaian text. The formulation of the first beatitude is very close to the redaction of the prophetic passage.[12]

Here we find a prophetic view of Jesus' mission. It is not just that a prophetic text is cited. The whole context of Christ's anointing, to which the passage applies, evokes the prophetic import of his ministry.[13] Here is the passage that Jesus reads: "The spirit of the Lord is upon me; therefore he has anointed me. He has sent me to bring glad tidings to the poor; to proclaim liberty to captives, recovery of sight to the blind and release to prisoners; to announce a year of favor from the Lord" (Isa. 61:1–2).

Jesus did not go on reading the text of Isaiah. His additional words would infuriate those listening to him. The text made him aware once again of the presence and power of the Spirit in him as he carried out his mission. Experience of the Spirit and the proclamation of the kingdom go hand in hand. "Today this Scripture passage is fulfilled in your hearing" (Luke 4:21). Jesus' consecration is his total dedication to the task of telling the poor that the kingdom is near, indeed in their very midst. The signs enumerated by Jesus, which he borrowed from Isaiah, are not tokens or mere calling-cards. These real-life changes in the lives of captives, prisoners, and others are already the kingdom that is on its way. The year of favor is credible precisely because the promise is already a reality in them. The universal perspective of the kingdom is inevitably fulfilled in and through a specific class of people, the poor and wretched of the land.[14] It is in them that the good news of salvation is verified. The year of favor retains its full social and historical import.

While there are exegetical difficulties to be resolved here, we can say that the program spelled out by Jesus here evokes the standards of judgment described in Matthew 25: e.g., giving food to the hungry, clothing the naked, and visiting those in prison. That is the good news

---

11. See J. Jeremias, *Teología del Nuevo Testamento*, Spanish trans. (Salamanca: Sígueme, 1974), 1:128–29; Eng. trans., *New Testament Theology* (New York: Scribner's, 1971). Also see Dupont, *Les Béatitudes*, 2:92.

12. See the detailed study of Dupont, ibid., pp. 92–98.

13. See I. de la Potterie, "L'onction du Christ," pp. 230f, 235 (footnote 31), and 251–52. Also see Dupont, *Les Béatitudes*, 2:134–36.

14. See I. Hermann, "Initiation à l'exégèse moderne," in *Lire la Bible* (Paris) 12 (1964):126f. Also see Dupont, *Les Béatitudes*, 2:216.

converted into real life and historical praxis. To do those things is to immerse oneself in the dynamism of God's love, to live by the power of the Spirit whether one realizes it or not, and to give concrete social embodiment to the Lord's year of favor.

The prophetic passage read in the synagogue at Nazareth establishes the christological content of the relationship between experience of the Spirit and liberation. The mission task becomes the place for life and growth in the Spirit. There is no holiness apart from the carrying out of justice. We must eliminate hunger, give drink to the thirsty, suppress oppression and exploitation, and fight against the poverty of the poor. To be the good news, evangelical proclamation must not only go by the way of the poor; it must also entail the transformation of their social, historical, and political reality.

This is the mission to which Christ feels he is consecrated because it truly is good news. It is in this task that he grows increasingly aware of being the redeemer and a brother. His mission is a spiritual experience. In his program Jesus makes it clear to us that the proclamation of a year of favor cannot be dissociated from the liberation of those in captivity. There is no joyful experience of God apart from the experience of human liberation. There is no life in the Spirit apart from consecration to the poor. It is because the poor are liberated that I experience the Spirit upon me as well. This, indeed, is what contemplation really means. It means experiencing the Spirit at work transforming us insofar as the face of the earth is renewed for the lowly and the dispossessed. It means recognizing and admiring the presence of the Spirit as a prophetic force in the very heart of the mission, among those who are inheritors of the kingdom.

What is ultimately at stake here is the love of God, which can be recognized in love for the oppressed. It opens us up to universal brother-hood, and also to the full and total realization of his love. The fundamental point is that God liberates human beings gratuitously. The experience of life in the Spirit is to be found in the liberation of the afflicted. In short, it points us toward the cross. Thus the liberation of human beings presents itself to us as an experience of the Spirit.[15]

---

15. See the valuable remarks of S. Galilea, "La liberación como encuentro de la política y de la contemplación," in Concilium 96 (1974): 313–27. He maintains that contemplation should be regarded as the deepest dimension of liberation, not as a functional tool of it. Also see Galilea, "Contemplación y apostolado," IPLA (Bogotá) 17 (1973): 46.

Holiness as Liberation Praxis

The experience of Christ just described above and the rest of his preaching shows us that he took great pains not to push his listeners into practicing virtues. That was the idiom of his enemies. Perfection is not the practice of virtues as it was for the Greeks, the Stoics, and other masters of philosophical schools.[16]

For Jesus, holiness means entering the kingdom and the dynamic thrust of its socio-historical exigencies. That is something very different from competing with others to adorn one's heart with the largest possible number of virtues.[17] Those who posed as the most virtuous people of his day were the object of Jesus' harshest attacks. Christ was against any religion that concentrated on the accumulation of virtues. His message is for the unvirtuous, for those who know that they can be just only if God in his infinite love makes them so. The holiness to which Jesus summons his followers is not the result of ascetic practices; it is a total openness to the demands of the mission, an unshakable fidelity to the task of proclaiming the good news to the oppressed.

There is no holiness unless we change our project. We must shoulder as our own the evangelical project that Christ proclaimed in the synagogue of Nazareth. We must consecrate ourselves wholly to the poor, joining them in their struggles for justice. Otherwise the good news that the kingdom is at hand will not be believable, nor will the experience of the Spirit be meainingful for the lives of human beings. Life in the Spirit ceases to be that when it loses its dynamism and fails to transform human beings.[18] Holiness means transforming the history of injustice and exploitation into a history of love and brotherhood. And this is done from the

---

16. See H. Urs von Balthasar, "El evangelio como criterio y norma de toda espiritualidad," in *Concilium* 9 (1965): 7–25; Eng. trans., "The Gospel as Norm and Test of All Spirituality in the Church," *Concilium* 9, pp. 7–24. He stresses that Christ constitutes the dynamic unity of every human spirituality because he surpasses them. Thus the gospel message is their norm and critique.

17. See O. Bauernfeind, article *"areté,"* *TWNT*, 1:457–61; Eng. trans., *TDNT*, 1:457–61.

18. See P. Fontaine, "Vida religiosa y experiencia de Dios," *Testimonio* 28 (1975): 5. He notes that the experience in question is a historical one. To invoke the name of God while failing to serve the alienated people of our society would be to fall into idolatry.

standpoint of the poor, the lowly, and the needy. Holiness which does not find expression in a love that transforms the history of the forgotten people on our continent is a corruption of the Spirit's gifts.[19]

The liberation praxis of the poor is not just the sign that reveals the presence and growth of the kingdom to us. It is also the mediating factor that gives life to our faith and makes our hope operative. In that sense liberation praxis is the decisive factor in our love for God and in the sanctifying action of the Spirit.[20] It is not a matter of taking advantage of this praxis and using it to present and spread the message. It is in this very praxis that the message is rediscovered and explored. It is in this praxis that the newness of the Spirit at work there is proclaimed.

The plain fact is that a relationship to liberation praxis is intrinsic to our faith, our experience of the Spirit, and our mission to proclaim Christ as the savior. If we turn the historical liberation project of the poor into the guiding norm of our lives, that should not separate or distract us from our life of faith, prayer, or our experience of the Spirit.[21] The action of the

---

19. See X. Leon-Dufour, "Bulletin d' Exégèse du N.T.," *Recherches de Science Religieuse* 62 (1974): 288. In commenting on the excellent work of C. Spicq (*Vie chrétienne et pérégrination selon le N.T.*, Paris, 1972), Leon-Dufour reminds us that the primitive catechesis constantly related holiness to *filadelphia*, to "brotherly love" and charity.

20. See P. Jacquemont, "¿Es la acción una oración?" in *Concilium* 79 (1972): 349; Eng. trans., "Is Action Prayer?" *Concilium* 79, pp. 39–51: "Mary's attitude shows us that action is not self-sufficient if it is to be meaningful. The action of serving another derives its meaningfulness from that other person, who was welcomed by the sisters and who enabled Martha to serve. The wellspring and meaning of our action are rooted in the other person, but the totalitarian thrust of action tends to make us forget or ignore that fact." See also Maurice Boutin, "Evangélisation comme projet dans la culture," in *Les religieux et l'evangélisation du monde*, Canadian Religious Conference, 1974, Collection Donum Dei, no. 21. Boutin uses this basic and decisive framework to point up the relationship between faith in Jesus Christ and culture, and also to get beyond the framework of exterior versus interior, absolute versus relative.

21. See J. Leclercq, "Culture and the Spiritual Life," in *Review for Religious* 30, no. 2 (1971): 167f. He reminds us that the monks of the Middle Ages also had to confront the problem of relating their spiritual life to profane realities; and that they discovered the latter through the study of Latin! Today things have gotten more complicated and our perspective has changed. The basic problem today is to relate our spiritual experience to the struggle for liberation. And we come to this struggle not through Latin but through the socio-political sciences. We are beginning to become more familiar with the latter.

Spirit overflows history, but in no sense does it ever put history in parenthesis. As the work of the Spirit, holiness overflows historical praxis precisely because it persistently confronts this praxis with the total project that this praxis is seeking to turn into a reality. Here the New Testament idea that doing works of justice means experiencing God (1 John 2:29) takes on its full evangelical weight and its historical bite. It brings out the fact that liberation praxis is the path to holiness.

The liberation activity of the exploited aims at turning human beings into one single people. That is impossible today unless we radically transform the existing social, political, and economic order. Only in that way can we establish a new pattern of relationships between human beings and nations. Understanding the message of the good news does not mean simply opening up to others and being with them. It also means striving to make sure that our relationship with others will be different; and the qualitative difference in this new form of social relationship derives from the project of liberation. Thus liberation is a collective experience of what it means to be a people and to make ourselves free in an ongoing process.[22]

Holiness is nothing else but communion with our fellow human beings and the communion of all human beings with God. It has a collective, communitarian character. As Comblin puts it: "Biblical man denies any attempt to set up a distinction between public life and a mass of individuals restricted to a private life. The 'people' is a form of life in common, and God is its witness and support. . . . The new covenant rules out the distinction between what is private and what is public, between the individual and the collective group."[23]

Things might be less complicated if holiness were a matter of inner fidelity on the part of the individual. Once we discover the social reality and the public, historical structure of life in the Spirit, however, we cannot but be suspicious of any forms of holiness that have left unchanged a world filled with injustice and exploitation.

The saints who will be most important for the history of our continent, who will inspire and motivate the lives of human beings here, will be those whose witness of fidelity to the Spirit takes the form of unswerving fidelity to the movement for the people's liberation. There will be such saints, though they will never be raised to canonization on our altars.

---

22. J. Comblin, "Libertad y liberación, conceptos teológicos," in *Concilium* 96 (1974): 397.

23. Ibid., pp. 396–97.

They will stay down below because the "miracle" of transforming a continent by relentlessly fighting oppression does not fit in well with the neat rungs on the ladder leading to officially recognized sanctity.[24]

The spirituality that animates such individuals, and even whole communities, finds its inspiration in certain aspects of the Exodus experience. Liberation spirituality and its mystique has a "Mosaic" character. Moses did not enter the promised land. He believed in it, but more in the sense that he believed it nearer and tried to bring it nearer. He labored for that land, but he himself reached it only in and through those who fought and won the wars of conquest. Our experience today is akin to that of Moses. It expresses our dedication, our concrete commitments, our relentless militancy, our "incredulous faith," and our lucid realization that what we hope for is the full measure of the reality we are already living now.

Will we ourselves see the new society as a collective experience of truly fraternal freedom? Our conviction that this will not be the case in no way cripples our present experience of the new human being and the new society, however fragmentary it may be. On the contrary, the harsh reality sharpens our faith, shores up our confidence, and recharges our liberation praxis. This aspect of our militant experience and our spiritual life revives in us Christ's own experience on Calvary and his promise that the Spirit would finish the work he had only begun. The dawning light of some coming morning, when our people will experience brotherhood and justice, reminds us constantly how critically important our dedication today is.

When we say that liberation praxis is the path to holiness, we are saying that it provides the historical context for our prayer life and our sacramental life. They must be explored and deepened from the standpoint of that context.

The origin of what we call the "liberation approach" to theology, spirituality, and pastoral work lies in the life of Christian communities that came into existence in and through the liberation movement of the common classes. There is only one way in which the liberation approach can vivify the greater community known as the church and give living expression to the present-day exigencies of the struggles of the Latin

---

24. See A. Plamadeala, "Le monachisme dans la société moderne, à partir de l'expérience orthodoxe," in *Collectanea Cistercensia* 35 (1973): 19–37. He concludes that if he were God, he would never canonize a human being who became holy by living in a cloister off the work of others!

American people. That way is "the redemptive way of the cross." It cannot be done by magisterial explanations, authoritarian imposition, or facile manipulation.

The message that Christ preached and the kingdom that he inaugurated here proved to be liberative only through the power of the cross, the witness of his death, and the strength of his generosity and total self-surrender. Liberation theology will serve as a new breath of the Spirit only with the help of a holiness lived out in the flesh. There must be existential witness, which may well be given in "traditional" or "classic" categories too: e.g., obedience, fidelity, austerity, the cross, and death. Without the support of these signs our message will not be credible. It will not summon people to conversion or transform history. The perspective that comes from the poor does not find its strength in the erudition or the orthodoxy of the learned. Its fruitfulness lies in its ability to transform history. Its future rests on the holiness of those who turn the struggles of the poor and the oppressed into the locale for their following of Jesus Christ. This is the most urgent task and the most perduring concrete challenge that faces our generation.

Conclusion

Their concern for the work of evangelization has led Christians to a better understanding of the gift of salvation. Starting off from the dictum that "there is no salvation outside the church," they have come to see that love is the basic requirement for salvation both within and outside the ecclesial institution. Thus their dictum now is that "there is no salvation outside the circle of human love."

Reading the gospel message from the standpoint of solidarity with the oppressed classes on our continent, we have come to specify this dictum even more. We now see and believe that there is no salvation apart from love for the poor, the hungry, the suffering, and the oppressed. Christ, the poor human being, is the focal principle for understanding the good news. Today we gain strength and inspiration from such passages as Chapter 25 of Matthew's Gospel, the beatitudes, and Jesus' programatic discourse on liberation in the synagogue at Nazareth (Luke 4:16–21). In the poor, the Indian, and the aborigine of our lands the Lord is calling us religious to renew our consecration and to become heralds of the good news.

The revitalization of the religious life must come by way of our option for the poor classes on our continent. It is there that the following of Christ will find its embodiment in real history. The future of the religious life on our continent does not reside in the possibility that men and women from the common people will fill our convents and congregations. New ways of following Christ are already being lived out by many militant Christians. Dedicated wholeheartedly to the struggles of their class, the common people, they are living the following of Christ in Christian communities composed of these people. If a people is capable of overcoming exploitation and building a fraternal society, in that very process it will be creating new forms of consecration to Christ and fidelity to our baptism. From there we will get a theology of the religious life that truly expresses the Spirit who renews the face of the earth.

Index of Authors